BUSINESS IN JAPAN

The logic of an airline presenting itself as a business information service and source of business intelligence on Japan may, initially, have been viewed by some rather sceptically. We hope, however, that in the last two years Japan Air Lines' Executive Service for businessmen interested in exploring the Japanese market has demonstrated its validity and proved worth while to those for whom it was intended. Within this scheme we introduced a booklet series entitled *Business in Japan: guidelines for exporters*. The world-wide success of these booklets encouraged us to bring the whole series together in book form. This book, *Business in Japan*, prepared in collaboration with The Macmillan Press, is the result. It is our earnest hope that this volume, containing much new material, will contribute to the greatly needed fund of knowledge and insight which individuals and businesses all over the world need in their endeavours to develop the Japanese market.

BUSINESS IN JAPAN

A GUIDE TO JAPANESE BUSINESS PRACTICE AND PROCEDURE

Edited by
PAUL NORBURY
and
GEOFFREY BOWNAS

M

First published 1974 by
THE MACMILLAN PRESS LTD
London and Basingstoke
Associated companies in New York
Dublin Melbourne Johannesburg and Madras

Printed and bound in Great Britain by
Redwood Burn Limited
Trowbridge & Esher

'What is of the essence is the capacity to communicate oneself and one's business objectives within Japan's own terms of reference.'

Contents

Editors' Preface

When Japan Air Lines invited us to prepare their business booklet series, *Business in Japan: Guidelines for Exporters,* on which this volume is largely based, we set ourselves two principal objectives.

First, we aimed to relate the Japanese business world with its often rather unfamiliar practices to its natural setting – the society and its traditions in which business evolved. We tried to identify the intangibles that would face the foreign businessman in his dealings with Japan, and we promised ourselves that we should never mystify, and thus avoid the accusation of fostering that unease and nervousness which sometimes assails the visitor coming face to face with Japan's idiosyncratic world for the first time. Nor, on the other hand, should we go too far in the opposite direction – over-simplify and promise facile success in a booming market as a reward for diligent application of the advice given by our contributors.

Our second principal objective was to provide as much practical help and guidance as possible, rather than to construct fluent analyses of strategies and structures. A consideration of business strategies, of course, is part of our brief; but we have left theory and theoretical format to those who have already employed it far more expertly and effectively than we could. Our task we regard as indicating to the exporter or businessman who knows little or nothing of the Japanese market the many inescapable problems that face him once he has taken the decision to explore this new field. We suggest how that first approach might be made, how some of the preliminaries can be tackled at home, and where information and help can be obtained before setting out. We introduce the trading house, both Japanese and western, as a potential first go-between, and we examine the advantages and drawbacks of the different modes of entry – trading house or other agency, licence, joint venture, and so on. We explore some aspects of doing business in Japan (such as the often-maligned marketing and distribution system), the myths about which have been inhibiting many potential exporters for far too long. We also investigate hitherto poorly-charted territory, such as business and the law and the role and functioning of the advertising industry.

A fundamental guiding principle has been to produce something that is not only interesting and readable, but something that will offer food for thought and reflection as your business associations with Japan develop; something, perhaps, that might offer the clue to understanding that disturbing episode at an earlier business meeting once you are back in your hotel after a frenetic day. We hope also that, in addition to providing practical help on a day-to-day basis, the contents of this book will help create a more informed and realistic picture of the Japanese businessman, set in the foreground of his own business world against the backdrop of his society at large.

Throughout the series it has been our good fortune and privilege to have worked alongside an advisory group, with each member contributing valuable time and even more valuable expertise. Advisory editor, *Robert Ballon*, a professor at Sophia University, Tokyo, and chairman of the University's Socio-Economic Institute, has to be thanked especially for spurring our enthusiasm and supplying the personal insights and richly competent analyses that have been so valuable at each stage of the venture. We must also thank him for introducing us to so many of his business friends and associates around the world who have all helped to make sense of a very ambitious programme. *Hans-Bernd Giesler*, director of the German–Japanese Economic Institute and director of the German–Japan Society, has given us the benefit of his wide contacts and know-how in German business circles. *Gil Holdsworth*, director of Dodwell & Co., has been doing business with Japan for many years and has brought to his advisory role the experience and specialist knowledge of one of the oldest trading companies in the world. *Michael Isherwood*, assistant to the London director of the Mitsubishi Corporation, and in the rare position for a westerner of having his finger on the pulse of a representative giant of the Japanese business world, has been able to interpret for us some of the unspoken or more obscure tenets of that world, as well as giving us new ideas concerning the meaning of business relationships in Japanese society. *René*

Lehmann is currently advisor to Mitsui & Co. in Paris, but has some twenty years of direct, practical experience of running an enterprise in Japan; his own remarkable sensitivity and interpretative talent has helped bring the depth we have sought in all our observations. *Sadao Oba*, deputy general manager (economics and market research) of Mitsui & Co., London, for four years, is yet another of our practitioners well versed in the problems facing both importer and exporter, anxious to promote Japan in Europe and push Europe in Japan, yet never shrinking from sharp criticism of timidity, or brutal exposure of the causes of failure. *Charles Smith*, Far East correspondent of the *Financial Times* and now the paper's bureau chief in Tokyo, has an expert knowledge of Japan's financial world and is unrivalled as a foreign commentator on Japan's economy. Our thanks are also due to *Gene Gregory*, who, although a late arrival to the team, contributed valuable references and material based on his experiences as an American businessman in the Far East and today as a consultant in Japanese business affairs.

As we write this preface, at the end of December 1973, Japan and Western Europe appear the most cruelly hit and the most dramatically affected in the long term by the world oil and energy crisis. Long cherished dreams of new life-styles have vanished, carefully planned growth-targets lie thwarted or, perhaps, in pieces.

Yet we know that there will always be business with Japan, and that Japan will remain one of the world's foremost trading nations. We are confident that the Japanese strengths which we have tried to analyse in this book will prove to be even more powerful influences in the restructuring, rephasing and renaissance of industry that must be bravely planned and surely executed under these new circumstances.

The crisis happens to coincide with the entry of the Japanese into a very individualistic and very creative period. As they themselves like to put it, they 'settled down' in the late 1950s (after considerable preoccupation with western values) to re-examine their own indigenous canons and traditions. The 1960s saw the emergence of a fluent synthesis with which most Japanese were able to identify; but today, in the mid-1970s, in many artistic and cultural fields and in the whole range of industrial and technological development, there is an emergent and thrilling individuality and inventiveness. This mood could even prompt the breakthrough towards a new and distinctive technology which is hinted at by Yujiro Hayashi in his chapter in this book.

Such is the spirit and flavour of Japan; the country of interminable contradictions and astonishing juxtapositions, archaic in so many of her traditions yet a professional of ruthless determination and efficiency when applying herself to a purpose. We hope this book will go some way in helping you sense and savour this for yourself. More important, we hope the book will play a part in helping you establish that *complete* relationship with Japan and the Japanese which our contributors never tire of stressing as the only real and lasting basis for any successful business encounter.

30 DECEMBER 1973

Paul Norbury
Geoffrey Bownas

Foreword

In an article I contributed to Japan Air Lines' own quarterly on Japan, *Tsuru,* published in November 1972, entitled 'Japan and Europe: an Economic Analysis', I made the point that it was vital that we in Japan and the West, particularly Europe, should try to create an environment of greater trust and understanding based on knowledge and mutual respect. 'It would be a bad thing', I said, 'if Japan and Europe worried so much that they placed restrictions on imports. It goes without saying that it is to the benefit of the whole world for the Japanese to be able to buy English woollens, French brandy and Italian shoes cheaply, and for the Europeans to be able to buy, equally cheaply, Japanese consumer goods. The reason why such a situation does not exist is to be found partly in the strong internal opposition from industry in the various countries. But it also lies in the level of ignorance which one country has of another. Between countries with widely differing manners, customs and ways of thinking, the slightest misunderstanding can be the seed of conflict'.

Happily, since that time Europe and Japan have begun to develop a closer understanding and a more tolerant commercial relationship. The massive import crusade of the Japanese government, the 100 per cent capital liberalization, further reductions of tariffs and quotas have been very positive moves from the Japanese end. What is more, specialist consultancies in Japan, involving representatives of Japanese industry, have been set up to provide particular guidance to certain foreign countries in their export endeavours. Indeed, such was the success of the government's import policy that Japan's balance of payments has turned into deficit since March 1973. Though there remain pockets of indignation over certain Japanese trading practices (and I do not deny that we have not reached a perfect norm) there is every reason to believe that some solid progress towards a common understanding has been made. It is my belief that a continuing and growing exchange on the cultural, business, academic and tourist levels between our countries is the most important single factor in our mutual search for knowledge, trust and respect. Hopefully, the funds that are being made available through the Japan Foundation, inaugurated in fiscal 1972, will help support and encourage this exchange.

News that this volume was being planned was obviously of particular interest to me. During the course of the last eighteen months, in fact, I have had the pleasure of reading the individual booklets .that Japan Air Lines in Europe promoted throughout that region in four language editions, and subsequently in other parts of the world–such was the quality and authority of the contents and comment. Although, there exist many books on business strategies in Japan, which are excellent for their data analysis and structured observations, the interpretative, practical comment contained in the Japan Air Lines booklets, and now in this volume, is of special interest and merit.

I take great pleasure, therefore, in recommending this volume to the busines world and to others who are seeking a practical introduction to Japan's business life-style. Individuals and companies who are planning entry into the Japanese market will find the book especially rewarding. But I also might suggest that companies already established in Japan would find these pages a valuable source of reference, offering perhaps new insights and knowledge which could well enhance their existing business relationships.

JANUARY 1974

Hisao Kanamori
PRESIDENT
JAPAN ECONOMIC RESEARCH CENTRE
TOKYO

Glossary

amakudari	move of retiring bureaucrat to directorship in similar line of industry (see p. 99)
asobi	'play', business entertainment
bon	religious festival holiday, usually four days, mid to end August
bu	department
bucho	department head
bun	status-role
ch'an	sect of Buddhism (see *zen*)
daimyo	feudal lord
denwa	telephone
gaijin	foreigner, outsider
geisha	hostess
gyosei shido	administrative guidance
haiku	short traditional poem
haragei	'stomach art', gut feeling
harakiri	ritual disembowelment
hashi	chopsticks
hashigozake	entertainment ladder
hisho	executive assistant (to president)
honne	'real intention' (see *tatemae*)
ichiban	'number one', best, top
jomu	managing director
jomukai	executive committee
ka	section
kabuki	traditional drama
kabushiki kaisha	joint stock company
kacho	section chief
kafu	'house style'
kaicho	chairman of the board
kaigi	conference
kaisha	company (see also *yugen*, *kabushiki*)
kansa hojin	auditing corporation
kansayaku	statutory auditor
Keidanren	Federation of Economic Organizations
kobun	'client', subordinate
kogaisha	'child company', offshoot company
kojin	owner driver (of taxi)
ku	ward, city district
kuchikomi	'word of mouth' communication
kunigara	national characteristics
Kurashi no Techo	consumers' journal
kyoso	competition
meibutsu	local product (food, etc.)
meishi	visiting card
noh	traditional drama
oyabike	prearranged purchase of new shares (see p. 81)
ringisho	document circulated for consensus (see p. 106)
saitori	securities dealers (see p. 79)
sake	rice wine
samurai	knight, warrior
Sanken	Council for Industrial Policy
sashimi	raw fish
semmu	senior managing director
sensei	'teacher', often used of a master of his field
shabu-shabu	meat, vegetables dipped in boiling water
shacho	president
shafu	'company style', ways
shingikai	joint consultative committee
shinto	indigenous religion
shokuba	work-place
shukko	transfer of employee to related company
sogo shosha	general trading company
sukiyaki	meat, vegetables, etc. cooked in soya sauce
sumo	Japanese wrestling
sushi	rice rings with raw fish filling
tatami	thick straw mat, 6 ft by 3 ft, used to measure floor area
tatemae	attitude, stance (see *honne*)
tempura	fish in batter, deep-fried
tokonoma	'alcove' in traditional Japanese room
torishimariyaku	director
yugen kaisha	limited liability company
zaibatsu	(prewar) business conglomerate
zen	sect of Buddhism

Note: The term 'billion' refers to US billions (one thousand millions) throughout.

1 The Japanese Market

INTRODUCTION

One of the most compelling examples of the spending power of the Japanese consumer is to be found in the department stores which handle some 11 or 12 per cent of all the retail trade in Japan. These stores are immense establishments rising to six or seven floors and are packed with high-quality consumer goods. Typically, they are more than just a store–they are a complete customer service complex and include travel agencies, hairdressing salons, children's play centres, restaurants and exhibition galleries. The sheer variety, quality of display and evident pressure to buy is stunning–certainly by European standards. Western goods, such as furniture, furnishings, fine art, tableware, clothes, cosmetics, footwear and a great assortment of household/kitchen equipment are well represented.

In this first chapter we have set out to try and crystallize the vast marketing potential that exists in Japan for the western trader; it is a subject, of course, which is examined frequently within different contexts throughout the book. Even so, it is by no means an easy market to break into although trading conditions have improved markedly since the 1960s. That Europe as a whole has barely established itself in Japan is a fact that astounds even the Japanese. Today, Japanese society is vigorously adjusting itself to western-style living patterns both in the structure of the family unit and in home life. Thus the Japanese require all the domestic and personal accoutrements that go with this new scale of values. But they demand only the best quality in western goods and are prepared to pay the very high prices involved.

The uninhibited opulence displayed in the department stores is no sales gimmick: it is simply a sign of the times. The prospective trader should make a point of discovering these places for himself; he will see at once, at least in the consumer field, what is meant by 'the Japanese market'.

THE MARKET PROFILE

In many ways the market profile of Japan reflects the classic export ideal: its size is very substantial and its potential considerable. It has a young to middle-age consumer group with growing earnings and disposable income. It is in the process of both cultural and social change, a context which fosters consumer interest in trying out different, even novel, products. It is multiplying its domestic family units (there is a growing tendency for the tightly knit Japanese family circle to split up). Relative to its size the consumer group is concentrated geographically–a major factor in the economics of marketing and distribution.

Knowing this, what should the marketer be asking himself? For Japan, as for any other export market, his questions might be:

1 Who distributes products competitive with ours in Japan?
2 What marketing channels do they use?
3 How many people handle the product before it reaches the consumer?
4 What credit, commission and compensation terms are extended by the manufacturer to the distributor and on down the line?
5 Do manufacturers have their own sales forces? How are they organized and compensated? And who handles transportation?
6 How much investment is there in this product field in advertising and promotion, and how is it handled?
7 How do the competitive products get to the market? If imported, who are the importers? What credit, pricing and other terms are offered by the foreign supplier?
8 If manufactured locally, what are the licensing terms?
9 What share of the market is held by each competitor?
10 How do prices of competitive products compare?

Such questions will help focus attention on essential information requirements. Obviously, those questions which are special to an individual's product needs will best be answered through personal research and a spirit of enterprise.

The fact that 75 per cent of the total population and 85–90 per cent of purchasing power are clustered in five major areas–Tokyo, Kyoto-Osaka-Kobe, Nagoya, North Kyushu and South Hokkaido–offers precisely that kind of selective, concentrated marketing and distribution pattern which is so typical of Europe.

International marketing in the 1970s, of course, is not just about the classical methods of export and import. In Japan, as elsewhere, the exporter's potential strategy may–and in some cases must–include alternative approaches, such as licensing know-how or a joint venture arrangement supported by capital investment.

Finally, much as he wants his short-term sales, the marketing strategist increasingly needs to examine a particular market, not in isolation, but for its longer-term regional marketing prospects. There is no doubt that wide areas of Asia have already become what, according to Herman Kahn, is now the Japanese 'economic hinterland'. The rate of growth of the Japanese economy will determine the business cycle in most markets in East and South-East Asia. The Japanese market, therefore, should be seen both as a significant growth area itself and as a route to the wider marketing possibilities of Asia.

POINTERS TO SUCCESS (AND FAILURE)

Sadao Oba

At the beginning of 1972 the director of a major British tea company announced that his company had sold US$1,800,000 of tea in Japan in 1971. This was only seven years after the company got down to serious business, and the total represented a 50 per cent increase over 1970.

There are many other success stories. European companies, for instance, have long held a major share in various sectors of the food and drink market. If the Japanese want a prestige watch, they buy Swiss. If they want to buy top-quality silk they go to Italy, and for perfumes they go to France. German machinery and Swedish ball-bearings hardly need mentioning, and Japan is the biggest overseas market for British woollen products.

Japanese manufacturers and distributors imported 1843 patents and licences in fiscal 1972, on which they spent US$572 million. There was a substantial increase in patents and know-how related to consumer products and distribution techniques. For instance, Japan bought 272 designs, patents and techniques for the manufacture of clothing, an increase of 42 per cent over fiscal 1971.

There is a steep increase in the social demand for quality patents and designs in step with the rising standard of living in Japan. Also, life in Japan is based more and more on western models. Thus, the number of patents and techniques linked with home appliances, packaging, furniture and cosmetics purchased in 1972 was 104 per cent more than the 1971 figure. Such patents and techniques come mainly from the USA, Britain, Switzerland, France, West Germany and other European countries. To quote an unusual and perhaps surprising example, a Japanese woodworking plane manufacturer recently bought a patent for an automatic plane from Portugal.

Reasons for success

The most fundamental reason behind these successes is Japan's staggering economic growth of more than 10 per cent per annum in real terms throughout the 1960s. Japan's rapid economic expansion has been spurred by the introduction from abroad of sophisticated capital goods (equipment and machinery), know-how and raw materials. These ever increasing imports brought several foreign exchange crises in the 1950s and 1960s, but they were successfully overcome by domestic fiscal measures and an increase in exports, partly attributable to imported equipment and know-how.

The net income of the individual Japanese more than doubled in the 1960s. As a result, demand for consumer products has become considerably diversified and sophisticated. To quote a few examples:

In 1972, paintings and antiques worth more than US$9·3 million were shipped to Japan from Britain.

One of Sweden's leading manufacturers of recreation cottage-type timber houses shipped 750 Swedish pre-fab houses in early 1972 (special tea-room attached), an order worth about US$3 million.

A Japanese shoe-cream manufacturer concluded a sole agency agreement for shoe-trees made by a London-based manufacturer.

Isetan Department Store, one of the biggest in Japan, is selling handprint cloth made by a famous manufacturer in Helsinki.

Over 100,000 oil-filled radiators were shipped from the UK to Japan in 1971.

Economic growth is forcing changes in the patterns of daily life in Japan. More and more women (including housewives) go out to work. The Japanese eat more meals outside their homes; there is an increasing demand for quick and inexpensive but highly nutritious meals. More and more, the western diet of bread and meat replaces the traditional rice and fish. To meet these demands, world-famous catering chains from Britain and America and even Czechoslovakian state organizations have established joint ventures with Japanese partners and are adding to the number of establishments in their chains.

These success stories in Japan indicate that the Japanese still believe the old saying 'foreign-made products are of good quality'. A century ago, the distance between West and East and the highly selective sense of the Japanese importers meant that only top-quality European consumer products entered the Japanese market. And today the Japanese are still sensitive to the good feel and high quality of European products. The Japanese have a weakness for top-quality and known brands. In a group-orientated society, a Burberry coat or a Ronson lighter, which few possess, are the roots of prestige; for the same reason, it is often a must for the élite to drink Scotch, smoke a Dunhill and wear a Bolsalino hat.

Failures

But there is the other side of the coin, for foreign enterprises have not always enjoyed such success in Japan. Many prominent companies have curtailed their activities or withdrawn completely from Japan.

To list a few examples:

A large multinational food corporation lost its Japanese partner in a baby-food joint venture because of loss of business.

A tyre manufacturer withdrew from Japan because of marketing failures.

A chewing-gum maker introduced over-rationalized marketing systems which were ill-adapted to Japanese conditions.

A watchmaker lost out in competition with Japanese watchmakers.

A monorail maker failed because of the excessive noise of its system.

Reasons for failure

Neglect of the special characteristics of marketing in Japan, such as the role of trading companies and wholesalers, and the very complex structure of the distribution system.

Disregard of the peculiarities of personnel management and labour relations in Japan. The seniority system still dominates the personnel administration of most Japanese companies; foreign companies may be required to do as the Japanese do.

Inadequate knowledge of Japanese business practices. For example, the takeover, very common in the West, is very rare in Japan; a takeover by force is generally regarded as unfair and disgraceful practice.

Underestimation of the strength of competitors. The Japanese are more sensitive to the activities of foreign enterprises than are Europeans, and will wage an all-out campaign for survival when confronted with competition. There are examples of large foreign enterprises being unable to secure markets occupied by smaller Japanese competitors and being forced to withdraw from the market.

Refusal to make the effort to understand the Japanese mentality or to listen to Japanese advice. This can lead to the wrong choice either of the Japanese partner or of the foreign representative sent to Japan.

European products, know-how and capital

In 1973, of Japan's total imports of materials and products worth US$38,303 million (calculated on a customs clearance basis),

US$4061 million (10·6 per cent of total imports) came from West Europe. Foods and beverages increased 84 per cent over 1972. Japan is the second biggest importer of Scotch whisky. Clothing, woollen goods, jewellery etc. increased 147·3 per cent over 1972.

High-quality goods, licences and know-how are in high demand. Once a foreign product has established a sizeable market, there is a natural tendency to start local manufacture. Capital investment into Japan has now been liberalized 100 per cent in principle. Japanese business circles already anticipate that more foreign capital will be invested in Japan.

Japan is not a far-away market. It is a most promising outlet for overseas exporters if only it is tackled in the right way.

BUSINESS JAPANESE-STYLE

Michael Isherwood

Doing business in Japan is not necessarily more difficult than doing business elsewhere, but it is different and it is essential for the western businessman to appreciate the reasons why. Business relationships in Japan are complex and almost unique and resist to a remarkable extent any outside pressure that threatens to disturb their delicate balances.

Japanese people are very conscious of being different; this difference derives from the distinction between a set of Confucian and Christian values and has been emphasized by Japan's historical isolation. Of course, the normal procedures of business life are basically the same as elsewhere and present the overseas visitor with little difficulty. It is rather the responses and motivations of the Japanese people that are frequently more than a little difficult for the foreigner to understand.

Japanese people tend to think and act as a group rather than as individuals. This is a basic concept of society quite different to that of the West where emphasis is given to individual self-sufficiency and the development of a strong, competitive personality. In Japan the opposite is required. The Japanese are trained to subdue their personalities, to conform strictly to group norms and to adopt a conciliatory approach to problems.

The lifetime employment system makes the working group the most important group in life. After school or college the new employee joins such a group, roughly corresponding to a department or a business section and comprising about ten to twenty people. He will be closely connected with them for years after and, because he will always remain with the company, he will personally identify himself with the progress and success of his particular group and the larger organization of which it is part. In return for being looked after and protected he gives complete loyalty and devotion.

The Japanese company man does not think of his relationship with the company in contractual terms as is usual with the western employee. It is more like belonging to a family to which by far the most important part of his life will be devoted. His own family, sheltered by the protective mantle of the company, will receive much less of his time than would be normal or even acceptable in the West. Evenings and weekends will often be spent in the company of his business colleagues–the members of his group.

The Japanese possess a high degree of emotional sensitivity. By this I mean that they are better at feeling things than they are at analysing them rationally. The Japanese language has much to do with this. It is imprecise by comparison with European languages–it tends to force one to allude to things, to suggest obliquely, to convey the feeling of the moment. Western languages encourage a way of thinking that is far more clear and exact. Japanese is concerned less with the meaning of words than with the emotional overtones or implications they suggest.

The restrictions and conventions of group behaviour, coupled with a high degree of emotional sensitivity, place great pressure on the individual who becomes preoccupied with relationships and the subtleties of personality within his working environment. As a result, Japanese people feel it important to conceal their emotions as much as possible for it would be considered most impolite and inconsiderate to impose one's feelings on others. The stranger from overseas, of course, may never realize what a significant role personal feelings play in Japanese behaviour.

The stability of the working group takes precedence over everything. The golden rule is to avoid at all costs unnecessarily embarrassing or offending others, particularly within one's own group. Harmony in human relationships is a recurring theme in the Japanese way of life. For these reasons the Japanese will avoid direct confrontations or disagreements at all costs and will always seek ways to conciliate. Failure to compromise is seen as weakness and an embarrassing loss of face.

Since it is almost impossible to express unqualified refusal in Japanese, foreigners are frequently confused by the Japanese inability to say no. In fact, people will often say yes when they mean no. Western businessmen, experienced in the ways of Japan, learn to read the negative response signs – hesitancy in speech and facial expression or an unwillingness to be more specific. But the unwary can be easily misled, sometimes with serious consequences.

It is also important to mention the decision-making process common to all Japanese companies and government organizations, for this is often the source of a great deal of misunderstanding and frustration for the unsuspecting businessman from overseas.

Problems arise when it is assumed that because Japanese companies seem to be organized along similar lines to those in the West (they have, for example, a formal management structure that looks encouragingly familiar) they actually *operate* western-style. In reality they work through their own unique group system.

The role of senior management is to act as mediator between the various groups (departments, sections) and to co-ordinate activities according to general policy. They are far more involved with personal relationships than with business expertise and it often surprises westerners that they lack the knowledge and authority of their western counterparts.

The differences in decision-making can best be summarized by saying that in western organizations most of the major decisions are made at senior executive level and are imposed downwards. In Japanese organizations, the decisions originate at the lower levels where day-to-day business is done and are then co-ordinated and approved by senior management.

The process of decision-making does take a long time and can prove very frustrating for westerners engaged in business negotiations. The reason is that everyone who will be concerned in or affected by the final outcome must be consulted and his opinion taken into account. The pressures on the individual do not come from above but rather from his working colleagues in the group. In the context of this decision-making process the Japanese have developed a remarkable ability to modify individual opinions in order to reach a consensus. In practice, everyone will now give the matter his fullest support and so the implementation of the decision will go ahead very quickly and smoothly. The speed of action after the decision-making period often fully compensates for the slowness beforehand, and often astonishes western observers.

VISITING JAPAN: SOME DO'S AND DONT'S

1 Exchange business cards–a formality as important as shaking hands. Go to Japan armed with an ample supply, about two or three hundred. They should give the full address of the company and your position in it. (In Japanese companies, titles indicate rank rather than function.)

2 Introduce yourself by your own family name. Avoid the use of first names even if invited to. Japanese always use the family name when addressing one another (except in the close family circle) and first names or nicknames tend to be an embarrassment. If you want to establish a more friendly relationship, add *-san* to the end of the family name (e.g., Matsumura-san).

3 Remember that you will always be faced with several people whenever there are discussions; everyone will need to be convinced of your proposals. There will also be other people to convince whom you will never see, so any prepared information you can offer will be much appreciated. It is useful to include information of a general character about your company such as the company brochure, annual report and information about products.

4 Invariably, you will find one person on the Japanese side who will do most of the talking, either because his English is the best or because he knows most about the subject under discussion. However, remember to acknowledge the senior man in the group.

5 Get into the habit of speaking clearly, slowly and for not more than a minute or two at a time. Emphasize your main points by

expressing them in several different ways so that the meaning is clear. Use words and expressions that are simple and avoid slang expressions.

6 The Japanese are apt to remain quiet while they mull over what has been said and what alternatives are open to them when they next speak; they may remain silent while they wait for others to reach conclusions they have come to already. Westerners usually find such pauses acutely embarrassing and feel obliged to say something unnecessary to relieve the supposed tension. At best, what is said may appear ridiculous; at worst, you might make a quite unnecessary concession in the belief that this is the reason for the silence. If the silence is caused by the difficulty of solving a problem, the Japanese will happily postpone the meeting to give everyone time for further reflection.

7 It is considered impolite in Japan to interrupt someone who is speaking. Foreigners often become impatient at the slowness and difficulty with which the Japanese speak foreign languages (usually English) and find it difficult not to butt in.

8 Make the most of your interpreter if you are using one. Brief him beforehand and give him any notes you may have on the proposals you intend to make. Allow him plenty of time to make his own notes during discussions and to clarify points where he thinks the meaning is obscure.

9 The Japanese will not do business with people they dislike, no matter how attractive the deal appears. High profits are not their chief priority; stability, sustained growth and good personal relations come first. It is, therefore, of the utmost importance to establish a harmonious and trustful atmosphere in business negotiations. The Japanese use meetings to sum up people and to gauge the desirability of long-term relations, so your reactions to situations will be keenly observed.

10 Entertainment in Japan plays a major role in any business relationship. When offered it should always be accepted and, in due time, reciprocated. Golf should be encouraged whenever possible. It is very popular and is played at all levels of the company hierarchy.

POINTERS TO JAPANESE MARKET DEVELOPMENT

Geoffrey Bownas

Japan's growth and trading policies have suffered profound fluctuations since the beginning of the 1970s. The late 1960s witnessed the longest ever continuous postwar boom (1967–70)–a boom that was based on buoyant exports and a flourishing home market. But from the end of 1970 it became painfully obvious that Japan was heading for a major recession, deriving mainly from over-investment. Then, as the Japanese sat through 1971 waiting for demand to catch up, the shock measures of the Nixon Administration's dollar defence programme, directed primarily at Japan, bit deep into Japan's economic and trading policies, sparking off the first yen revaluation, a massive swing to an 'import crusade' and a curb on export growth.

The surge out of the recession during 1972 was made possible not so much because of a revitalized export policy (as had been the case previously), but because of several straightforward domestic factors, led by the consumer and construction boom. However, the following year, 1973, made it clear that the boom was going to be short-lived because, as the Japanese like to call it, that was 'the year of shortages'. It was the year when record bonuses were paid to the work-force, when inflation became a major problem, and when low investment levels in plant and equipment during the recession produced shortages throughout industry. It was also the year when the growing labour shortage became even more critical and a persistent consumer boom created long waiting lists for the most popular status symbols, such as cars and air-conditioners. There was an acute scarcity of land for housing development, and the land that did become available was offered at astronomically inflated prices. Building materials, too, were scarce. At the height of the summer there was an electric power crisis–due, in no small way, to the strength of the environmentalist lobby which successfully opposed plans for new power station building, preventing starts on about four-fifths of the plant needed to meet the demands estimated for 1975–6.

Meanwhile the 'import crusade'–the build-up of overseas

investments and the drop in export growth–had been creating, as early as April, a balance of payments deficit; finally, the oil crisis struck and before the year was out official voices were calling for a full return to export growth.

Demand for know-how

None of these past fluctuations should have hindered the determined would-be exporter from getting his product into the Japanese market. Nor should he feel any more daunted today–whatever Japan's export policies might suggest. Although there is to be a cutback in public spending in 1974, the demand for know-how will certainly not diminish: know-how to help develop new energy sources and restructure industry and communications systems, control pollution and reassess the relationship of man and the environment–thus withdrawing from today's reliance (the greatest of all the advanced industrial nations) on the heavy and chemical industries.

On the question of pollution, it is no accident that Japan's new international airport at Narita, some 40 miles north-east of Tokyo in Chiba prefecture, has been standing idle and empty since its completion two years ago. It is an environmentalist issue of great magnitude where private citizens have grouped together to outwit and outmanoeuvre the government with astonishing success. Even the citizens of Osaka are presenting local and central government with considerable headaches concerning the future of Japan's second-largest operating airport. And for some time flying in and out of Tokyo's Haneda airport after 11.00 pm has been prohibited. Suddenly in mid-1970, it seemed, the ordinary Japanese woke up to the fact that he was living in the most polluted land on earth; today, the anti-pollution movement, as a national issue, has united the Japanese as effectively as any in the last 25 years.

Quality of life

There is another feeling, clearly defined, that although Japan's growth rate has been for years the highest in the world, the Japanese worker who helped bring it about has fared not at all well in terms of improving his quality of living. The standard of public services for example, particularly roads, housing, drainage and sewage, is very low compared to that of other advanced industrialized nations. And although there is to be less public investment, there must be some allowance on the part of public planners for these growing expectations.

Status

Again, the people once derogatively referred to as 'economic animals' now want to savour the more essential fruits of affluence. This is evident from the progression of top status symbols since 1960. Initially, these were a record player, a good-quality camera, a refrigerator and an electric washing machine. By the mid-1960s, the top target was the 'three C's'–car, colour TV and 'cooler' (i.e. some form of domestic air-conditioning unit). In 1970 the 'three V's' emerged. The first 'V' is for villa, for weekending in the hills or along the coast. The second is for visa, for a trip abroad. Several reliable sources estimate that there could well be three or four million Japanese 'doing' Europe each summer by the end of the decade. The trip to Hong Kong or Honolulu has already become an aspect of company fringe benefits (the reward for 25 years' devoted service, for instance), and it may not be long before the trip to Europe is a regular item among the top status symbols. The third 'V' denotes a 'visit' to the much larger, better equipped and better built home of a colleague or workmate. It was found, in a recent survey, that 90 per cent of Japanese today regard themselves as middle class: they want the tokens of this status – leisure and the tools of leisure, such as the 'three V's'.

There were mass consumer crazes for nearly all the top status symbols until 1970. These crazes brought diffusion rates almost to saturation point for black-and-white television, refrigerators and washing machines. Many of the status symbols later became the basis of a new Japanese export drive – transistors, cameras, tape recorders, televisions, pianos and cars.

Average wage

Wages in Japan doubled twice during the 1960s. (Including all the fringe benefits and the twice-yearly bonuses, the average Japanese wage is now as high as in Europe.) From 1960 to 1964, there was the deliberate 'income doubling plan' of the Ikeda

Government; then between 1966 and 1970 workers in their twenties and thirties again found their pay packets doubled. Since 1970 wage increases have been of the order of 17–19 per cent per annum, but even this high rate has not been enough to keep the Japanese worker ahead of an inflation that became one of Japan's major problems in 1973. There is also a steadily growing number of households in which married women return to work and add a full- or part-time wage to the family budget.

Yet, despite all the consumer spending sprees of recent years, the Japanese still remain the world's best savers. More than 20 per cent of their disposable income is put into savings, usually in the form of deposits which are then put to work by the banks in industrial investment. This habit of thrift is helped by the bonus system, where amounts of up to three or even four months' basic wage are paid out in June and December. This makes a total of an additional eight months' wage in the year, if the company is doing well. Lump sums of this order are ideal, of course, for savings and down-payments (private consumer credit has grown in volume by 30 per cent a year).

One category of the growth industries of the 1970s is that linked with pollution control. The acute shortage of resources (both in land and labour) will channel development into the non-resource sectors, into capital technology. A major growth sector will be communications equipment, automated transport and storage, data processing and storage, information retrieval, time-sharing and numerical control. But all sectors linked with computer development are to be strictly cocooned by the Japanese authorities and protected, for a limited time, from would-be foreign investors. As with the labour-intensive industries that boomed in the sixties, capital liberalization in this sector will be delayed until the domestic manufacturers have grouped themselves together in the strongest position so as to leave only the pickings.

Target export areas

The following list summarizes the likely developments that will be preoccupying Japan over the next few years:

1 Pollution control and the environment in its widest sense: anything from the largest and heaviest plant to the tiniest gadget that makes life cleaner, quieter and safer.

2 Communications equipment etc., as noted above.
3 Pharmaceuticals.
4 Aerospace and marine technology.
5 Resource security and development of cyclical resources.
6 Recycling technology.
7 New energy technologies, including all-out research on solar, subterranean and other sources.
8 The pursuit of the life of quality.

This last sector concerning the quality of life is highly susceptible to the prestige- and luxury-consciousness of the Japanese. The term 'de luxe', in fact, has never been so thoroughly exploited as in Japan during the last six or seven years. And there is no doubt that there will be a developing market for:

1 All manner of leisure goods and sports equipment, from skis to cabin cruiser accessories, but especially anything connected with golf which is a business and social must. Quality sports shoes and clothes etc., will also find a ready market. Remember that the Japanese always wear the full and correct 'uniform' whatever they are doing.
2 The travel trade, serving maybe five million Japanese travellers abroad by the end of the 1970s.
3 Clothing–fashion and top-quality western clothing, particularly as women emerge in all areas of life. In fact, the Japanese now want to wear, to eat, to drink, to display in their homes, exactly what the fashion-conscious are wearing, eating, and so on in New York, London and Paris. A well-made replica is no longer good enough.
4 Household goods, as the Japanese turn more and more to western-style furniture and decor. Antiques, western art, carpets, fittings (top-quality shelving, for instance), together with the conventional bathroom appliances and accessories for Japanese western-style bathrooms. Prestige glass and tableware.
5 Quality foods and drinks.
6 Giftware.

This is by no means an all-inclusive list. In general, if you have a product in these sectors that sells well in Europe or America, there is no reason why it should not be just as attractive to the Japanese.

The total of new houses built has been running at approximately 500,000 annually. Demand should remain high as the old three-generation household (grandparents, their married eldest son and his children) gives way more and more to the new social pattern of the two-generation unit. Planners expect that by 1985 the average number of members per household will fall to three. There is also much rebuilding and improvement to be done–nearly a quarter of the houses in Greater Tokyo were found to be substandard in a 1969 survey and more than one-third of Tokyo's householders are dissatisfied with their present housing conditions. If nothing else, they certainly ought to grumble at the miserable average of seven square yards of living floor space per person.

All these trends will take the Japanese in the direction of the 'three S's' seen by one large Tokyo securities firm as the signposts to the major roads of the 1970s. 'S' for 'sense' (the restoration of the old taste in Japanese life, in place of some of the brashness of recent years); 'S' for 'safety'–the control of pollution and the safeguarding of the environment; and 'S' for 'systems'.

'S' for 'sense', among Japan's 108 million consumers (45 per cent of them under 35), could well make them into the marketing man's ideal. They have a firm eye for value and quality. They have a fine regard for the prestige product, and they have the purchasing power to back up their judgement.

2 Industrial Policies in Japan

YUJIRO HAYASHI

INTRODUCTION

The history of Japan's recent industrial past clearly shows that the planning of her postwar development was expertly conceived and beautifully executed. At the root of the success story lies what many commentators now refer to as *Japan Inc.* – the confederation of government, industry, commerce, the banks, the trading companies and, of course, the single-minded Japanese people themselves. This confederation has proved to be one of Japan's most vital strengths; starting with a wasteland, the planners channelled resources first into power industries, then into labour-intensive and later into capital-intensive industries.

More recently, the emphasis has moved to the knowledge-intensive industries. Japan's industrial planners, in fact, will be putting increasingly greater stress on a swift and comprehensive swing to the knowledge-intensive sector, moving beyond the resource-intensive phase. One of the main reasons for this is Japan's urgent need to rid herself of pollution; for the outcry against the destruction of the environment has become an issue uniting Japanese opinion perhaps more solidly than at any other time since 1945. Again, 'aptly adapting herself to the circumstances', Japan will move with the times and accommodate herself to the new ground-rules dictated by the energy and resources crisis challenging the world.

As a former President of the Economic Research Institute in the Economic Planning Agency, Professor Hayashi is eminently qualified to discuss Japan's industrial policy-making. As he looks forward to further developments springing from the knowledge-intensive sector, he defines a new concept, a new plane in which the dehumanising processes are countered by what he calls 'soft science'. Taking due account of human behaviour and human desires, 'soft science' will create a 'societal software' which could be more humane, emit greater warmth and be less dispassionate than the West's cold and indiscriminate technology. Such is the vision of Japan's President of the Institute for Future Technology.

POLICY CONCEPT AND PRACTICE

I remember speaking to an executive of an international business organization after he had made a study of long-range planning by Japanese private enterprise. He said there was one thing which he simply could not understand.

'Every enterprise, including the government', he observed, 'always sets itself just one target whenever a plan is drawn up, and this target is always expressed as a single value, never as a flexible set of values. Japan has what is known as a free economy, it is true, and private enterprise generally enjoys a high degree of freedom and autonomy. Japan's economy, in fact, appears to have a tremendous amount of elasticity and dynamism, and not infrequently, as we all know, growth far exceeds targets set up in both the public and private sectors. And, from what I have heard, both the government and private enterprise use plans simply as guideposts.

'Thus, if plans are intended to be guideposts, wouldn't it be more appropriate to leave a certain margin of freedom for the actual goals? Yet there is no such planning margin. What puzzles me, therefore, is the fact that every plan is built around a fixed target leaving no room for manoeuvre. Is there any explanation for this phenomenon?'

In reply I said that the concept of the fixed target, the single value, was one of the characteristic features of Japanese society. In fact, it is precisely because Japan's economy is extremely elastic and dynamic that the projected targets, which we use as guideposts, have to be confined to one single target. For a Japanese businessman there is nothing contradictory about this.

First of all, when a goal or target is proposed in Japan, no one accepts it unreservedly. When the target is specifically set up as a guidepost, it is recognized from the outset that it contains a degree of flexibility, a margin of tolerance. However, interpretation of the actual degree of flexibility obviously differs from one person to another: and since this degree is not spelled out, the overall target assumes a variety of interpretations. On the other hand, if targets were originally presented with a specified degree of freedom, it would, on the contrary, be more difficult for everybody concerned to set up his own goals within the target area. In other words, because the socio-economic system of Japan is so extremely flexible and dynamic, narrow and very specific targets seem to flourish.

'Aptly adapting oneself to the circumstances' is a common Japanese expression and, as a people, the Japanese are exceptionally good at modifying their own standard of behaviour to fit changing circumstances. It might even be suggested that this behavioural characteristic is a basic national trait.

Generally speaking, in order to design a system of social adaptation which can react to any number of given changes in the external environment, we would have to rely on what are known as operation research methods. Luckily, for the Japanese it is much easier and simpler to adapt subconsciously rather than to follow a set of superimposed prescriptions. Thus, there is simply no point in providing for a degree of flexibility in long-range planning: it will automatically be assumed and interpreted accordingly.

During the last twenty years, therefore, long-range plans with single-value targets have continued to be used by governmental agencies, private enterprise and industrial organizations in spite of the fact that the targets frequently differ from the end result. This may appear strange to the casual observer, but the fact is that this form of planning has been found to be both useful and effective.

Centralization

Somewhat ironically, Japanese often refer to their prefectures (local government authorities) as having only a '30 per cent autonomy', suggesting that the financial independence of local government goes only about a third of the way. There is no denying that in overall terms a strong inclination towards power centralization exists in Japan.

France is also known as a state which revolves around centralized power – probably more so than any other country in Western Europe. The patterns of power centralization in Japan and France, however, differ greatly. To clarify this point, consider the long-range plans prepared by the governments of France and Japan respectively.

M. Pierre Massé, formerly Commissaire Général du Plan, commented on France's economic plans by saying that they were not quite as forceful as commands nor quite as timid as recommendations. He proposed instead that planning be described as *planification active.* While it is true that no peremptory orders are issued about production targets to individual private firms, it is also certain that the plans of the French government do more than serve as guideposts.

To begin with, the role of the French parliament in planning is quite clear, with well-defined limits of responsibility over the plans. All governmental economic plans must be brought before parliament for its approval, a prerequisite to implementation, and once these plans are approved the government supervises the limits on investment as appropriated in the budget plan. Even accepting the fact that France possesses a great number of nationalized enterprises, the central role played by parliament appears to be a characteristic peculiar to the French political structure.

The state in France is equipped not only with authority over all matters bearing on the national budget, such as financial investment, but it possesses also powerful tools to control private investment plans. For instance, companies requiring funds are serviced (through such agencies as the Fond de Développement Économique et Social–FDES) on a priority basis, which favours economic activities in line with the government's plans.

The situation in Japan is very different. The government, for example, is not required to obtain approval from the Diet (parliament) and in fact the Diet's role in the national budget is by no means clear. There is also no such organ as the FDES, and Japan's Economic Planning Agency is not vested with French-type guiding power to bring about plan targets. On the whole, the situation in Japan is more ambiguous and indefinite than it is in France, and even the government maintains the view that plans are guideposts for economic activity. M. Massé would no doubt say that planning in Japan has hardly gone beyond the stage of recommendation. However, Japan's economic plans are not at all insubstantial. Even though there is no institutionalized guiding system as such, effective guidance can still be given over economic activities.

The Economic Council, the organization which formulates Japan's economic plans, is much more simply structured than its French counterpart, and the economic plans themselves tend to be generalized and macroscopic. For this reason, the number of businessmen elected to the Council as representatives of industry is not large. Nor are there any official channels for exchanging information between industrial circles and the Economic Planning Agency, which acts as the secretariat for plan formulation and has administrative authority over plan implementation.

The Economic Planning Agency traditionally has had two characteristic features:

More than half its staff consists of personnel seconded from other governmental ministries and agencies.

A large number of personnel are delegated by private business organizations to work on the staff of the Agency.

Both private and public sectors are thus represented on the staff and they generally work together quite harmoniously. The personnel representing private enterprise come from almost all the key corporations in Japan, and serve as a kind of invisible information channel built in between the EPA and business circles. The importance of this invisible information channel as a catalyst in effective decision-making will be obvious–both for the government and for the private sector. There is another popular Japanese expression which goes, 'neither too close, nor too remote', and aptly describes the relationship between government and the private sector.

Decision-making in a homogeneous society

The term 'industrial policy' has only recently found its way into the documents of the Organization for Economic Co-operation and Development (OECD) and other official sources; this fact tempts one to assume that the idea behind the term is somewhat foreign to the western mind. On the other hand, the Japanese expression *sangyo seisaku* (industrial policy) has been well rooted in the Japanese language for many years.

In a free market society (which, let us assume, has reached maturity) one would expect to find an established market structure conforming to the principles of a capitalist economy, which would include the principle of fair competition. In such a society, there would be no need for the government to interfere with industrial activities; indeed, any such interference could well prove harmful. All this is tantamount to saying that any such free market society might well be expected to have established economic policies for social welfare but probably no form of industrial policy.

In a country like Japan, which has been trying to catch up with the West for about a hundred years, the circumstances have been different. Even if we focus just on the postwar era it is obvious that Japan could not have left its economy fully to the free play of the market mechanism. The need in postwar Japan was for continued rapid economic growth side by side with a shift of the industrial structure to the heavy and chemical industries.

The term 'industrial policy', applied literally, means governmental interference in business activities, and presupposes the existence of two mutually opposed groups. In Japan's case, however, governmental and business organizations tend naturally to work well together; there is a similar harmonious relationship between management and labour, which again is rather different from western practice. This feature is undoubtedly one of the distinguishing characteristics of Japanese society.

Labour unions in Japan are company-based, presenting a rather striking difference from the industry-based unions of the West. In Japan, one cannot really conceive of a union going so far as to force its company into bankruptcy; throughout the entire Japanese business world, from the smallest to the largest enterprises, management ordinarily spends considerable sums of money on health and welfare facilities solely for the benefit of the employees.

The recent demonstrations of 'people's power' in Japan, growing out of opposition to environmental destruction, are protests, more often than not, against the products and by-products of the heavy and chemical industries, or against the policy of rapid economic growth itself. However, it was not until the late 1960s that the respective interests of the state, of private enterprise, and of the individual came to be regarded as necessarily conflicting and contradictory.

THE FUTURE INDUSTRIAL STRUCTURE

Industrial development, therefore, obviously became the leading factor in Japan's search for economic development, even though the scarcity of indigenous natural resources meant that Japan launched itself into a new industrial era at a grave disadvantage as compared with the other industrialized nations of the world. Since Japan had to depend on imports for most of its raw materials, industrial facilities came to be located in coastal areas around the main ports, and there was a high price to pay for transport costs.

However, in the long run the location of industry largely along the coastal areas was to prove a great advantage. Consider the fact, for example, that both the Ruhr district in Germany and the Five Lakes district in the United States are located inland and have to depend, for the most part, on overland transport to ship finished products to domestic as well as to overseas markets. Even though such industrial areas do not incur high transport costs for the raw materials they consume, delivery shipment costs put them at a considerable disadvantage compared with the easy shipment facilities of Japan's coastal industries. Product shipment from coastal industrial areas goes mainly to marine transport, which, compared with overland transport, costs relatively little when the number of units shipped is high. Thus, even though Japan had to fund the importation of raw materials, it gradually gained a position of advantage in local transport terms relative to those western countries whose industrial centres were largely located inland.

Herein lies one of the main reasons why the Japanese iron and steel industry, which depends on imports for both iron ore and coal, has edged out many western countries from the international market-place in spite of their more abundant natural resources. In other words, Japan's scarcity of natural resources has, in the long run, turned out to be something of a natural advantage.

In itself, a large population means a high potential for domestic expansion. In the postwar period Japan's major objectives were demilitarization and democratization; the Japan Housing Corporation and Japan Highway Public Corporation, founded in the mid 1950s, played an important role in the shift of Japan's industrial structure to the heavy and chemical industries, in the rapid growth of industrial production capacity, and in the overall high tempo of economic development which continued unabated until the early 1970s.

The Japan Housing Corporation constructed large-scale apartment housing projects in all the main cities, and the Japan Highway Public Corporation modified and extended highway networks throughout the country. The government's investment in public enterprises clearly favoured the construction of highways and housing facilities, and one of the vital factors that made this huge building programme possible was the volume of spare cash released as a result of demilitarization. Labour unions were organized on a wide scale, but their struggles had limited economic objectives involving few political overtones, and this, too, bolstered the rapid rise in general living standards.

The homes of industrial workers, especially those living in public housing facilities, created a vast market for home electrical appliances, while the expanding highway networks augured well for the motor industry. In addition, Japan's 100 million population was an enormous and very attractive domestic market. These factors, together with the rapid growth in exports, gave Japan its competitive edge in world markets and contributed, of course, to increasingly greater demand for the products of the heavy and chemical industries.

In relation to supply, Japan's limited land mass proved highly advantageous. As previously mentioned, demilitarization accelerated the funneling of financial resources to public enterprises, which led to the breakthrough and the massive economic progress of the 1960s.

Private enterprises competed strongly in equipment investment in order to expand production capacity, since the larger the production volume, the larger the market share and thus supremacy in the market-place. The main competitive arena was in the field of plant and equipment investment, and commercial banks were ready to supply the required funds.

This company fund-raising operation has been another important, and also somewhat unusual, aspect of Japan's industrialization, for far from acting in a passive role, Japanese banks have virtually stood at the back doors of companies and actively fed funds into them. Such indirect financing through banking institutions is another strictly Japanese feature, one that can be traced back to the immediate postwar period.

Immediately after the war, Japan converted its currency to a new yen. Cash payment of salaries was limited to yen 500 a month, with the remaining portion frozen until otherwise decreed by the government. Thus, workers' deposit passbooks merely showed a growing amount of 'unexpendable savings'.

According to the official explanation, the intention underlying the measure was to reduce cash in circulation to control inflation, but in fact inflation was unaffected. Superficially, then, this particular government measure appeared to have no effect whatever, but it was in fact an industrial policy, and one which achieved great success. The assets frozen in this way were not really 'unexpendable', but were used to the best advantage by companies to develop their production capacity.

Although all the manufacturing companies were dismembered by the allied forces after the war, commercial banks were left virtually untouched. It is true, for instance, that Mitsubishi Bank changed its name to Chiyoda Bank at that time, but this was a change in name only. The Mitsubishi Bank remained the same in substance. Accordingly, the channels of access to the banking institutions remained open and, with the reserve of funds still being pumped in, the banks made combined use of both contacts and financial assets to reopen their services, now that they held a dominant position *vis-à-vis* the dismembered and weakened manufacturing companies. These circumstances present an interesting contrast with the situation in West Germany, which shared a similar fate during the postwar period. On the surface West Germany, too, implemented a currency conversion to a new mark and its conglomerates were also dissolved; but here the parallel stops.

The method adopted in West Germany for raising plant and equipment investment funds was an internal or self-financing method, and this contrasts with the indirect or bank-routed financing which has been prevalent in Japan. Thus a cause-and-effect type difference between production efficiency or equipment funding has come to distinguish the two countries.

Since the latter half of the 1960s, the internal and external environments of Japan have begun to show significant change. In specific terms, there is a shortage of young workers which upsets the traditional undercapitalized and labour-intensive structure of the economy and which, at the same time, is pushing the country closer to the western structural balance. Internationally, progress has been made by the Asiatic countries in the commencement of their own industrialization processes, and advanced countries elsewhere have regrouped under a number of new alliances such as the Organization for Economic Co-operation and Development (OECD). Japan, too, has shared in this change by joining OECD, and this resulted in new demands facing the country, such as the need for prompt capital and trade liberalization.

The move to knowledge-intensive industries

Industries are customarily grouped into categories such as iron and steel, chemicals, machinery, textiles, and so on. This classification is based on the flow of raw materials to finished products, and it is generally viewed as a vertical classification. But how would a horizontal classification be presented?

When industries are divided roughly into processes, they fall into three phases–the raw material stage, the processing stage and the assembly stage. The iron and steel industry, for example, may be considered to consist of a raw material stage covering iron ores, steel ingots and rolled steel, a processing stage in which steel materials are fabricated into machine parts, and an assembly stage in which various machine parts are combined to make up different machinery systems. It is generally true for industrialized countries that the growth of shipment at the processing stage exceeds that of the raw material stage, while the growth of shipment at the assembly stage is even greater than that at the processing stage. Japan is no exception. However, Japan's growth differential at the various stages is somewhat less sharp than that of the United States or West Germany, and it is conceivable that the differentials may widen in the future.

The raw material stage, the processing stage and the assembly stage may be characterized and distinguished in terms of the interrelationships with other external elements, as is shown in the following chart:

	Raw material stage	*Processing stage*	*Assembly stage*
Relation with cities	minimum	medium	maximum
Amount of information, know-how and software	minimum	medium	maximum
Outbreak of pollution	maximum	medium	minimum

The raw material stage is the one most likely to cause harm to the environment in the form of air or water pollution, and generally speaking this is less likely at the processing stage and least likely at the assembly stage. The raw material stage is also distinguished by being the most generalized in terms of knowledge, and as we proceed to the higher processing and assembly stages there tends to be more intensive and specialized application of information and know-how. In other words, the higher the stage, the higher the software content. Finally, as large cities tend to pool greater supplies of information and knowledge, industries become more predominantly urban in character as they move up from raw material to processing and then to the assembly stage. The chart above is a synoptic representation of these distinguishing features.

Japan has achieved its economic growth, therefore, on the basis of heavy and chemical industries in coastal areas in the vicinity of large ports, most of which are located in the neighbourhood of large cities. In relation to the classification set out above, the heavy and chemical industries place greater relative importance on the raw material stage.

This pattern is, however, extremely undesirable, since the proximity of these industries to urban areas creates concern about industrial pollution and inevitably results in the formation of anti-industry movements. Raw-material stage industries, therefore, should have been located in places more remote from human habitation. Of course it is easy to be wise after the event; on the other hand it was by no means obvious during the 1960s that these industrial locations were undesirable. On the contrary, as noted earlier, coastal location of industry was extremely well-suited to Japan's postwar growth.

For Japan, industrial development has led to industrial pollution and to the formation of anti-pollution movements; and in support of the anti-pollution movements the idea of the *polluter pays principle*, the so-called PPP rule, has gained considerable support, partly due to pressure from industrialized foreign countries for Japan's industries to take a more responsible environmental role. The PPP rule means that parties emitting pollutants are obliged to remove the pollution at their own expense, and if all countries follow it there will continue to be a basis for fair competition among the industrialized countries.

It also has to be admitted that, the more faithfully Japanese industries observe the PPP rule, the less powerful will be their international competitive capacity, for eradicating pollution is a gargantuan task in Japan.

It will be increasingly unrealistic for Japan to expect the primary product producing nations to supply their raw materials to Japan under the same arrangements that prevailed in the past, for most of these countries are developing countries, and this means that their basic desire is not raw material export but industrialization.

Japan is now faced with the need to review thoroughly the existing direction of its industrial policy–giving predominant emphasis, as it does, to the heavy and chemical industries which form the core of the industrial structure. Japan must adapt to the changing external and internal conditions now facing her.

The Industrial Structure Council, an advisory organ to the Ministry of International Trade and Industry (MITI), in a document entitled 'Industrial Policy for the 1970s', concluded that knowledge-intensive industries should dominate the industrial structure from now on. Converting the industrial structure towards knowledge-intensive implies a fundamental re-evaluation of the relative importance of the whole industrial system–or, more properly, a reassessment of the importance we place on each stage of industry–away from the raw material stage and towards the processing and especially the assembly stage: this is horizontal not vertical thinking.

What will be the future of the raw material and processing stages as progress is made in converting to knowledge-intensive industries? Neither of these stages will ever become irrelevant to or be entirely eliminated from Japan's industrial system. What is to be expected, however, is that these stages will gradually be transferred to those developing countries which have been supplying Japan's raw materials. In the process, the transfer must not be made in a form that could effectively amount to an export of pollution. Whatever the cost, the two stages should be transferred in a clean, pollution-free form and one which is adapted to the principle of recycling.

Distribution systems

The shift in the industrial structure towards knowledge-intensive industries will apply to the whole industrial gamut, primary and tertiary, as well as to the secondary 'assembly' sector.

In the distribution industry, which falls into the tertiary sector, the shift towards a knowledge-intensive structure has resulted in certain 'systematization' concepts. What does this mean? Formerly, for example, goods which were fed into the distribution stage as input remained the same goods when they emerged as output; in most cases goods did not change in shape or quality at the distribution stage. Today, however, it is no longer feasible or satisfactory simply to transport hardware from one place to another; it is now essential to introduce software techniques into the distribution system.

Yet a review of the present state of affairs reveals ironically that the shift of the distribution industry to a knowledge-intensive structure has so far failed to meet adequately the particular needs of individual consumers. In other words, the hard reality of poorly designed services runs quite contrary to what one might have expected. There is a good example in the case of cooling systems; the old electric fan was perfectly capable of being flexibly deployed and adjusted in any direction to meet any one individual's particular requirements (within the scope of the fan). But as fans were replaced by air conditioners, and air conditioners by central cooling systems, there has been a progressive increase of rigidity in the ways in which the equipment can meet the needs of any one individual. In short, the equipment reflects a progressive dehumanization. The implication here, *vis-à-vis* the distribution system, is that as things stand at present the software techniques that are being introduced into the distribution system are not particularly well designed.

It is clear that systems development in so many fields has not reached the full maturity of true systematization, although it is true that some remarkable progress has been made in the application of computers to the needs of society.

The reason for the still immature state of the systems serving society lies in the inadequacy of available software. In order to overcome this shortcoming it is essential to bring a much deeper meaning and interpretation to the existing software concept, and to develop what may be called 'societal software' in greater variety and volume. Such an attempt will necessarily call for fundamental studies on such themes as the relation between human behaviour and human desires and the relation between human desires and those organized functions serving society. Studies in this area of research are called 'soft science'.

To sum up, it is now essential to provide for the development of 'societal software' on the basis of soft science, to design various forms of societal systems that fully incorporate such societal software, and to integrate as fully as possible such societal systems into society at large. This calls for a new area of technology – 'soft technology'. A rapid development and introduction of 'soft technology' could help solve some of the major problems that confront Japan today.

3 Business and the Law

EUGENE H. LEE

INTRODUCTION

For the ordinary citizen, including the businessman, understanding the role and application of law in his own country is frequently a tortuous, perplexing exercise. But in so far as the businessman operates within a specific framework of law it is his business to familiarize himself with its tenets where they are relevant to his affairs. Often enough this legal knowledge and perspective is established for him by a professional legal consultant.

In Japan, however, this form of indirect 'acquaintance' with the law is inadequate; whatever the business arrangements–a tie-up with a trading company, the export of know-how, a direct investment–a clear personal grasp of both the facts and the psychology of the law is essential. It is essential because its logic is just as 'foreign' as the Japanese language itself.

As Eugene Lee states in his opening section, from a western point of view one quickly becomes convinced that the law, as a way of life, does not exist in Japan. In that western law is based on fundamental *rights* pertaining to the individual and to society, Japan has no law. Rather, it has responsibilities, *duties*, incumbent on both the individual and on the community. It is in this way that Japanese justice is achieved. And justice is achieved in the West–but the route and the reasoning have no parallel.

This chapter also traces the historical development of law in Japan and identifies the various western codes that were adopted and translated in their entirety towards the end of the last century and after the Second World War. Thus, Japan can be said to possess all the accoutrements of western codes of justice. This is a fact. But it is also a fact that Japan has fewer lawyers per head of population than any other advanced industrial country. Litigation, which implies a confrontation over 'rights', is instinctively shunned by the Japanese.

The great healer in Japan is not the law and the public legal thoroughfares of the land, but the private paths of compromise and conciliation. This constant appeal to mediation is as much a part of business, government and daily social life as it is of traditional legal practice.

JAPAN'S UNWRITTEN LAW

Perhaps the most significant thing about the role of law in business in Japan is its relative unimportance.

What is difficult for the foreigner to understand is how a 'free' nation can operate in a fair, efficient manner without law playing a central role. Yet some of the most innovative and complicated financial and business sorties the world has yet witnessed are now being pioneered in Tokyo–generally with little reference to law and no consultation with lawyers. Business terms, for example, can be changed rapidly and pragmatically to suit changes in circumstances, and the largest financial deals can be closed without ever questioning the credit of the borrower or requesting security to support the transaction.

Until very recently, Japanese companies have not used western-type contracts for their ordinary transactions and even today some organizations place only minimal significance on the written agreement, believing that a good mutual relationship will sort out any misunderstandings or required amendments. Traditionally, in fact, Japanese lawyers have not provided business counselling services as do lawyers in the West.

What is it then, that provides the frame around which Japan's surging business world revolves?

The inherent contradiction of a highly integrated and orderly society operating without a clearly structured legal system obviously comes as a shock to western minds.

First-hand experience with Japan, however, soon shows that the Japanese way of life is itself not conducive to the development of independent advisers and counsellors. Three obvious reasons come to mind:

The close ties that exist between employer and employee.
The tradition of encouraging employees to be generalists and not specialists.
The concept of personal 'duties' as opposed to individual 'rights'.

Business is a 'family'

In Japan the company functions as a family; automatic loyalty and lifetime membership are expected from the employee in return for a secure position and a warm sense of belonging. The company is not only the centre of work, it is the centre of life itself–the heart of all the social activities of its members. Work in the western sense is merely one facet of the company. The employee's natural family assumes a role secondary to that of the company because it is not part of one's company group and is, therefore, an 'outsider'. It is the exclusivity of the company group that makes it so difficult to deal with outsiders, including placing confidence and trust in outside advisers. The family's future planning is the family's responsibility and an outsider is not likely to have the same degree of concern for its welfare. Thus as a family the company keeps its own counsel, mobilizing its own dedicated ranks to provide the research and evaluation necessary to undertake new projects rather than relying too much on outside consultants.

Generalists

Surprisingly, the system of lifetime employment has not led to the development of specialists* within Japanese companies. On the contrary, great pains are taken to develop competent generalists capable of handling any job function within the

*Many young Japanese graduates are today requesting opportunities to specialize within business or industry in order to satisfy personal talent and inclination. The larger international companies appear to be recognizing a need to develop more 'individual' specialist operators.

organization. This process begins at school and college. The first half of a university course is of a 'general studies' character: every student, whatever his speciality, takes mathematics and a science through to university level. Further 'generalist' training continues at work in a company through regular job rotation and training programmes, which seldom have any relationship to specific job assignments.

The need for outside specialists, therefore, is minimal. The professional generalist is accustomed to plunging into unknown fields to accumulate the information required to make a decision and takes his daunting task for granted.

Advisers

Except perhaps for the role traditionally played by elderly men as mediators and advisers, Japan has almost no tradition of personal advisers. In fact there were no lawyers or official legal representatives in Japan until the late 1800s. Even today one of the largest groups of consultants/advisers is made up of retired government officials and senior company executives who follow in the tradition of offering the services of age and experience for guidance and conciliation. These 'elder statesmen' are often engaged by a company or company group. In the absence of lawyers in Japan, the smooth running of the system, the constant attention to all the details involved in maintaining a steady relationship, take the place of the law as we define it.

'Duties' and 'rights'

What is likely to cause a great deal of confusion for the foreign businessman is his insistence on the 'rights' due to him in his dealings with government or any other body. The concept of 'rights' in Japan is still relatively underdeveloped. In place of rights, duties are the dominant concern. In other words, each party knows his duties and is extremely concerned about performing them properly. Failure to do so could result in a loss of face. The Japanese system is based on the view that if everyone properly performs his duties, there is no need for rights as such to be exercised and this emphasis is still predominant.

BACKGROUND TO THE LEGAL SYSTEM

In the 1870s, after more than two centuries of isolation, the new Japanese government sponsored missions to leading western states to study their legal systems and make recommendations as to how Japanese law should be revised. At the same time leading foreign legal scholars were invited to Japan to study its needs and make recommendations. This analysis resulted in the adoption of a Criminal Code in 1880 (and in 1882 the adoption of a Code of Criminal Procedure) along the lines of the French *Code Napoléon*. In effect, the Japanese codes were direct translations of the French codes. The scholars involved in the translation found great difficulty with the words 'rights' (a term at the very heart of western legal concepts), since no such word existed in Japanese. After years of debate between proponents of English and French law, the government compromised and adopted the German Civil (1898) and Commercial Codes (1899) instead. These laws were also translated into Japanese in their entirety.

The technique of adopting foreign law was well suited to the purposes of the Japanese leaders–it enabled Japan to boast it had a modern legal system, and strengthened its claims for membership of the circle of the world's advanced countries. In practice it was left to actual dispute resolution to rationalize the differences between Japanese social custom and the new modern legal system. The gap between these two is undoubtedly one of the reasons why westerners have so many difficulties in adjusting to the law in Japan.

The next most powerful outside influence on Japanese law came from America during the period immediately following the Second World War. The most dramatic and influential of these developments was the new constitution, drafted along American lines, which guaranteed a wide range of human and personal rights that had never really been a part of Japanese thinking. All the major legal codes had then to be fully revised to make them consistent with the new constitution. Additionally, some laws, such as the Corporation Act, were replaced with new laws that followed the American model. Many new laws, such as the Antimonopoly Law and the Securities Act, were also enacted at that time.

Features of Japanese law

As a total system, the Japanese legal code continues to resemble the European continental civil law system far more closely than Anglo-American common law. As in continental Europe, the basic codes comprise the core of the laws, and these codes still resemble most closely their French and German models. The judiciary is well developed with a very professional career judge corps. In theory, previous court rulings do not constitute a binding precedent on current cases as they do in England or the United States; but, in practice, judges carefully research previous court decisions and act accordingly.

Scholarly opinion is looked to as a source of law and is widely cited in court as persuasive evidence. This practice is much more common than in the United States or England. General principles of equity are set forth in the codes and call for good faith and justice to prevail at all times.

The administration of justice in Japan is 'judge-orientated' rather than 'lawyer-orientated'. In the United States or England one is treated to the spectacle of competing lawyers cleverly representing their clients' interests before a judge whose role is largely limited to refereeing the competition between the lawyers. In Japan, the primary goal of judges is seen as a search for the truth. They take an active role in interviewing the parties and witnesses, suggesting new witnesses who should be called to testify, or even researching the legal background for the lawyers. This system tends to protect the interests of litigants from being damaged by mistakes made by their own lawyers and promotes the function of a trial as a search for truth. Furthermore, it fits nicely into the Japanese paternalistic system. In fact, there are no jury trials; the judge is left with primary authority and responsibility.

Conciliation

The administration of justice in Japan is based on conciliation. Traditionally, and still today, conciliation is the preferred means of dispute settlement and the courts are used comparatively seldom. Instead, in the case of a dispute, Japanese normally prefer to work through a go-between. Training in law would not be a requisite qualification for such a person. Most importantly, he should be someone respected by both sides. Normally, he is an older person, perhaps retired. His function is to listen to both sides, suggesting areas for possible compromise and eventually working out a solution which both parties can accept.

The legal system in Japan, therefore, involves comparatively few people: Japan has only one lawyer for every 12,500 people, compared to West Germany with one lawyer for every 3000 people, or Switzerland with one lawyer for every 2400 people. The judiciary is also proportionately small. This difference in numbers reflects the fact that Japan still uses traditional techniques for solving the problems that lawyers solve in the West. The small number of lawyers practising in Japan is almost entirely 'trial lawyers' and no one would think of consulting a lawyer until a problem has become so acute that litigation is imperative–a situation that rarely occurs.

LAW AND THE GOVERNMENT

Other sources of law in its broad sense, and certainly in the sense that interests businessmen, are the various administrative agencies of the Japanese government. The government agencies normally initiate draft legislation; they also have the authority to enact whatever regulations are felt necessary to interpret formal laws and this authority is usually unlimited. Usually, there is no need for government agencies to make available the guidelines of the standards they apply in deciding certain cases; for that matter there is no requirement that they have standards at all. There is no such thing as an administrative court to hear appeals from administrative decisions, nor is it usual or even advisable to take a lawyer along when visiting officials. Japanese companies succeed by appealing to the agency's *sense of duty*; they do not demand their *rights*.

There is no requirement that a government agency give reasons for its decisions, nor is there a convenient procedure for challenging an administrative decision. Basically, the government has broad, discretionary powers. These discretionary powers, however, can also be beneficial to the foreign investor since the government is not stopped from liberalizing certain industries to foreign investment on a *de facto* basis before these industries have been included in the announced liberalization programme.

Liberalization

The formal restrictions on foreign business in Japan can be formidable, although these restrictions have been considerably relaxed over the past few years. In 1967, for example, in the area of direct capital foreign investment, Japan embarked upon a liberalization programme of selected industries. Initially only a handful of industries was opened to 100 per cent foreign investment, while a somewhat larger number of industries was opened to 50 per cent foreign investment, which, of course, means the use of joint venture companies. Following the last round of liberalization policies (1 May 1973), all lines of industry are to be opened to 100 per cent foreign investment except those involving agriculture, leather, petroleum and retail businesses having more than eleven stores. (However, there still remain a further seventeen lines, currently limited to 50 per cent foreign investment, but scheduled to be fully liberalized by 31 March 1976.) Investment in the relevant liberalized industries is granted what is called 'automatic approval'. This does not mean that the approval is granted on the spot. First, formal and detailed applications are submitted to the appropriate government agencies through the Bank of Japan. If, after study, no special difficulties are found in the application, approval will be forthcoming within approximately 30 days of submission of the application. It should be noted that the liberalization guidelines apply only to companies to be newly established and not to investments in existing companies.

'Irregularities'

A variety of 'irregularities' can result in an application being removed from the automatic approval system. For instance, an automatic approval for establishing a joint venture company may not be forthcoming where the prospective partner has had no experience in the same business as the proposed company.

Sony was once considered inexperienced in the record industry and denied automatic approval of the establishment of a joint venture company with the Columbia Broadcasting System (CBS). Automatic approval may also be refused in cases where the investment is in an already established company instead of a company to be newly established, or where the Japanese partner is expected to transfer some of its own facilities to the new company as its contribution.

The size of the investment must conform to the government's unwritten standards. If the investment is too large there may be a fear that the new company will endanger existing operations in Japan and the government may insist that the amount of proposed capital be reduced. Additionally, in the case of joint venture companies, the authorities take great care to ensure that the foreign partner will not be able to exert his influence in a way inconsistent with the regulations limiting the amount of the investment of the foreign side to 50 per cent. In practical terms, this means that the foreign side cannot have greater participation in management than its share ownership warrants.

In spite of increased international pressures on Japan to liberalize, it still takes time for liberalization (in a western sense) to get under way because of the 'duty' of government to protect those under its care. It is worth keeping in mind that liberalization is not the basic issue; the intimate co-operation between government and industry in Japan naturally leads to a position in which government is given the authority to review and approve a wide range of business proposals. A wide-sweeping liberalization would not reduce the role of the government in domestic business. The foreign company in Japan must learn to live with 'administrative guidance'–*gyosei shido*–and this is not an easy task.

Administrative guidance

The term 'administrative guidance' is used to refer to the way in which government, in one form or another, directs business along certain paths. In effect, it provides the lubrication that keeps all the working parts of the Japanese business machine in smooth operating condition. Foreign businessmen in Japan sometimes feel that administrative guidance is a tool devised to blunt the activities of foreign enterprises in Japan. This is certainly not the case. Administrative guidance has long been an integral part of the Japanese system. It is basic to Japan–and thus it is Japan itself that provides the challenge to foreign businessmen.

The first time the foreigner is likely to be confronted with administrative guidance is in connection with the filing of an application for permission to do business in Japan, say in the form of a branch office, joint venture company or wholly-owned subsidiary. Government approval to establish such offices is required by law; however, the procedure and standards for approval are part of the policies of the government agencies concerned. Sometimes the relevant policy may have been revealed in part to the public, i.e. the liberalization programme, but at other times no information has been made public at all and the government's policy is administered according to *naiki* (internal standards written only to guide the bureaucracy). Occasionally, it seems that not even such *naiki* exist and individual departments, or even individual officials, establish their own guidelines.

Where particular government policies have been publicly announced, unpublished exceptions to the basic policy may also exist and in practice substantially alter the announced policy.

LAW AND THE BUSINESSMAN

The easiest way to do business in Japan is to sell directly to a trading company or through a local distributor. Since perhaps the greatest difficulty in doing business in Japan is the difference in social and business customs, this indirect approach can certainly be the least frustrating. Tariffs in some industries, however, and the imposition of several levels of middlemen (each of whom takes his own profit before the goods finally reach the consumer) may make the imported foreign product no longer competitive.

Another point sometimes overlooked is that the ubiquitous trading companies may handle competitive products manufactured by several companies. If one of these companies is related to the trading company itself, which is often the case, it is not difficult to imagine which product is most vigorously promoted to wholesalers.

Local branch offices

If the company is engaging in 'commercial transactions' in Japan there is a legal requirement that a branch office be registered; this entails two separate formalities. One is the need to send a formal notification to the Bank of Japan. This notification has the nature of an approval since unless it is accepted by the government agencies concerned the second formality, registration at the corporate registry, cannot be accomplished. The registration of a branch makes good sense, even if the representative is not to engage in commercial transactions, since without registration the representative has no legal status in Japan and may confront difficulties in such simple matters as establishing a bank account, receiving funds from abroad, leasing office space, buying a car, etc.

Branches can be divided into two types: operating branches and representative branches. An operating branch will presumably make a profit from its activities within Japan and thus will be responsible for full corporate tax. Government screening of proposals to establish operating branches is strict; otherwise, it might be possible to achieve through a branch office what would not be allowed through a direct capital investment (see page 39).

The registration of a local branch office normally secures government acceptance relatively easily. However, the activities of the branch are strictly limited to what is approved in the application for registration and any extension or modification of activities must be specifically approved by the government. The local branch does have the advantage of providing a visible presence and gives an appropriate level of prestige and sophistication to the branch manager's functions.

Contracting

All international contracts must be filed with the Fair Trade Commission (FTC). Basically an 'international contract' is any contract between a Japanese and a foreign party. This filing does not presume that FTC approval is needed for the contract to be binding but rather allows the FTC to screen all contracts to determine whether a violation of the Antimonopoly Law* has occurred. Once an agreement is filed with the FTC it becomes a case of 'no news is good news', since the parties are never contacted by the FTC unless some violation is suspected.

Most of the problems that the FTC has found in reviewing international contracts concern licence agreements which convey technology or know-how to Japanese companies. The most common of these have involved either royalty-free grant-backs of technology (situations where the Japanese licensee must give the foreign licensor rights to any improvements on the technology that he creates), exclusivity requirements (under which the Japanese party is prohibited from trading in competitive goods), or other unusual requirements such as requiring the Japanese licensee to buy all his needs for raw materials or intermediate parts from the licensor (see also patent protection, page 45). During the postwar period Japan relied heavily on foreign technology licensing for swift industrial rehabilitation; these policies were felt necessary to prevent technology-hungry Japanese companies from agreeing to unreasonable restrictions. Basically, the FTC seems to be applying a sort of 'fundamental fairness' rule in evaluating agreements. If the proposed restriction is balanced by a like restriction on the foreign licensor, approval by the FTC might be given. However, if the restrictions are entirely against the Japanese licensee, the FTC is likely to ask that the parties revise the agreement to comply with its standards.

Marketing

Consumer interests are still not particularly well represented in Japan, although there have been some significant moves recently. Antimonopoly Law regulations do give protection to consumers through standards imposed on advertising and labelling, and the FTC has taken a positive stand to ensure that the public is better informed of the ingredients or components used in consumer products.

*The Japanese Antimonopoly Law, based on American legislation, was enacted soon after the Second World War. But since economic philosophy in Japan differs widely from the American approach, the development and enforcement of Japanese antimonopoly regulations vary substantially from the Americal format.

The channels of marketing in Japan are complex. Usually a multi-tiered distribution system is used whereby the product passes through several different wholesalers before finally reaching the retailer. The FTC tries to regulate relationships between manufacturer, wholesaler and retailer in order to promote price competition and protect consumers. For instance retail price fixing is generally prohibited, as are exclusive sales arrangements. Incentives to retailers to sell the products of a certain manufacturer, such as rebates, prizes, etc., are also carefully regulated. Foreign businessmen have sometimes mistakenly criticized the FTC for attacking foreign business. In fact, the FTC plays an important role in regulating the activities of Japanese firms as well.

Trademark protection

Japan has a well-developed trademark law which offers full protection to marks which have been registered in Japan. There have been reports of instances in which certain famous foreign trademarks have been registered by third parties in Japan and then offered for sale to the true owner of the trademark. Despite the publicity, the instances of this happening are rare enough. On occasion, the Japanese courts have even stepped in to prevent the misuse of well-known foreign marks in order to avoid confusing the Japanese consumer. Even so, if trademark protection is desired, it is wise to register the mark with the Patent Office as soon as possible.

Once a trademark has been registered, the trademark owner can use either the trademark itself or license it to a third party. The licensing of a trademark from a foreign licensor to a Japanese licensee technically requires approval from the Bank of Japan (BOJ). In recent years, approval of trademark licences has been easy to obtain as long as it contains no 'unusual' provisions. In the past, trademark licences have often been granted to sole distributors of foreign products in Japan. Through his trademark licence the distributor was able to prevent importation into Japan of products bearing marks infringing upon the registered trademark or even genuine products imported by another party. This system gave the sole distributor a virtual monopoly of the product in Japan and sometimes tempted the distributor to take advantage of his sales monopoly by maintaining high prices. Under a recent court decision, exclusive trademark rights can no longer be used to prevent parallel importation of genuine products into Japan. This decision has opened the way for retail outlets, such as department stores, to by-pass exclusive distributors of foreign products in Japan and to import genuine goods directly from abroad.

Patent protection

Patents are obtained in Japan through registration with the Patent Office, and foreign applicants are entitled to the same treatment as Japanese. Patent rights can be enforced by actions for damages, suits for injunctions ordering cessation of acts of infringement, and, where relevant, petitions to customs authorities to disallow importation of infringing goods. Patent litigation is a long and difficult ordeal anywhere, and Japan is no exception. The very process of this type of litigation gravitates towards compromise and Japanese judges seem to encourage private compromise settlements where possible. Naturally, all proceedings in the Japanese courts are conducted in the Japanese language.

Patents can be licensed either on an exclusive or non-exclusive basis. Where a foreigner is licensing his rights under Japanese patents to a party in Japan, prior approval of the Japanese government is necessary. These approvals can usually be obtained within thirty days of filing the application. In some cases, the screening of the licence agreement by the Fair Trade Commission can pose a larger problem than the search for basic government approval, since the FTC is the watchdog charged with preventing unfair business practices. In the case of licence agreements the FTC pays special attention to provisions which give the foreign licensor grant-backs of improvements of the licensed technology that may be conceived by the licensee, where the licensee is unreasonably prevented from dealing in competitive goods, or where there are restrictions on exporting licensed products from Japan. Where the FTC finds such restrictions are unfair, it may request the parties to amend their agreements accordingly.

Contractual choice of law and court

International business contracts normally determine how the law is to be applied in case of a dispute over contracts, and, less frequently, select the court which is to resolve any disputes arising out of the agreement.

Japanese law permits a certain amount of autonomy to the parties concerned in the choice of law (i.e. the legal code of any country) which is to govern the contract. Clearly, the code of law which is chosen should not conflict with Japanese public policy.

Arbitration

International contracts involving business in Japan normally provide for arbitration in case of future disputes arising from the agreement. The existence of such an arbitration clause is enforceable and can be used as a defence in a court action over the contract.

Once the arbitrators have rendered an award it is very difficult to challenge it. Court procedures can be invoked, of course, to enforce the arbitrators' judgement. Yet, in spite of the widespread use of arbitration clauses in international contracts concerning Japan, there has been surprisingly little use of arbitration as a technique for the settling of disputes. The Japan Commercial Arbitration Association provides rules and facilities for arbitration hearings; but it appears that nearly all disputes are settled before arbitration awards are actually rendered. Thus in arbitration as in litigation private conciliation and settlement are the most commonly used techniques for actually resolving a dispute.

The business contract

Negotiations are a difficult part of any business transaction and for the foreign businessman in Japan they pose some special problems. As can be seen in Chapter 7 (see especially pp. 135–42), there is a fundamental difference in attitudes towards contracting–highlighted by a recent comment from a Japanese that the 'trouble with foreign businessmen is that they try to negotiate a contract while Japanese try to negotiate a relationship'. The Japanese seek a *relationship* that is continuing and dynamic. Then problems can be solved on a case by case basis out of the framework of the relationship. Westerners, while concerned with good relationships, emphasize *the contract* as the vehicle for interpreting and solving problems related to the transaction and thus emphasize the text of the contract during negotiations.

This difference in objectives can lead to difficulties during the course of negotiations. While the Japanese side is striving to 'get to know' the foreign negotiators and the organization they represent in order to determine the nature of the relationship that can be developed, the foreign negotiators invariably approach the discussions intent on finalizing a business 'deal' and, eventually, a contract. As negotiations drag on, with little being accomplished in western terms, the visiting businessman may sometimes feel that the Japanese side is simply not interested and is too polite to say so. In actual fact, the Japanese side is probably playing for more time to evaluate the relationship and to let these evaluations pass through a complex decision-making process (see Chapter 1, p. 9). However, once the decision to proceed is made, the foreign businessman often finds that he cannot move nearly as quickly as the Japanese in ironing out details and implementing the agreement.

The difference in attitudes towards contracting can also lead to different approaches in interpreting the transaction or in resolving disputes. For instance, if a change in circumstances affects the negotiated transaction, the Japanese side (thinking in terms of a relationship rather than a contract) is often quick to request a change in terms so that the transaction can continue to be attractive. The fact that a hard bargained contract has already been signed seems only incidental. Meanwhile, the foreign side equates the concept of 'contract' and 'morality' and is shocked by the request for a change in terms.

This reliance upon the 'relationship' is a matter of Japanese custom and not law. In terms of law the situation in Japan is substantially the same as in the West and it is almost impossible for one side to force the revision of a contract because of a change in circumstances. This is an example of an area in which one hundred years of living under western law has neither changed Japanese traditional values nor produced any real harmony between borrowed law and traditional concepts.

Conclusion

There exists a legal framework, based almost entirely on European and American models, which provides a familiar foundation for commercial transactions. The judiciary is well educated, honest and at least as free from discrimination as fellow jurists in other countries. However, the difference in Japanese attitudes towards law, as illustrated by the infrequent use of lawyers and the courts, points to a very different social ethic regarding 'law' and its uses. Japanese companies look to government to provide positive action and to fulfil its *duty* to look after those under its care: this understanding generates an interdependence between government and business that can survive healthily without any reliance on western-style administrative law, based on individual *rights*.

4 Japan's Banking and Investment Systems

IWAO HOSHII

INTRODUCTION

The financing of Japan's enormous postwar economic expansion has been a hardly less significant accomplishment than the build-up of the country's productive apparatus and worldwide distribution system which have made Japan one of the leading industrial nations. At times, the financing operations relied on for promoting economic growth have been highly unorthodox and monetary policy has had to bear more than its fair burden in the periodic adjustments necessitated by the overheating of the economy. Despite its shortcomings and weaknesses, Japan's financial system has proved itself equal to the task.

To a certain extent, financial capitalism preceded industrial capitalism in the development of modern Japan and financiers played a significant role as initiators of industrial and commercial ventures. Because of the low standard of living of the farmers and the industrial workers, thrift institutions grew more slowly than the industry-orientated banks and contributed little to the improvement of social conditions, although they responded to the traditional frugality of the people.

The emphasis of the city banks on retail banking has somewhat altered their big-business image but has not changed their position as economic power centres. Basically, Japan's economy remains very much compartmentalized, despite the recent flurry of diversification, and the banking structure reflects the neatly circumscribed segments of the economy.

There is a fundamental difference between the Japanese system and the British 'stock-market-orientated' system because Japan's stock market is closer to Monte Carlo than to

Threadneedle Street and has hardly been used for strategic acquisitions. Again, unlike the German bank-based conglomorates, the Japanese groups are not the result of bank-directed investment strategy and bank-supervised corporate management. There is some similarity between Japan and France in the influence of the bureaucracy on the financial system, but while the Japanese Ministry of Finance and the Bank of Japan have a powerful influence on the daily working of all financial institutions, the business leaders have a decisive voice in all important policy decisions of the government affecting business and finance.

The West may have nothing to learn from Japan's experience but an understanding of the country's somewhat complex financial organization may be of some use to the businessman who has commercial or financial connections with Japan.

FINANCIAL INSTITUTIONS

THE BANK OF JAPAN

The Bank of Japan, founded in 1882, was modelled on the statute of the Banque Nationale de la Belgique. In 1942 the original BOJ Regulations were modified by a 'Bank of Japan Law', which greatly strengthened the supervisory powers of the government.

An amendment to the Bank of Japan Law, passed in 1949, established a Policy Board for formulating the basic bank policies, fixing the official discount rate, determining loan collateral and regulating the deposit reserve requirements. The board consists of seven members: the Governor of the Bank of Japan and one representative each of the Ministry of Finance, the Economic Planning Agency, the city banks, local banks, commerce and industry, and agriculture. The last four members are appointed by the cabinet with the approval of both houses of the Diet for a term of four years.

A revision of the Bank of Japan's structure has been debated off and on since 1957, but, so far, all reform plans have foundered on the problem of the 'neutrality' of the bank, i.e. its independence of the government. In practice, decisions concerning changes in the official discount rate and the deposit reserve requirements are always taken in consultation with the Ministry of Finance and the bank's credit policies follow rather than precede the government's economic policies. Traditionally, the post of governor has been held alternately by an official of the Bank of Japan and the Ministry of Finance although, occasionally, private bankers have been appointed to this post.

Note issue

The Bank of Japan, which is both the government's bank and the banker's bank, is the country's sole note-issuing institution. The legal restrictions on note issue, however, have become meaningless. According to the provisions of the Finance Law of 1947, the Bank of Japan cannot subscribe to public bond issues and give loans to the government (except if the Diet agrees to make an exception), but the bank can purchase national bonds once they have been issued. Credit transactions with the government consist mainly of short-term advances against Treasury bills, so-called food bills (bills issued by the Food Control Special Account for financing the government's rice purchases) and foreign exchange fund bills (issued for financing purchases of foreign exchange).

Only the city banks, the long-term credit banks, a limited number of local and mutual banks, the securities finance corporations and the short-term money (call money) brokers have access to direct central bank credit. Through these institutions, however, the Bank of Japan also lends to other corporations, particularly in the case of 'relief financing' (rescue operations) under Article 25 of the Bank of Japan Law. During the 1950s, central bank credit provided a considerable part of the funds required for economic expansion which resulted in the 'overloans' of the city banks. Although the Bank used changes in the official discount rate and high penalty rates for regulating credit, it relied mainly on its 'window guidance' (direct credit controls) for curbing the advances of the city banks. But in view of the spiralling loan balances (in May 1962, the BOJ's outstanding loan balances, yen 1301·2 billion, exceeded the note circulation–yen 1258·8 billion), the bank switched to a system making open market operations the main form of money supply.

Credit regulation

Between 1967 and 1971, the Bank regulated credit to the city banks by what was called 'position guidance', i.e. the increase in lending was regulated on the basis of the total of internal funds and borrowings of each bank. When the city banks relied increasingly on the call market for raising loanable funds, the Bank of Japan gave short-term loans to call brokers and also used Treasury bills for market operations involving call brokers. In early 1973, the Bank increased the rate of reserve deposit requirements three times in order to reduce the loanable funds of the city and local banks.

With the appearance of the large surpluses in Japan's balance of payments in 1968, central bank credit began to lose much of its significance for the money supply, but the Bank's direct credit control in the form of ceilings on the expansion of bank lending fixed for each quarter still plays an important role in the banks' anticyclical monetary policy. At the end of March 1972, bank borrowing from the Bank of Japan was down to yen 599·5 billion compared with a peak of yen 2365·8 billion at the end of January 1971.

PRIVATE FINANCIAL INSTITUTIONS

Depending on their legal foundation, Japanese banks are divided into *ordinary banks, long-term credit banks,* and *foreign exchange banks.* The division of ordinary banks into *city, local* and *trust* banks has no legal foundation although the older trust banks were originally organized on the basis of the Trust Company Law. City banks were so called because of the location of their head offices. Now the term has become a label for banks treated as a group for administrative purposes.

Savings banks

Japan has no savings banks in the strict sense. In 1921 savings banks had numbered 636, but at the end of the Second World War only four were left and they were reorganized as ordinary banks. The mutual loan and savings banks are derived from a popular form of credit institution peculiar to Japan called *mujin*, a combination of instalment savings and mutual loans distributed among the participants through drawings or biddings.

The postwar banking system was supposedly based on the separation of short-term from long-term financing. Before the war, long-term credit was chiefly supplied by the so-called special banks which were permitted to combine the acceptance of deposits with the issuance of debentures. The Occupation authorities insisted on the abolition of these banks. A number of special banks were converted into ordinary banks while the remaining institutions were liquidated. Since the institutional arrangements for the supply of long-term funds were insufficient, the government enacted a law giving banks authority to issue debentures. Outwardly the law applied to all banks (because of the principle of legal equality) but the government's real intention was to make the issuance of debentures possible for institutions that had actually been emission banks. Since this situation was somewhat too untidy to be solved by 'administrative guidance' (see Chapter 5, p. 96ff.) the Long-Term Credit Bank Law was enacted in 1952 and three banks have been organized on the basis of this law (see below, page 55).

Foreign exchange banks

The revival of the prewar special bank system was completed in 1964 with the passage of the Foreign Exchange Bank Law. During the Occupation, the foreign exchange business was largely in the hands of the Japanese branches of foreign banks but with the increase in foreign trade, the 'authorized foreign exchange banks', designated by the Minister of Finance on the basis of the Foreign Exchange and Foreign Trade Control Law of 1949, were able to expand their foreign business.

In order to justify the government's preferential treatment of the Bank of Tokyo, the Foreign Exchange Bank Law was enacted in 1954 and the Bank of Tokyo became the only bank organized under this law. In 1962 the law was amended so as to authorize the issuance of debentures up to five times the bank's capital.

The Law Concerning Mergers and Changes of Status of Financial Institutions, passed in 1968, permitted existing institutions to remodel themselves and made possible mergers of financial institutions organized under different laws. The first mutual bank to take advantage of the law was Japan Mutual Bank (then the largest) which became an ordinary bank and assumed the name of Taiyo Bank.

City banks

City banks now number thirteen (including the Bank of Tokyo) but the Bank of Kobe and Taiyo Bank have concluded a merger agreement which went into effect on 1 October 1973. Roughly speaking, the city banks account for one-third of all offices and 60 per cent of the funds of all commercial banks. As of 31 March 1973, the city banks had 51·5 per cent of all accounts and 59·9 per cent of the deposit balances of all banks, the local banks 47·2 per cent of the accounts and 32·7 per cent of the deposit balances, which means that, on average, the deposits of the city banks per account were much higher than those of the local banks (yen 570,507 as against yen 339,989).

Most city banks have a nationwide network of branch offices. The head offices of most local banks are located at the seats of the prefectural governments and most of their branch offices are in the prefecture in which their head office is situated (Japan is divided into 47 prefectures). This system is the outcome of a deliberate policy of concentration pursued by the government between the two world wars resulting in a dramatic cutback in the number of banks down from a peak of 1867 in 1901 to 61 at the end of 1945. The pattern which the government created by this consolidation conformed more or less to the principle of 'one prefecture, one bank' and only the expansionary thrust of the city banks gave the provincial towns a choice of banks.

In addition to the trust banks and insurance companies belonging to their respective group, the leading city banks also have close relations with certain local and mutual banks, on which they rely particularly for the supply of funds. All large enterprises are clients of one or more city bank and over half their outstanding loan balances exceed yen 100 million.

Local banks

The business sphere of the local banks is limited, their main customers being medium-sized or small local enterprises. As of 30 June 1973, deposits by individuals accounted for 49·3 per cent of their deposit balances, and while the difference in the overall share of time deposits in local banks (59·8 per cent) and city banks (54·2 per cent) was not large, individual deposits accounted for 58·4 per cent of the time deposits of local banks, against 42·0 per cent of those of city banks. The share of the time deposits of general corporations was 51·3 per cent for city banks and 31·9 per cent for local banks.

Because local banks often lack sufficient investment opportunities, they buy relatively more securities than city banks, and, prior to the monetary relaxation of 1971–2, they used to be very active as lenders in the call market. Monetary stringency affects local banks less than the city banks so that large enterprises occasionally turn to them for supplementary funds.

Long-term credit banks

As mentioned above, the Long-Term Credit Bank Law of 1952 was enacted in order to create banks which could raise capital mainly through the issuing of debentures. The three banks organized under this law are the Industrial Bank of Japan, the Long-Term Credit Bank and the Nippon Fudosan Bank. These banks can issue debentures up to twenty times the aggregate of their capital and reserves but can accept deposits only from the government, public bodies and firms to which they extend credit or for which they act as trustees in floating bonds. They can supply working and investment capital to enterprises by loans, discounts and guarantees; they can also purchase (but not underwrite to) government, public and corporate bonds, stocks and other securities.

Trust banks

Of the seven trust banks now in existence, Mitsui, Yasuda, Sumitomo, Mitsubishi and Nippon Trust & Banking Co. go back to the trust companies founded in the 1930s.

The trust banks have to keep banking accounts (their business as ordinary banks) and trust accounts (their business as trust institutions) separate; this separation applies to both assets and liabilities. Money trusts are usually pooled and invested by the trust banks without distinguishing the individual trusts (this is referred to as jointly operated trusts). Dividends are distributed on the basis of the overall profits of the pool; the banks now agree, in fact, on uniform rates.

Individually operated money trusts are limited to funds with a minimum amount of yen 5 million and a trust term of at least one year; under the guidance of the Ministry of Finance, the trust banks fix a maximum interest rate (at present 6·21 per cent).

The most successful operation of the trust banks has been the loan trust business based on the Loan Trust Law of 1952. Loan trusts, for which the banks guarantee principal and interest, represent a kind of time deposit. They are accepted in units of yen 10,000 for periods of two and five years.

Financial institutions for small businesses

Private financial institutions for the small business are very numerous; they comprise the mutual loan and savings banks (total 72), credit associations (total 484), credit co-operatives (total 502), labour credit associations (total 47), and the Shoko Chukin Bank (Central Bank for Commercial and Industrial Co-operatives). The local credit associations and credit co-operatives are affiliated with national organizations, the National Federation of Credit Associations and the National Federation of Credit Co-operatives; the labour credit associations, which are organized on a prefectural basis, are members of the National Federation of Labour Credit Associations.

The mutual loan and savings banks are authorized to accept deposits and instalment savings, to give loans and make discounts, and to engage in the domestic exchange business (remittances).

The mutual banks as well as the credit associations have played an important role as lenders in the call market.

Securities companies

The postwar securities companies have been organized under the Securities Transaction Law of 1948 which, in Article 65, prohibits banks, trust banks and other financial institutions, designated by cabinet order, to underwrite, offer for subscription, or deal in securities. An amendment passed in 1967 replaced the registration system under which a simple notification to the Minister of Finance was sufficient for establishing a securities company by a licence system. This licence is given for four different functions: underwriters, brokers, dealers and distributors. A capital of at least yen 3 billion is the basic requirement for managing (general) underwriters: out of the 237 securities companies only eleven qualify as managing underwriters. The business of the securities companies as brokers (buying and selling securities at the request of customers) and dealers (buying and selling securities on their own account) is based on their membership in the stock exchanges; as of April 1973, 150 securities companies were members of the stock exchanges, but the 'Big Four' (Nomura, Nikko, Daiwa and Yamaichi) account for 55 per cent of all transactions and do most of the underwriting.

Because Japanese banks rarely provide credit for stock purchases, the securities companies had to shoulder the burden of financing credit transactions. But the financial resources of the securities companies were insufficient for this task and locally organized securities finance companies took over the credit function. An amendment to the Securities Transaction Law, passed in 1955, regulated their operations and the existing companies were consolidated in three firms, Japan Securities Finance Co. (Tokyo), Osaka Securities Finance Co., and Chubu Securities Finance Co. (Nagoya).

In practice, the securities finance companies need only relatively small balances of funds and shares, because to the extent that purchases and sales offset each other the transaction can be settled by mere book-keeping operations. Lending is restricted to the regular members of the stock exchanges but customers can obtain loans through their dealers if the dealer guarantees the loan.

FINANCIAL INSTITUTIONS OF THE GOVERNMENT

Government financing has played an important role in Japan's economic development. Although the Bank of Japan is the country's central credit institution, its funds remain outside the national budget; but there are a large number of financial institutions owned and operated by the government which support the collection, management and distribution of funds.

The central organ for fund management is the so-called Trust Fund Bureau, which is entrusted with the management of postal savings, the accumulated funds of special accounts and temporary surplus funds. All deposits accepted by the Trust Fund Bureau are time deposits with maturities ranging from one month to seven years. The interest rates paid on those deposits are fixed by law. The Bureau lends its funds to governmental financial institutions and other public agencies under the yearly fiscal loan and investment programme which is compiled jointly with the budget. For fiscal 1973, this programme amounted to yen 6924·8 billion–48·5 per cent of the size of the budget. Funds derived from the savings of the private sector, therefore, play an important role in the government's financing operations.

In 1953 the Industrial Investment Special Account was set up in order to make government funds available to industry and trade in the form of capital investment and loans. A large part of the initial funds was derived from the counterpart fund for American aid (GARIOA and EROA) which contributed greatly to Japan's postwar reconstruction.

In 1951, the Japan Development Bank was founded and given the following tasks: (1) to grant loans for equipment investment; (2) to subscribe to industrial bonds; (3) to guarantee financial obligations. The Japan Development Bank lends chiefly to large enterprises; in the beginning, the electric power industry and shipping received the largest share of the bank's funds but its field of activity has been greatly expanded by the successive inclusion of other sectors able to borrow from the bank, including the distribution system, private railroads, public parking, regional development, housing, private developers, hotels, and car dealers.

Medium-sized and small enterprises can obtain credit from the government's Small Business Finance Corporation, while little businessmen, artisans and shopkeepers turn to the People's Finance Corporation. In fact, there is a total of over 200 assorted governmental and semi-governmental organs many of which have no other purpose, it would seem, than to provide sinecures for retired government officials.

Of great importance for Japan's foreign trade is the Japan Export-Import Bank. It was set up in 1950, originally for supplying funds for export financing, and was called the Japan Export Bank. Import financing was added to the bank's tasks in 1957 and its name changed to the Japan Export-Import Bank. The scope of its business was further enlarged to include capital investment in, or stock acquisition of, foreign corporations by Japanese manufacturers or exporters, credits to foreign partners in joint ventures with Japanese firms, either abroad or in Japan, loans to domestic manufacturers for equipment required in their overseas manufacturing operations, credit for technical services, and loans to foreign governments or other agencies for development projects. The bank's operations include loans, discounts or rediscounts of drafts, and liabilities' guarantees of the parties entitled to credit. Usually the Export-Import Bank supplies only a part of the funds needed for a certain transaction and adjusts its share to the conditions of the money market. In the financing of ship exports, its share comes to 38·5 per cent of the total price but it may go up as high as 80 per cent. For overseas investments and enterprises, the bank may supply 70 per cent of the required funds without the co-operation of commercial banks and it may advance the entire amount of loans to foreign governments.

The Export-Import Bank used to be in charge of the administration of the government's Economic Co-operation Fund which was also used for financing private transactions deemed helpful to developing countries. The administration of the Economic Co-operation Fund has now been completely separated from the Export-Import Bank; the fund will be used exclusively for government loans and other aid while private projects will be financed only by the Export-Import Bank.

BANKING OPERATIONS

According to the Bank Law, the business of ordinary banks comprises the acceptance of deposits, lending of money, discounting of bills, remittances and ancillary operations. Banks are not permitted to underwrite securities; the emission of bank debentures is restricted to the long-term credit banks, the Bank of Tokyo, the Shoko Chukin Bank, the Central Bank for Agriculture and Forestry, and a number of governmental financial institutions. By administrative guidance, the trust business has been separated from banking. Administrative practice has interpreted ancillary operations to include the settlement of drafts and cheques drawn against current accounts, custodial deposits, safekeeping, money exchange, payment of dividends, collection of debts, guarantee of liabilities, acceptance of drafts, letters of credit, and purchase, sale and lending of securities. Banks have diversified into leasing, credit cards and consulting but they have established separate companies to engage in these activities.

Deposits

Demand deposits are either chequing accounts (called current deposits in the statistics of the Bank of Japan), ordinary deposits, which may be withdrawn at any time upon the presentation of the depositor's passbook, and deposits at notice, which must be left intact for one week and then may be withdrawn, usually at two days' notice. No interest is paid on chequing accounts, but the interest rate on deposits at notice is slightly higher than on ordinary deposits. Interest is calculated on a daily basis and credited to the depositor's account semi-annually. Special interest rates apply to interbank deposits; deposits of local banks and credit associations have supplied a considerable part of the short-term funds borrowed by city banks.

Time deposits must be left untouched for a stipulated period (three months, six months, one year, eighteen months, two years); automatic renewal is possible. Fixed deposits cannot be withdrawn during a specified period. Instalment savings are another kind of time deposit for which the depositor pays fixed amounts at certain intervals. When the banks moved into consumer credit, they were more interested in attracting new deposits than in financing consumer demand; hence consumer credit was tied to instalment saving for particular purposes such as housing, purchase of consumer durables (cars, pianos, electric home appliances), education, marriage and foreign travel. Deposits for tax payments cannot be used for other purposes; interest paid on these deposits is tax-free.

The banks have tried to make deposits more attractive and to retain the money paid out of deposits by a series of services which they perform for their customers without charge. Many banks have concluded agreements with enterprises for the automatic transfer of wages and salaries from the account of the enterprise to the accounts of the employees. To make the system sufficiently convenient, the city banks have supplemented their own network of branches by co-operation arrangements with other banks. In addition to credit cards, the city banks have arrangements with the large department stores under which they debit purchases to the account of their depositors on the basis of the bills sent in by the department stores. Preparations are now under way to convert the present arrangement into an on-line, real time system by connecting terminals in the department stores with the central processing system of the banks (which means that Japan will move into the era of a cashless society without having gone through the stage of cheques).

Other periodically recurrent payments made by the banks for their depositors include telephone, electricity and water bills, television fees payable to the official broadcasting system (NHK) and general taxes (all Japanese banks are fiscal agents for the exchequer). The on-line system has enabled the banks to let their customers make and withdraw deposits at any of their branch offices. On 9 April 1973, an on-line system went into operation which links some 7200 domestic offices of 87 banks (13 city banks, 63 local banks, seven trust banks, three long-term credit banks and Shoko Chukin Bank) and makes almost instantaneous remittances possible. The system replaces interbank transfer by mail, telegraph or telex.

Loans and discounts

Japanese enterprises rely largely on bank loans for working capital as well as investment. The enormous expansion of Japan's economy would have been impossible without the system of indirect financing. The funds available through depreciation and retained earnings were completely insufficient and the capital market would have been unable to absorb the issues of stocks and bonds which would have been required for raising the necessary capital. Two factors helped the banks to meet the fund demand of industry, i.e. the high saving ratio and the availability of central bank credit. During the 15 years from 1956 to 1970, net personal saving accounted for over 20 per cent of disposable personal income. As of 31 March 1973, personal financial assets amounted to yen 101,045·2 billion, an increase of yen 19,354·7 billion (equivalent to 19·2 per cent) over the previous year. In the personal sector the acquisition of financial assets was almost double the amount of net capital expenditures, and over nine-tenths of the financial assets took the form of indirect savings. Time deposits alone constituted over one-half of all financial assets.

The readiness of the Bank of Japan to give credit to the commercial banks eliminated the liquidity problem and made it possible to allow the so-called overloan situation not only to arise but also to continue for long periods of time without fear of panic or insolvency.

Consumer credit

The manufacturers of consumer durables have done their level best to transform Japan into a credit society, but so far without much success. Despite a strong increase in recent years, consumer credit plays a very minor role in Japanese banking. At the end of June 1973, outstanding consumer credit of all banks amounted to yen 2,972,463 million, equivalent to 3·97 per cent of the outstanding bank credit (yen 74,787,400 million, including advances on trust accounts). The largest part of the consumer credit, yen 2,524,017 million (84·9 per cent) consisted of housing loans.

Noteworthy is the tendency to tie consumer credit to fixed schemes or 'plans', usually combined with instalment savings, which then leads to a great proliferation of different 'plans'. Often enough, credit is only given for purchases from department stores or manufacturers belonging to the bank group, and 'tied' housing loans–limited to the acquisition of land or housing from a specified contractor–are given with preferential terms. (The practice exists because these loans remain with the banks as deposits of these firms and the banks further profit from financing the operations of the contractors.)

The Japanese credit card business started in 1960 with the introduction of *Diners Card.* Now there are two large systems. The first, called *Union Card,* is run by a company established jointly by Fuji, Mitsubishi, Dai-Ichi, Kangyo, Taiyo, and Saitama banks in 1968; the other, the *Japan Credit Bureau,* is supported by Sanwa, Mitsui, Kyowa, Daiwa, Kobe, Hokkaido Takushoku,

Yokohama, and Chiba banks. A few banks also issue their own credit cards.

Four institutions specializing in home loans have been established; two by city banks and one by the trust banks, and the fourth by mutual loan and savings banks.

Securities investment

Investment in securities by Japanese banks is not inconsiderable but it has little significance either as an investment method or as a source of income. The Antimonopoly Law limits the ownership of stock of any other company by financial institutions to 10 per cent (the Fair Trade Commission can permit exceptions). Within this limit most banks hold considerable blocks of shares of the enterprises belonging to their respective group. As of 31 March 1973, financial institutions owned 34·3 per cent of all listed stocks (based on market value); the share of banks and trust banks amounted to 15·9 per cent and that of insurance companies to 10·4 per cent. Individuals held 29·8 per cent of all listed stocks. Generally speaking, stock ownership is an expression of group membership rather than its foundation, but in some cases the acquisition of large blocks of shares has accompanied changes in group allegiance, both usually being previously arranged together. Since the largest part of the stock portfolio of the banks is made up of shares of related enterprises, yield is of no consequence in the selection of these shares. By the same token, banks almost never liquidate their portfolios in order to increase their loanable funds. Hence Japanese managers consider financial institutions as the most reliable stockholders and ask them to buy their shares in order to stabilize stock ownership and gain protection against takeover bids.

The situation is completely different for bonds. Banks are the most important buyers of certain bond issues, particularly bank debentures. Government bonds and government-guaranteed bonds are eligible for the open market operations of the Bank of Japan so that bonds play an important role in the adjustment of bank liquidity. Banks sometimes agree to take over a certain portion of the issues of bank debentures on the understanding that the issuing bank (e.g. one of the long-term credit banks) will give a corresponding loan to one of its clients.

Interest rates

Interest rates are regulated on the basis of the Temporary Money Rates Adjustment Law of 1947 which applies to practically all banks but not to the Bank of Japan or the financial institutions of the government. Interest rates of mutual banks, credit associations and credit co-operatives are regulated under the organic laws of these institutions and the rates of the postal savings system are treated separately.

For changes in interest rates under the Temporary Money Rates Adjustment Law the initiative lies with the Minister of Finance. Upon consultation with the Money Rates Adjustment Council, the policy board of the Bank of Japan fixes (or abolishes) the maximum interest rates on deposits and loans of financial institutions. The banks are free to fix their interest rates within the limits of the maximum rates. Not subject to regulation under the Temporary Money Rates Adjustment Law are interest rates on loans for longer than one year and short-term loans of less than a million yen (they are called non-regulated rates). For certain loans, the Federation of Bankers Associations has voluntarily lowered the interest rates below the legal maximum; these rates are referred to as 'voluntary' rates. The rate corresponding to the American prime rate is called standard rate; it applies to discounts and loans on bills of the highest credit rating eligible for rediscount by the Bank of Japan.

Actual fund costs are appreciably higher than the nominal interest rates. The banks often demand compensating balances and these so-called 'debtors' deposits' have run as high as 40 per cent of the loan. The Ministry of Finance has often tried to curb excesses but only with qualified success. For consumer credit the 'add-on' system is frequently used, not so much because it allows higher rates (the banks are required to indicate the real interest costs) but because it simplifies the administration of these loans (payment of interest and repayment of the loan are consolidated). For short-term loans the banks retain the interest when they pay out the loan.

Adding to the banks' fund costs is the reserve deposit system. This system was first enforced in 1959 but has been little used for regulating fund supply. It was only in the beginning of 1973 that the Bank of Japan, unwilling to raise the official discount rate, increased the rate of reserve deposit requirements in order to squeeze credit.

Foreign exchange and foreign trade financing

The foreign exchange business has long been hampered by the extremely strict exchange regulations. The central feature of the system was the concentration of foreign exchange which was accumulated in the Foreign Exchange Fund Special Account. The foreign exchange fund buys and sells foreign exchange against yen. The fund acquires the yen required for its net buying by borrowing from the Trust Fund Bureau, the emission of short-term paper (foreign exchange fund bills) and sales to the Bank of Japan of foreign exchange not required for current operations. All operations of the fund are carried out by the Bank of Japan through which the fund also intervenes in the foreign exchange market. The funds of the foreign exchange fund have also been used for import financing by the foreign exchange banks, first in the form of loans in foreign currency, and, since March 1971, in the form of deposits of foreign currency with the foreign exchange banks. In November 1973, the government began to reduce the deposit balances which, at that time, had reached about $5 billion (these deposits constituted a hidden foreign exchange reserve).

The concentration system was abolished on 8 May 1973, but the foreign exchange fund still buys and sells dollars against yen. Foreign exchange banks cannot sell other currencies directly to the foreign exchange fund; they must convert them in overseas markets in which these currencies can be sold against dollars.

In addition to the foreign exchange fund, the foreign exchange market includes foreign exchange brokers who act as intermediaries between the foreign exchange banks. Of the seven foreign exchange brokerage houses, four are also called market (bill) brokers. These firms do not engage in transactions on their own account; they cannot hold foreign currency and there are no cash and delivery transactions. The Bank of Japan, however, acting for the foreign exchange fund, uses the brokers for intervention in the foreign exchange market (e.g. buying excess foreign exchange for which the brokers can find no buyers).

In April 1972, a dollar call market was organized in order to make short-term loans in foreign exchange possible. The number of banks participating in the dollar call market rose from the original 41 to 81 banks in April 1973, the volume of monthly transactions from $130 million to about $2 billion in November 1973, and the balance of dollar call funds from $70 million to $600 million. The market has provided small banks with an opportunity to make use of their dollar balances while the large city banks have channelled the funds borrowed on the Tokyo market into Eurodollars when Eurodollar rates were high.

Documentary transactions involving export or import usances account for the bulk of foreign trade financing. Until 1971, the Bank of Japan maintained preferential rates for export financing, but in the course of that year the rates were made the same as the official discount rate and export financing has now been discontinued as a special interest category.

Since 1952, the government has deposited part of its foreign exchange reserves with the Class A foreign exchange banks which, through their foreign branches, or corresponding banks, made these funds available to Japanese trading firms as working capital for their foreign operations. In a gradual relaxation of the postwar regulations the foreign branches of trading companies have been given permission to retain and use funds in foreign currency, but the operations of the foreign branches of Japanese banks remain under various restrictions in order to check the inflow of short-term funds into Japan.

Under the 'yen-defence programmes' (i.e. measures to prevent a revaluation of the yen), funds of the foreign exchange fund were deposited with the foreign exchange banks for import financing. Import usance bills represent short-term loans mostly from foreign banks; their rates, which are based on the bankers' acceptance rate of the American banks, are fixed by a conference of the managers of the foreign departments of the city banks called *nisui-kai* (second-Wednesday meeting).

In order to promote imports from developing countries, the government instituted the system of 'import development financing', i.e. loans at preferential terms for developing products which can be exported to Japan. Special institutions, such as the Petroleum Development Corporation and the Overseas Mineral Development Co., make government funds (largely provided through the fiscal loan and investment programme) available for the development of overseas raw material resources. The role of the Export-Import Bank in foreign trade financing has been discussed above.

Under the system of foreign currency loans from the government's foreign exchange holdings which was started in September 1972, the government, until the end of March 1973, approved loans amounting to $1684 million, mainly for investment in mining, manufacturing and commerce.

CORPORATE FINANCING

Bank credit

The postwar inflation wiped out the monetary assets of most individuals as well as corporations. The revaluation of fixed assets did not provide Japanese enterprises with new working capital while funds were practically unavailable on the capital market. Industrial reconstruction, therefore, had to be financed largely by external funds, usually in the form of bank loans. (The role of the Reconversion Finance Bank has been mentioned above.) From 1949 to 1971, fiscal policy was based on budgetary balance and since, until 1968, the balance of payments was in the red (the surplus in 1965 and 1966 was too small to influence the money market), the increase in money supply required for the expansion of the economy came mostly from central bank credit which supplemented the funds that the banks collected through deposits. Until recently the banks paid little attention to consumer credit; basically, therefore, they acted as intermediaries collecting funds from individual savers and channelling these funds into industry.

In addition to central bank credit, the city banks relied on call money which was supplied mostly by local banks, mutual banks, credit associations and the agricultural credit co-operatives. Originally, these funds, too, came from individual savers, so that the Japanese system of indirect financing interposes several layers of financial institutions between the saver and the fund user.

Postwar corporate management became used to depending on external funds and since the situation was the same for almost all enterprises, reliance on external funds and a low equity-debt ratio did not impair the credit rating of an enterprise. Based on the financial reports of 389 companies listed on the First Section of the Tokyo Stock Exchange for the first half of fiscal 1973, the average ratio of equity capital to total capital employed was 16·78 per cent for all enterprises in the manufacturing industries. The ratio has undergone some fluctuations, but in the last ten years the basic trend has been downward.

This does not mean that Japanese management does not pay attention to financial ratios. But just as the performance of a Japanese enterprise is judged primarily by its market share rather than by its earnings, so its credit worthiness is based on its banking connections rather than its equity-debt ratio. The dependence on bank loans created strong bonds between banks and enterprises.

The leading city banks form the nuclei of the enterprise groups which have succeeded the former *zaibatsu*. Before the war, the *zaibatsu* relied as much as possible on internal financing but after the war the firms of the dismembered *zaibatsu* found themselves in the same position as the other credit-starved enterprises. On the other hand, each bank wanted to have at least one large enterprise in every branch of industry among its clients. During the periods of rapid expansion the city banks could not satisfy the entire fund demand of their clients, so that enterprises had to rely on a number of banks. As a result, Japan's leading enterprises have banking connections with several city banks although one bank is regarded as the firm's main bank. On account of the 'window guidance' by the Bank of Japan, the city banks usually consult among themselves and with the enterprise on the fund supply, without, however, forming special syndicates.

Today's *zaibatsu* groups (Mitsubishi, Mitsui and Sumitomo) are composed of a number of concentric circles of enterprises and some enterprises, like certain planets in the solar system, have their own satellite firms. The nucleus of each group is made up of the enterprises represented on the presidents' committee which constitutes the highest liaison organ of the respective group. The second circle comprises firms that traditionally belong to the group and with which the same kind of relationship prevails as with the enterprises of the inner circle, including mutual shareholding, interlocking directorates and financing by the financial organs of the group. The outer circle is composed of enterprises for which the bank or trust bank of the group is the main supplier of funds. In addition to the firms of its own group, Sumitomo Bank, for example, is also the main bank of some firms belonging to the Matsushita, C. Itoh and Kureha groups.

Groups built around other city banks have similar structures. The Fuji Bank Group (also known as Fuyo group) comprises enterprises formerly belonging to the Yasuda, Nissan, Asano, Mori, Okura and Kureha concerns, among them Marubeni Corporation, Nippon Kokan, Oki Electric, Nihon Cement, Showa Denko, Hitachi Ltd, Nissan Motor and Nippon Reizo. Daiichi-Kangyo Bank is the main bank of both the Kawasaki and Furukawa groups and of smaller groups such as Shibusawa, Meiji, Fujiyama and the former Suzuki Shoten. Sanwa Bank co-operates with numerous firms in the Kansai (Osaka) area not belonging to Sumitomo, among them Hitachi Shipbuilding & Engineering, Ube Industries, Osaka Gas and Teijin.

Although corporate fund demands for equipment investment and other special projects are most conspicuous, the largest part of the loans given by financial institutions to enterprises is for such commonplace needs as wage and salary payments, payment of bills, taxes and dividends, and advances to their suppliers. It is not unusual for corporations to finance their expansion (investment in fixed assets) by borrowing, and increase their capital once their larger sales permit them to pay the dividends on their larger capital.

Despite their dominant position, the city banks ordinarily do not interfere in the management of their groups. Interlocking directorates and mutual stockholding are quite common although there are considerable differences in the extent to which both are practised. The banks very often send their executives as presidents or managing directors to affiliated firms which are considered as subsidiaries, but it is only when an incompetent or dishonest management has wrecked an enterprise that the banks demand a 'rejuvenation' of the management. Under normal circumstances, Japanese corporate management is self-perpetuating and irresponsible (in the sense that there is no effective way of bringing it to account except in cases where outright violations of the law are discovered). Most corporate managers move up from the ranks. (To become president or at least a director of the company is the most cherished goal of every white-collar employee when he joins the firm.) In addition to the executives sent by the company's main bank, government officials reaching retirement age parachute* into large companies coming under the jurisdiction of the ministry in which they served, which strengthens the incestuous relations between big business and the bureaucracy.

A recent amendment to the Commercial Code abolished the provision that stockholders holding one-fourth of the shares of the company could demand cumulative voting even if the by-laws of the company stipulated that cumulative voting should not be used in the election of directors. Ostensibly, the change was made in order to protect Japanese firms against snooping by foreign directors; actually, it only protects the inbreeding and unresponsiveness in Japanese management.

Equity financing

The reliance on borrowing did not supersede the procurement of funds by stock and bond issues but direct financing accounts for less than 10 per cent of total fund supply to corporate enterprises. New capitalization by listed companies (all exchanges) rose from yen 43,690 million in 1951 to yen 712,175 million in 1961. Thereafter, new issues dropped sharply (1965: yen 117,361 million) and it was only in 1972 that the 1961 high was eclipsed when the capital raised by new share issues amounted to yen 1,034,214 million. Until recently, issues of new shares were usually allocated to existing stockholders at par but managers were reluctant to make stockholders a 'present' of the difference between face value and market prices. On the other hand secondary advantages connected with borrowing encouraged enterprises to rely still further on external financing; unlike dividends, interest payments are deductible as business expenses and loans can be scheduled according to actual needs.

Public offerings of corporate bonds are restricted to companies meeting certain qualifications so that only the largest enterprises can raise funds by such issues. In recent years, issues of convertible debentures and private bond issues have increased significantly.

*I use the word parachute deliberately: the Japanese use the word *amakudari*, literally 'to float down from heaven'.

Trade credit

Of enormous importance in corporate financing is trade credit. As of 31 March 1973, outstanding trade credit amounted to yen 69,503·5 billion of which the corporate sector owed yen 53,813·1 billion and the personal sector yen 12,090·4 billion. The outstanding balance of loans by private financial institutions amounted to yen 111,253·8 billion of which corporate enterprises owed yen 84,975·7 billion.

The financial role of trading companies

For most firms connected with the large trading companies, the financing of their transactions is almost as important as the distribution or supply channels provided by the trading companies. Through their credits the trading firms divide their own bank credit among their customers and suppliers and, at the same time, take over credit rating and risk. Financing by the trading firms is often more advantageous because they do not demand compensating balances.

While the banks insist on collateral in the form of deposits, securities or mortgages, the trading companies have to accept warehouse receipts, bills of lading and similar documentary security whose liquidation often involves losses. The banks stop their credits when the situation of their customers becomes risky but the trading companies often find it impossible to extricate themselves and suffer great losses from bankruptcies. The losses of the large trading companies are sometimes caused by the collapse of small or medium-sized traders who, in turn, have become insolvent on account of the difficulties of small industrial enterprises. In times of recession the financial needs of most enterprises grow rapidly while official policy restricts credits. Industry has to finance huge inventories accumulated through overproduction preceding the recession; moreover, the curtailment of production creates additional financial needs (chiefly because enterprises refrain from lay-offs).

In recent years, the large trading companies have become investment bankers. They have played an important role in the development of overseas natural resources (petroleum, natural gas, coal, iron ore, non-ferrous metals, salt, timber, agricultural products, etc.), in housing developments, high-rise apartment buildings, prefabricated housing, hotels, leisure facilities, retail chains, ocean development, and leasing.

For their financial needs the trading companies rely on bank loans and convertible bonds (straight bonds other than bank debentures are 'industrial' bonds secured by floating mortgages on fixed assets).

In the field of foreign exchange the large trading companies came under fire when they converted large amounts of dollars (collected as prepayments for exports) into yen prior to the floating of the yen in August 1971. Recently, they have been accused of enormous speculative land purchases and stock transactions. Since they control a large share of domestic and foreign trade and dispose of vast sums of liquid funds, they wield enormous economic and financial power and are able to exercise many financing and investment functions without any (or certainly without sufficient) regulation and control.

JAPAN AND INTERNATIONAL FINANCING

Foreign operations of Japanese banks

The close co-operation between Japanese banks, trading companies and manufacturers extends to foreign business and the customers of a particular bank prefer to deal with a representative of that bank wherever they do business. Financing of foreign trade was the main objective of the establishment of foreign branches, but with the development of the Eurodollar market the induction of foreign capital gained in importance. In recent years the banks have placed growing emphasis on the investment business while the securities companies have founded foreign subsidiaries or opened foreign branch offices for underwriting and investment in foreign securities.

The main forms used by the banks for foreign operations are branch offices, representative offices, subsidiaries, participation in or joint ventures with foreign banks, participation in foreign finance companies, and in consortium banking. Branches can engage in the usual banking operations while representative offices are not allowed to accept deposits or give loans, and must restrict their activities to liaison, information and negotiations. The banking legislation of the State of New York restricts Japanese banks to agencies or subsidiaries. Because of the restrictions on the deposit business of branches some Japanese banks have established subsidiaries in California and Chicago. In Australia, where branches or subsidiaries of foreign banks are banned, Japanese banks have acquired shares in Australian financial institutions. At the end of 1972, Japanese banks had 89 foreign branches, 67 representative offices (including those of the trust banks) and had an interest in 40 foreign financial institutions (including wholly-owned subsidiaries, participation in foreign banks and multinational financial institutions). In fiscal 1973, the Ministry of Finance gave permission to establish 16 new overseas branches and 24 representative offices.

Initially, the overseas offices largely served the financing of foreign trade and the induction of foreign capital into Japan. The activities of these offices were restricted in line with domestic credit policies. With the liberalization of capital transactions in recent years these restrictions have been relaxed. In August 1972, the eleven London branches of Japanese banks were allowed to issue certificates of deposits up to $15 million; in November the limitation was removed and the issuance of certificates denominated in pounds was allowed. Increasing importance has been attached to international medium- and long-term financing, including participation in syndicate loans to foreign governments and multinational enterprises. The Japanese securities companies have likewise moved from the sale of Japanese stocks and the flotation of foreign bonds of Japanese enterprises to participation in international underwriting syndicates. Japanese banks and securities companies have also been very active in related fields such as leasing and consulting.

Induction of foreign capital

The chief forms used for inducting foreign capital into Japan are direct inward investment (which implies the acquisition of stocks of Japanese firms for participation in management), foreign loans, sale of Japanese securities to foreign investors and the flotation of external bonds. Foreign loans are either tied loans, i.e. loans given for a particular purpose, or untied loans, usually called impact loans. Important in Japan's postwar expansion were the loans of the World Bank for so-called development projects and the loans granted by the US Export-Import Bank for financing imports of capital goods and agricultural products (e.g. cotton). Impact loans gained significance with Japan's rapid economic expansion in the 1960s when the development of the Eurodollar market opened up new fund sources unencumbered by the requirements of collateral, credit lines or compensating balances. Most Eurodollar loans were taken up by the London branches of the Japanese foreign exchange banks, sent immediately to the head office, changed into yen and used for domestic loans because the high Japanese interest rates enabled the banks to pay even higher than going rates on Eurodollars (the 'Japanese' rate was 0·125 per cent–0·25 per cent higher) and still make a profit. Because the inflow of foreign funds seemed to threaten Japan's monetary policy (the main anticyclical tool used by the authorities) restrictions were imposed on the induction of foreign loans. The implementation of the foreign currency deposit reserve system, ceilings on the increase in outstanding loan balances and on the conversion into yen were some of the measures taken to this effect. Stricter controls were imposed under the government's successive programmes for preventing a revaluation of the yen. On 15 December 1973, the government reversed its policy of restricting the inflow of foreign funds and encouraging the outflow of capital which had originally been adopted in order to avoid a revaluation of the yen. Restrictions on the conversion of foreign currency into yen were removed and the emission of external bonds and stocks by Japanese corporations were to be approved if the proceeds were invested abroad. Restrictions on the purchase of Japanese securities by foreigners and on other capital transactions had already been relaxed in November 1973. On the other hand, limitations were reimposed on the amounts of foreign currency individuals could take with them for overseas travel and the ceiling on non-commercial remittance was lowered.

Foreign investment in Japanese securities takes the following forms: purchase of Japanese stocks, bonds or investment trust certificates in Japan, purchase of Japanese stocks abroad, and purchase of bonds floated abroad by Japanese public agencies or private corporations.

Until the capital liberalization programme of 1 May 1973,

portfolio investment was limited to less than 10 per cent of the issued shares of one company for one investor; the ceiling on total foreign investment was below 25 per cent of the issued shares of one company in unrestricted industries, and 15 per cent in restricted industries. These restrictions have now been removed. Direct investment has also been decontrolled; investment in five sectors (agriculture, forestry and fisheries, leather and leather products, retail trade) remains subject to specific approval (automatic approval up to 50 per cent of retail store chains with less than eleven stores) and for the extraction of natural resources (mining), automatic approval of foreign participation remains limited to 50 per cent. A number of industries now subject to specific approval or to the 50 per cent rule are scheduled for complete liberalization in 1974–6. But the acquisition of a controlling interest in a Japanese firm (takeover bid) requires the consent of the firm's management.

The various programmes 'for the defence of the yen', adopted successively in recent years, severely restricted foreign investment in Japanese securities. In 1972, validated purchases of stocks of Japanese companies amounted to $3,988,448,000 (including $171,313,000 for participation in management), acquisition of beneficiary certificates to $692,000, purchases of public and corporate bonds to $468,924,000, induction of foreign loans to $993,700,000 and issues of external bonds to $31,032,000 (i.e. one issue of DM 100 million by the Industrial Investment Special Account). The most important foreign investors in Japanese securities are funds specializing in Japanese issues.

For the sale of Japanese shares abroad, the system of American depositary receipts (ADR), originally used for European stocks, was adopted for Japanese issues. In addition to ADR's, European (EDR), London (LDR), Curacao (CDR) and Hong Kong depositary receipts (HDR) have been adopted. There is a growing tendency to have Japanese stocks listed in foreign exchanges, not only in the United States but also in Europe and in Hong Kong.

Foreign banks in Japan

The first foreign banks to establish themselves in Japan after the Second World War were authorized to open branch offices by the occupation authorities; they obtained a business licence based on the Bank Law in 1949 and were also recognized as authorized foreign exchange banks. Their banking licenses do not extend to savings, trust business and secured corporate debentures. They do not belong to the Federation of Bankers Associations and are not bound by the 'voluntary' interest rates of the federation, but must observe the interest ceiling on loans fixed under the Temporary Money Rates Adjustment Law and the guidelines of the Bank of Japan on deposits. They cannot give loans under one year and their loan volume (including loans in foreign currency) is also regulated. As is the case with Japanese banks, a ceiling has been fixed on the increase in free-yen deposits and on foreign exchange holdings. They need case-by-case permission for lending in the call money market but can operate freely in the dollar call market.

In addition to banks, foreign securities companies have opened offices in Japan under a special law regulating the business of foreign underwriters and securities transactions, but foreign underwriters without a licence can obtain permission from the Minister of Finance to participate in the master contract covering the issuance of securities or engage in other specified transactions. As of 4 July 1973, 41 foreign banks (including the central banks of South Korea and Indonesia) had 65 branch offices in Japan; representative offices of foreign banks numbered 67 and those of foreign securities companies 15.

Japanese outward investment

Until recently, the main outflows of capital from Japan were deferred payments for exports while direct foreign investment, loans and the acquisition of foreign securities were rather limited. At the end of December 1972, Japan's total foreign assets amounted to $43,595 million; of long-term assets ($16,185 million), deferred payments for exports accounted for $5412 million, loans totalled $4546 million, direct foreign investment totalled $2574 million and investment in securities totalled $1950 million (the remaining long-term accounts were investments in international agencies and other assets, $1703 million). Direct foreign investment has been at a high level in recent years. It rose from $668 million in fiscal 1969, to $913 million in fiscal 1970, but dropped to $879 in fiscal 1971. In fiscal 1972, direct foreign investment amounted to $2338 million, bringing the cumulative balance at the end of March 1973 to $6773 million, spread over 108 countries (this balance is based on validations).

The large trading companies have a worldwide network of branches and subsidiaries; Mitsui & Co., for example, has 133 foreign subsidiaries and branch offices and each of the large trading companies has interests in over fifty foreign subsidiaries in trade and manufacturing. A few Japanese companies, such as Matsushita Electric Industrial and Toray, have operating subsidiaries in more than twenty countries.

Investment in foreign securities was first allowed in February 1970 when investment trusts were given permission to acquire up to a total of $100 million in foreign securities. In July 1971, individual investment in foreign securities through domestic securities companies was allowed and investment in foreign securities, including foreign investment trusts and domestic investment trusts made up exclusively of foreign securities, was completely liberalized in November 1972. Over-the-counter transactions in foreign stocks started in July 1972, and in February 1973, the Ministry of Finance published regulations for the listing of foreign stocks on Japanese exchanges. The actual listing of foreign stocks has been delayed by procedural difficulties, particularly by the insistence of the Ministry of Finance on the filing of separate statements (this requirement may be dropped and foreign as well as Japanese corporations permitted to submit consolidated statements). The first six foreign firms were listed on the Tokyo Stock Exchange on 18 December 1973.

International financing

The international financing activities of Japanese financial institutions now take a variety of forms. Loans in dollars, yen and DM are provided by bank syndicates, including international syndicates, and issues of stocks, bonds or convertible debentures are taken over by domestic and international underwriting syndicates. Often, private placements are preferred because they require no public disclosure and can be handled by banks (which cannot underwrite public offerings).

Loans to foreign governments by the Japanese government have been fairly numerous and the efforts to reduce Japan's foreign exchange holdings led to the purchase of bonds of the US Export-Import Bank by the Japanese government, loans by the Bank of Japan to the World Bank (International Bank for Reconstruction and Development), loans by the Japan Export-Import Bank in co-operation with commercial banks to the Inter-American Development Bank and to Argentina's State Industrial Bank. Consortia of commercial banks extended loans to the Korea Exchange Bank and the Central Bank of the Philippines, and in December 1971, a syndicate of five Japanese banks and the Tokyo Branch of Morgan Guaranty Trust Co. concluded an agreement for a yen 5 billion loan with Trans-ocean Gulf Oil Co., a subsidiary of Gulf Oil Co. In May 1973, a syndicate of eighteen Japanese banks gave a yen 14·7 billion loan to the National Iranian Tanker Co. for financing the construction of two tankers. (The form of a loan was chosen in order to avoid OECD's restrictions on deferred payments for ships.)

The most prominent step in the emergence of Japan as an international capital market was the emission of yen bonds by foreign institutions. In December 1970, the Asian Development Bank floated a yen 6 billion issue (issue price yen 99, coupon rate 7·4 per cent, maturity seven years with redemption starting in 1973, yield to subscriber 7·619 per cent) of which financial institutions took over 80 per cent. The World Bank issued its first yen bonds in June 1971 (issue price yen 99·50, coupon rate 7·75 per cent, yield to subscriber 7·839 per cent, redemption 1977 through 1981). So far, the World Bank has floated six issues of yen bonds in Japan, the Asian Development Bank three. Altogether the World Bank has raised a total of yen 500 billion in Japan, including yen 392 billion in loans from the Bank of Japan, and yen 180 billion raised on the capital market through public offerings or private placements. By November 1973, thirteen issues of yen bonds with a total value of yen 164 billion had been floated.

At present, total financing on Japan's capital market comes to about $20 billion a year, comprising $3 billion in equity financing and $17 billion in bonds (national bonds, municipal bonds and corporate bonds). The potential of the Tokyo market for foreign financing, including equity and debt, has been estimated at 10 per cent of this amount, about $2 billion. The absence of an efficient distribution market remains a great obstacle to the functioning of Japan's international capital market. Foreign issues are absorbed almost entirely by institutional investors while general investors have so far shown little interest in bond issues (except convertible bonds). Although the uncertainties of the world's currency system have slowed the tempo of Japan's 'internationalization', the integration of Japan's capital market with the capital markets of the world will be of far-reaching significance for Japan's position in the international community.

THE CAPITAL MARKET

STOCK EXCHANGES

There are eight stock exchanges in Japan, located in Tokyo, Osaka, Nagoya, Kyoto, Hiroshima, Fukuoka, Niigata and Sapporo. Since 1961, the Tokyo, Osaka and Nagoya exchanges have contained two sections: the First Section specialising in large company stocks (capital at least yen 1 billion) and the Second Section handling stocks which previously have been traded over the counter. In the meantime, however, a new over-the-counter market developed which resulted in the Tokyo Stock Exchange opening up a special trading centre for such stocks.

As of 11 December 1973, 849 companies and 869 issues were listed on the First Section of the Tokyo Stock Exchange; the capital of the listed companies amounted to yen 7833·7 billion and the market value of the listed shares to yen 35,146·8 billion. On the Second Section, 523 companies and 545 issues were listed; the companies' capital totalled yen 430·2 billion and the market value of the shares yen 2014·8 billion.

The official term for stock exchanges is 'securities exchanges' because, in addition to domestic and foreign stocks, they handle all kinds of bonds and beneficiary certificates of investment trusts and loan trusts.

Exchanges are organized on the membership principle. Regular members (limited to 99 corporations, but actually involving 83 securities companies) are securities dealers engaged primarily in the securities business; *saitori* members (limited to twelve corporations) are securities dealers acting as intermediaries between regular members in their business on the floor of the exchange (brokers' brokers).

Trading posts on the Tokyo Stock Exchange are arranged by industries; a separate post handles the so-called 'specified' stocks and a 'special' post handles the stocks of bankrupt or delisted firms. There is no official odd-lot market.

Four types of transactions are possible: cash transactions (settlement on the same day), regular-way transactions (settlement within four days for stocks and within fifteen days for bonds), seller's option transactions and when-issued transactions. Practically speaking, 95 per cent of all transactions are regular-way transactions. Margin transactions are only permitted for stocks traded on the First Section. Shares with a face value of yen 50 (the vast majority of Japanese stocks) are traded in blocks of a thousand shares; those with a face value of yen 500 in blocks of a hundred shares. Bond transactions on the exchange are in blocks with a face value of yen 1 million, but convertible bonds are traded in units with a contract value of yen 100,000. Commission rates depend on the price of the stock and the number of shares involved.

Only the issues for which margin trading has been specifically sanctioned upon consultation between the stock exchanges, the securities companies and the Ministry of Finance will be accepted by the securities finance companies as collateral. There is a ceiling on the credit given to the securities companies but no ceiling on the credit given by the securities companies to their customers. Frequently, margin requirements (normally 40 per cent) are raised for issues trading in which the authorities anticipate speculative dealing; they are lowered when the stock market needs stimulation.

Listing on the exchange requires a certain capital (yen 1 billion for listing on the First Section, yen 300 million for the Second Section) and a certain distribution of the shares (Tokyo Stock Exchange: sale of 300,000 shares plus 5 per cent of all issued shares). In 1972, 29 new listings (including transfers from other exchanges) were recorded for the Tokyo Stock Exchange, 25 for Osaka and 16 for Nagoya. Greater prestige and easier access to credit (not necessarily through stock or bond issues) are the main motives of Japanese firms for listing.

Special regulations have been adopted for the price formation of newly listed stocks; factors to be considered are net assets per share, net profit per share in the year before the listing, net dividends per share in the same period, and stock price of similar companies in the same field.

Stricter regulations for the marketing of newly listed stocks made the public offering of all newly listed shares obligatory and prohibited the so-called '*oyabike*', i.e. the prearranged purchase of newly issued shares by the investors (usually financial institutions) designated by the issuing company. Support buying, which became problematic with the increase in issues at market prices, must be reported to the Minister of Finance and publicly announced; the announcement must specify the price at which support buying will be undertaken and the name of the securities company in charge of the operation. Takeover bids (offers to buy 10 per cent or more of the shares of a company from present stockholders outside the stock exchange) must be filed with the Minister of Finance together with a statement specifying the conditions of the offer and a certificate showing that the capital required for the takeover has been deposited with a bank. Ten days have to pass between the notification and the beginning of the stock purchases. The first takeover bid under the new rules took place in April 1972 when Yamaichi Securities Co. on behalf of Bendix Corporation bought 20 per cent of Jidosha Kiki, a manufacturer of braking equipment listed on the Second Section of the Tokyo Stock Exchange.

Convertible debentures became popular in 1970 and, in December 1972, the first unsecured convertible debentures were issued since the end of the war (all straight bond issues are secured bonds). The Tokyo Stock Exchange has a special trading post for convertible debentures (169 issues were traded as of 11 December 1973), but both straight and convertible bonds are also traded over the counter.

THE EMISSION MARKET

In 1972, new issues of stocks listed on Japanese exchanges for which payment was made numbered 492; total payments amounted to yen 1,034,214 million of which yen 651,734 million represented premiums (difference between face value and market price). The issues comprised 177 issues to existing stockholders (yen 280,120 million), 271 public offerings (yen 661,654 million) and 44 private placements (yen 92,440 million).

Gratis distributions of shares (stock dividends) numbered 189 valued at yen 69,481 million. There were 31 issues of convertible bonds amounting to yen 131,000 million.

Stock subscription rights were made transferable by an amendment to the Commercial Code enacted in 1966, which also made endorsement of the stock certificate unnecessary for transfer and provided that the transfer of shares to a particular party can be blocked by a vote of two-thirds of all issued shares (a provision aimed at preventing sales to foreigners).

Issues at market prices began to attract attention in the latter half of the 1960s and assumed large proportions in 1972. Individual stockholders as well as the insurance companies strongly opposed issues at market prices because Japanese stock prices had always discounted the capital gains accruing from new issues allocated to stockholders at par value. Moreover, Japanese dividend rates are based on the face value of the shares and not on the actual earnings of the companies. In December 1972, the average dividend rate of the 705 companies listed on the First Section of the Tokyo Stock Exchange and paying dividends (including special dividends and distributions) was yen 6·61 per share (13·2 per cent p.a.) but the average yield was 1·8 per cent.

In order to make issues at market prices more attractive to investors, the securities companies came up with the idea of 'returning the premium to the investor', i.e. compensating the stockholders for the premium by a higher dividend rate or stock dividends. A recent study showed that, until the end of March 1973, twenty companies which had issued new shares at market prices in 1969 (issues of a million shares or more) had 'returned' an average of 21·5 per cent of the premiums to the stockholders. The notion that the stockholders are the owners of the company has lost all practical significance. Under normal conditions the general meeting of stockholders of a Japanese company is a meaningless ceremony (in recent years protest attempts by the victims of industrial pollution have enlivened the proceedings of some companies and at times the so-called *sokaiya* – extortionists or blackmailers – embarrass the management). Management considers issues at market prices as a source of 'cheap' funds whereas, by contrast, new issues to existing stockholders at par would involve a 'gift'.

In 1971, the Tokyo Stock Exchange prescribed that dividends

must be stated in yen instead of percentages of the face value and that the announcement of the dividend should contain a statement of earnings per share. This may be a first step toward non-par value shares but it has not changed the dividend policy of Japanese companies. Because the dividend rate is part of the corporate 'image', firms of the same standing in a particular branch of industry tend to maintain the same dividend rate. The relation of the dividend rate to earnings is purely negative: it is illegal to pay out a dividend if the balance sheet shows a loss. The price–earnings ratio has no significance for Japanese stocks.

In order to facilitate large issues at market prices the issuing companies and the securities companies persuaded the banks to subscribe to large portions of the public offerings of new shares (which the banks can do because it is different from underwriting). But when the banks increase their shares in subscriptions to capital increases, the result is the same as an increase in bank lending. In December 1972, therefore, the banks (city banks, long-term credit banks and trust banks) were prohibited from taking over more than 50 per cent of new shares or more than proportional to their holdings of such shares, and in February 1973, the ceiling was reduced to 40 per cent. The four large securities companies made a dividend rate of yen 5 (10 per cent p.a.) for the last two terms preceding the capital increase and a ratio of at least 20 per cent of net profits after tax to capital a condition for taking over issues at market prices.

In October 1973, the eleven general underwriters agreed to demand a pay-out ratio of at least 20 per cent for companies issuing new shares at market prices, and to interpose intervals of one year between stock issues at market prices and of eight months between issues of debentures convertible at market prices. In the case of these issues being allocated to third parties, the interval will be extended to two years.

At the end of 1972, 170 bond issues were listed on the Tokyo Stock Exchange. Bonds issued by the central government comprise long-term national bonds, short-term bills (Treasury bills, food bills, foreign exchange fund bills) and external bonds (last issue in 1968).

Treasury bills are issued with maturities of 60, 90 and 180 days. The volume of issues of short-term government bills is decided for each week on the basis of the fund demand of the issuing accounts (new demand and conversion or refunding of bills already issued). Each Friday, details (type of issue, amounts, discount rate, issue and redemption date) are given to the Bank of Japan; issue dates are Monday, Wednesday and Friday. Financial institutions, securities companies and short-term fund brokers entitled to central bank credit can subscribe to these bills but because the discount rate is below other comparable short-term rates (call money rate, bill discount rate) public subscription is very low (between 5 and 12 per cent). The Bank of Japan automatically takes over the remaining portion.

Public offerings of municipal bonds are restricted to eight local governments (prefectures and cities) but there are numerous private placements often taken over by local banks. Government-guaranteed bonds are issued by eighteen public corporations, including the Japan National Railways and Nippon Telegraph and Telephone Public Corporation. Short-term government bills (60 days) are usually taken over by the Bank of Japan and the Trust Fund Bureau but financial institutions, securities companies and short-term fund brokers entitled to central bank credit can subscribe to them. Bonds issued by local governments are often taken over by local banks; guaranteed bonds of public corporations are issued by the Japan National Railways and Nippon Telegraph and Telephone Public Corporation (the latter issues interest-bearing and discount bonds). Bank debentures are issued by the Industrial Bank of Japan, the Long-Term Credit Bank, Nippon Fudosan Bank, Bank of Tokyo, Shoko Chukin Bank and the Central Bank for Agriculture and Forestry; these institutions issue both interest-bearing and discount debentures. The former are underwritten almost entirely by financial institutions although discount debentures are offered to the public through the securities companies.

Bonds of non-financial corporations are usually called industrial bonds; they are secured by floating mortgages on the fixed assets of the enterprise issuing the bonds. Since October 1972 industrial bonds are divided into four classes, AA, A, BB, B depending on the net worth and the dividend rate of the issuing company. Each issue is rated independently. The maturity of national bonds was changed from seven to ten years in January 1972 and the same change was effected for industrial bonds in July of that year. Municipal, government-guaranteed and corporate bonds are issued each month upon consultation between the underwriting syndicates and the depositary banks (which are entrusted with the collateral securing the bonds).

When the government resumed the large scale emission of long-term bonds in 1965 a new syndicate was formed which comprised thirty parties.

At present, the underwriting syndicate of the securities companies for national bonds comprises 53 firms; the lowest subscription unit is yen 50,000. The emission of local bonds is regulated by the Home Ministry.

Public offerings of securities (stocks and bonds) require an application to the Ministry of Finance (with supporting documents) and the publication of a prospectus; for private placements a notification to the Ministry of Finance is sufficient. Moreover, the underwriting syndicate has restricted public offerings of bonds to companies meeting certain qualifications (minimum requirements: capital yen 4 billion, net assets yen 7·5 billion, dividend rate 10 per cent p.a. for the previous six consecutive terms, ratio of net worth to total capital employed 25 per cent, ratio of total assets to net worth 150 per cent). The banks welcome private placements because they can take over these issues; furthermore, no commission is paid to the securities companies so that the return on these issues is higher.

In 1972, 36 issuers floated 102 bond issues with a value of yen 6,579,485 million. The average yield rate was 6·72 per cent.

THE CALL MONEY MARKET

The call money market is operated by six short-term money brokers (bill brokers) who act as intermediaries between lenders and borrowers. Unlike the foreign exchange brokers, the call money dealers may trade for their own account. Throughout the postwar period local banks, trust banks, mutual banks, credit associations, etc. were the chief lenders and the city banks were the most important borrowers. In times of monetary stringency the Bank of Japan has supplied funds to the short-term money brokers through market operations. The Bank of Japan decides daily what position it will take in the call market after learning from dealers the market situation.

The types of loans on the call market are overnight loans (repaid the following day unless renewed) and unconditional loans (called at will with one day's notice by the lender or repaid by the borrower). There used to be half-day loans (repayment on the same day) and over-the-month loans (repayment on a fixed day in the following month) but these forms have been discontinued.

All call money loans are secured by collateral such as government-guaranteed bonds, local government bonds, bank debentures, prime industrial bonds, bills eligible for rediscount by the Bank of Japan or ordinary commercial bills.

On account of their almost chronic fund shortage the city banks became permanent borrowers of over-the-month funds which used to constitute about 90 per cent of all call money. The call money market, therefore, lost its function of adjusting short-term fund imbalances and, as pointed out above, corrected the structural fund dislocations in the financial system. With the monetary relaxation in 1971, the city banks shifted from over-the-month to unconditional loans which, on account of the lower interest rate, were less attractive for the lenders. In May 1971, therefore, a bill market was organized to take over the long end of the call market. The parties are exactly the same as in the call market, the city banks are sellers and local banks, mutual banks and credit associations are buyers of bills. The bills comprise commercial paper (drafts drawn by manufacturers or traders), first-rate one-name notes and drafts drawn by financial institutions to their own order collateralized by commercial paper discounted by the banks.

Export and import bills are excluded. Eligible paper must mature in more than two but less than three months from the date of sale or purchase. As in the case for call money, the smallest transaction is yen 10 million; actually, most transactions are of the order of yen 100 million.

The call rates are negotiated between the call brokers and *sammei-kai,* a committee on which all city banks are represented. They must be approved by the Bank of Japan, which has exercised a certain control over the call money rates.

Call rates have always been higher than the official discount rate and have gone up sharply in times of credit restraints. The interest rate on unconditional loans is 0·25 per cent higher than that on overnight loans and the rate for the borrower is 0·125 per cent higher than that for the lender (the differential represents the broker's commission). Interest on call loans is paid when the loan matures but bills are discounted so that the actual costs are higher than the nominal rate.

INVESTMENT TRUSTS

Investment trusts take two forms, closed- and open-end trusts. For the first type, also called unit trusts, a specific sum of money (e.g. yen 4 billion) is raised by public subscription and invested for a specific period of time (e.g. five years). The term can be shortened or lengthened, with the approval of the Minister of Finance, in order to protect the interests of the investors. Once a year the income of the fund is distributed among the investors; a certain portion of the capital gains is retained in order to increase the redemption value of the fund.

No definite ceiling is set on the amount of an open-end trust and certificates can be bought at any time. Dividends are paid twice a year and a larger portion of the capital gains is distributed than in the closed-end type. This keeps the price of the certificates low and ensures greater marketability.

5 Understanding Japanese Management Techniques

ROBERT J. BALLON

INTRODUCTION

When Japan entered the technological age just over a hundred years ago, after two centuries of self-imposed isolation, there was no startling revolution in the social structure–no destruction of the old to bring about the new–which the West experienced. The mighty industrial machine which Emperor Meiji inspired his people to create and exploit was founded on the centuries-old strength of communal effort, integration and will-power–above all on the existing hierarchy and scale of values. In this chapter Robert Ballon explores these values and the related principles governing Japanese business practice, and helps to remove some of the general ignorance and common misconceptions that still cloud the western businessman's understanding of the way the Japanese work and think.

THE JAPANESE STYLE OF MANAGEMENT

It is easy to assume that, since people are people everywhere, management is management wherever it may be. But it is more practical to make no assumption and simply start from the facts. Japan's history and culture, not to speak of her recent successful economic performance, has caused Japanese managers to develop a style of management which is their own and is, generally, very successful–at least by Japanese standards, and indeed by some of our own. Corporate debt, government regulations, personnel administration, etc. are used in a way that might be rightfully questioned outside of Japan. However, they are part of what the Japanese challenge is all about.

The interpretation of the past is often coloured by current circumstances. In prewar Japan, it was customary among scholars to consider business managers as the descendants of the *samurai,* who for centuries had dominated society as the nation's elite. After the Second World War, to be more in tune with modern trends, managers came to be described as the descendants of the merchants who, in feudal times, made it possible for society, including the *samurai,* to survive. It would probably be nearer the truth to describe the prewar and postwar business executives alike as the descendants both of the *samurai* and the merchants.

Before the Meiji Restoration (1868) the acquisition of wealth, though officially frowned upon, was the real goal of both the higher social class, the *samurai,* and the lowest class, the merchants. But it was rather as the head of the extended family acting on behalf of his own personal family, that an individual desired wealth. The concept of property was depersonalized, in the sense that property belonged to the extended family personified in the family head.

The acquisition of wealth, though a prerequisite for Japan's industrialization, was not its cause, since the first faltering steps towards industrialization were taken by the political leaders of the Meiji Restoration rather than by any future captains of industry. By origin, therefore, Japanese industrialization is different from that of the West. It was only after more than a decade of hesitation, in the early 1880s, that the private sector finally awoke to the new opportunities; surprisingly, too, the government was happy to turn over to the budding industrialists most of its rather dismal attempts at industrial development.

The West was to be the model as far as industrial technology was concerned. However, industrialization was not the end but merely the means by which Japan would be able to take her place in the world. Thus there was no question of modifying Japan's spiritual values in the industrialization processes. The dichotomy was tersely expressed in the slogan, *wakon yosai,*

Japanese spirit and western skills. To this day the slogan remains at the root of Japan's success, if not also at the root of the international misgivings about her success.

THE JAPANESE ENTERPRISE

The economic success of postwar Japan remains a puzzle as long as it is analysed according to western norms. The key is not to be found in identifying so-called favourable circumstances which, after all, were at the disposal of other industrial nations, but rather in something that could be considered and described as typically Japanese–something which allowed Japan to capitalize on these favourable circumstances. This 'something' is particularly evident in the structure of the Japanese enterprise.

In the eyes of western management, after due tribute has been paid to social responsibilities, the main practical purpose of a company–the acid test–is to provide a worthwhile return on investment. The point is not so obvious in Japan. As her Commercial Code was imported from Germany, the Japanese translation for Aktiengesellschaft (the English 'Limited' or French 'Société Anonyme') is *kabushiki kaisha*, abbreviated as KK. But, outside of the Commercial Code, in real life, KK does not stand for AG. With some academic pedantry, Japanese scholars point out that a KK is not a *Gesellschaft* but a *Gemeinschaft*.

The nature of the Japanese enterprise can be examined from three basic viewpoints: its employment system; its capitalization and, finally, its competitive position.

Employment system*

In industrial terms a Japanese does not identify himself by his profession, occupation or skill, as a westerner would. He identifies himself and is identified by society at large, according to his work-place (*shokuba*), i.e. the company that employs him. In the context of industrial society what the westerner sees as the role of a profession or occupation and the expectations

*See Chapter 6.

he attaches to it come to the Japanese from the enterprise. It is from the enterprise that the Japanese derives both security and satisfaction. Employment, therefore, is not regulated by a contract that hires a skill; it is a life relationship that attaches a man to a specific organization. Labour contracts are indeed the exception in Japan.

In the context of the work-place, there is also no fundamental distinction between management and labour. The company employs managers and managed alike. The image of a coin comes to mind: one side of the coin is management, the other is labour; they are definitely different, but they converge to make the coin, the company. In that it assumes not a divergence but rather the convergence of different interests, the style of management in a Japanese enterprise will not be readily comparable to, nor imitable in, the West.

A striking illustration of this unique Japanese outlook on the enterprise is given by the type of labour organization. Japan has no 'labour union' in the western sense; she has a peculiar form of labour organization called an 'enterprise union'. This union restricts its membership to all regular employees of the enterprise and, as a rule, excludes outsiders to the company from its bargaining with management. When an employee quits, his union membership is automatically dropped, and if the company were to go bankrupt it would also mean the end of that particular labour union. It does not mean, however, that 'enterprise unions' are mere 'company unions', in the sense that they could be or are dominated by management. Conflict there is, but it tends to be resolved within the context of the company (*Gemeinschaft*) rather than outside the company or on ideological grounds.

Not less striking is the fact that, in general, the same salary system applies to ordinary employees and to operating managers, including department heads. The result is that at the bargaining table the managers involved are, in fact, negotiating their own remuneration. These negotiations usually take place at a pre-set time, the so-called annual 'Spring Wage Offensive'. In postwar Japan, the spring is heralded not only by the cherry blossoms, but also by wage struggles! As a result of this annual recurrence over the last twenty years, wage levels are raised simultaneously throughout industry–thereby having little impact on the competitive relationship among firms: and, of course, the production schedule is readily adjusted to allow for some spring problems.

All this goes a long way towards explaining why the Japanese, in western eyes at least, appear to be 'hard-working' people. In fact, it would be more correct to state that they work 'longer' as testified by comparative statistics on working hours around the world. But you would be right in assuming that two entirely different work ethics are involved here. Not even a Japanese enjoys work for the sake of work; the difference in output, as it were, results from the fact that work is considered less as a punishment or a form of exploitation and more as the normal way of acting. It could probably be said that a Japanese does not work for a living; he considers work a way of life. One does not have to be enthusiastic or to be motivated towards life as such, but there is evidently deep satisfaction in being alive. A Japanese is motivated not so much by the job he does as by the work environment where that job happens to be performed; motivation too is not described in terms of occupation but in terms of the work-place. Thus automation, rather than being considered a threat to the work force, is actually expected to improve the work environment and enhance the chances of survival of 'our' company!

Capitalization

It is well known that whereas western companies need something like 40/60 debt–equity ratio, Japanese companies thrive on a 80/20 ratio. In sociological terms, the 60 per cent equity stands for western corporate individualism, i.e. the independence of the individual corporation. The way to strengthen this equity is by profit maximization, as a better price–earnings ratio promises increased access to the securities market. On the other hand the 80 per cent debt in Japan should not be interpreted as control by the banks; it stands for the interdependence of all corporations. This contrast of independence versus interdependence might be visualized in the following manner.

The western 'group' is basically composed of individuals (persons or companies). At a given point a group emerges with its own set of dynamics. By adding up these individuals, the following equation can be imagined:

$$1 + 1 + 1 + 1 + \cdots = \text{GROUP}$$

Adding or subtracting an individual will change the nature of the group. The emphasis is not put on the group so much as on the independence of the individual.

The group-orientation of Japanese individuals (persons or companies), rather than starting from the individual, starts from the group itself. However, the equation given above cannot simply be inverted. If the original group in Japan is called WE, the equation could be imagined as follows:

$$1 \times 1 \times 1 \times 1 \times \cdots = \text{WE}$$

In this last equation the individual is present, but as an individual he does not really count. What is essential here is the multiplying sign tying the individuals together, in other words the interdependence of the individuals.

The debt position of Japanese corporations, notwithstanding the Commercial Code, explains why Japanese top management does not feel really accountable to shareholders, who could give it its independence of action or . . . dismiss it altogether. Top management, especially the company president, plays it safer by involving itself with the application of interdependence, as expressed by the predominance of industrial groups, the major role of trade associations, the partnership with government agencies and, last but not least, by the debt position. It is thus not the banks that 'control' debt; banks are but part and parcel of the system.

Although the debt–equity ratio in prewar Japan was similar to that current in the West, the present 80 per cent debt (which to a westerner would mean courting bankruptcy or takeover by the banks) has meant rapid expansion in the postwar years. Progressive companies had to double their operations every two or three years. In most cases this would hardly have been possible out of retained earnings; it required fresh capital in abundance. This form of massive capitalization was not sought on the stock market as long as custom required that new shares be issued at par value.* On the other hand, besides the fact that loans are acceptable as a deductible business expense, the banks by their loans and the discount of promissory notes,† backed up by the

*Issuance at near market price has spread since 1970. The bond market is still much under-developed.

†Somebody stated that 'Japan is floating on a sea of (commercial) paper'. Whereas a non-Japanese would put the stress on 'paper', a Japanese would put it on 'float'.

Bank of Japan, were most anxious to contribute their funds to industry. These funds in turn were largely provided by individual depositors (the general public) whose saving rate is, today, over twenty per cent of disposable income. And so here we are back again at the Japanese 'WE'.

Corporate management is not particularly interested, therefore, in maximizing profits that improve the price–earnings ratio. It is much more concerned about minimizing the cost of borrowed capital, not by refunding the debt but by expanding its market share and thus maintaining the imperative of RAPID growth.* This concern for the corporate market share is not reserved to managers; the work-force itself is extremely keen in its regard for this objective as it defines the company's industrial and social ranking.

Competition

It is thus to be expected that the relationship between Japanese companies is extremely ambivalent–at once competitive and co-operative. It should be remembered that there is really no Japanese equivalent for the western word 'competition'. Last century when Yukichi Fukuzawa, scholar and school administrator, largely responsible for the introduction of business administration into Japan, was translating an English textbook on economics, he ran into the word 'competition'. He rendered its meaning by fabricating a new word, *kyoso* (*kyo* meaning race, and *so* fight); he was criticized not so much for his semantics, but for introducing an 'un-japanese' value!

Even today the term is not fully accepted. When Japanese businessmen use the term *kyoso* they always prefix it with *kato*, which means 'excessive' competition. The implication appears to be that competition, which in the West stands for the normal relationship between enterprises, in Japan is simply considered as an excess. This 'excess' derives precisely from the dynamics of growth and the drive for market share: it leads corporations into expansive investments in facilities, not justifiable today, but required for tomorrow. The same 'excess' is at work among the sub-groups that compose any large group, be it the company,

*Foreign companies in Japan are no exception. See Norihiko Shimizu, 'Financing Foreign Operations', *Foreign Investment and Japan*, ed. Robert J. Ballon (Tokyo: Sophia/Kodansha, 1972) pp. 211–23.

industry generally or the economy at large. It is further compounded by the social technique of 'crisis', so prevalent in Japanese society. Again let us compare this situation with the human family. For most human beings it is a daily experience to live in a family; but an explicit consciousness of family life is revealed at a time of crisis. This is exactly what happens in any Japanese community, be it social or industrial. If an emergency can be construed or is actually on hand, the crisis atmosphere calls for the mobilization of all energies within the organization. Sacrifices are then accepted without question, and petty rivalries are overlooked; the emotional commitment reaches its peak.

All this has little to do with the western concept of competition, but in the Japanese organizational context it stands for *kato kyoso*, excessive competition. It is an active ingredient of the almost overwhelming dynamism of corporate growth as well as of national economic growth. Speaking of monetary policies, a Japanese government official has stated that, whereas in western countries the talk is about stop-go measures, in Japan one should speak of walk-or-run policies! This brings us to another aspect of Japanese-style competition, one that–to put it mildly–leaves the non-Japanese businessman almost permanently bamboozled: the partnership between government (i.e. bureaucracy) and business. This partnership is completely remote from the classic planned economy; it may be described as the workings of a 'concerted economy'.

> The essential characteristics of the concerted economy are, first, that a common ground be recognised where the government, representing the public interest, the private enterprises expounding private interests, can discuss common problems, exchange information and study the prospects together; second, that private industry pledges to put into practice the policies agreed upon, and the government promises to grant various favours to make implementation possible. Thus a bilateral nexus is created. In other words a promise is given to private industry to direct efforts towards achievements related to the public interest; and on the side of the government, a public promise is made to provide conditional favours to private interests. The result is a dynamic give-and-take relationship for the realization of mutually-agreed future objectives. Yet, the

purpose of such mutual agreement is never anything else than a striving to achieve public interests which are considered desirable from the viewpoint of the national economy as a whole.*

The crux of the matter, therefore, is a question of continuous interaction between government and business, for which the foundation is not the written text of the law, but the imperative of Japanese social dynamics. This pattern has been set by tradition, namely the tradition of the warrior-bureaucrat of the Tokugawa Era (1603–1868) who made, interpreted and administered the 'law' ('law' to be understood not as a written text, but as a rule of equity). The poles of this continuous interaction are administrative guidance and consensus, both effect and cause of the 'equity' role of bureaucracy.

Administrative guidance

Administrative guidance (*gyosei shido*) as provided by Japanese bureaucrats to industry has no legal basis,† and therefore no legal sanction. The penalty for not abiding is not direct but indirect, precisely through the mechanism of continuous interaction. It is essentially a case-by-case problem solving process.‡ The matter could probably be best understood by comparing it to traffic regulations. That traffic runs either on the left or right side of the road is an apparent universal principle; but it makes sense only if and when there is traffic, namely if and when two cars drive in opposite directions. . .

Administrative guidance is not so much the actual application of some universal principle, it is rather the manifestation of a direct initiative taken by the bureaucracy, sometimes arbitrarily but mostly controlled by consensus.

Consensus in Japanese society does not stand for acquiescence or unanimity nor does it stand for an inherent unity of

*Yoshihiko Morozumi, '*Sangyo Kyocho Taisei-ron*' (A discussion of Co-operative Industrial Systems), in MITI Research Section (ed.), *Tsusho Sangyo Kenkyu* (Studies on Trade and Industry), no. 100 (Tokyo: 1962).

†The Fair Trade Commission supports this view but MITI opposes it, arguing that administrative guidance is based on the enabling laws supporting the functions of the various government departments. Eds.

‡In recent years, the Government has been taken to court several times for not announcing administrative standards. Interestingly, however, all these cases concerned individuals, not corporations.

views in regard to broad objectives. Consensus is a style of life, not a mental process. When consensus is reached it does not mean that all parties involved speak with one voice, but that a given issue (as was the case for the previous issue, and will be the case for the following issue) is under consideration by all concerned; it means that execution is taking place. The consensus is formally achieved in joint consultative committees (*shingikai*)* and in trade and industrial associations. For example, MITI (Ministry of International Trade and Industry) regularly reviews the annual investment plans of such capital-intensive industries as steel and synthetic fibres. The matter has been discussed in the industrial association, and is discussed again in the *shingikai*, where the key members of the association meet with the appropriate government officials and private experts. MITI contributes its own views and acts as conciliator and industry responds in view of its own needs and the ability of the ministry to service these needs. More rarely the conciliator turns into an arbitrator and establishes a rule of conduct that will be enforced, such as when cartels or the minimum capacity of any new plant are involved. In all cases bureaucracy remains an active participant in the consensus process.

The Japanese manager

Given the context of Japan's business world, the Japanese manager has two powerful allies, government officials and his own counterparts.

It would appear that government officials, especially those at the Ministry of International Trade and Industry and at the Ministry of Finance, play a predominant role in the economy. This is not exactly the case. Their role is 'predominant' in the sense that:

these officials are among the very best brains of Japan, and their views are articulated with insight and vigour;

they thus express what they see to be in the best national interests;

*These committees often appear to be a waste of time since they form a ready excuse to the bureaucracy for justifying their opinions and the resulting reports are rarely adopted in government policy. The main result is frustration. Eds.

and they are able to back up their views with considerable political and administrative pressure.

However, it would be a gross exaggeration to say that they 'run' the economy. Industry, for its part, is also outspoken about its own views. The best brains in the private sector are gathered together in the *Sanken* (Council for Industrial Policy) and in other economic organizations, where it is made very clear that the formulation of national policies is not an exclusive domain of officialdom, and where views are expressed that repeatedly clash with the official views. What puzzles the foreign observer most is the small relevance of the political process itself. Business policies are, by and large, kept outside the political arena, certainly more so than in western industrial countries. It was all admirably stated by Lockwood:

> The metaphor that comes to mind is a typical Japanese web of influences and pressures interweaving through government and business, rather than a streamlined pyramid of authoritarian control. Perhaps it is just as well. Business is somewhat shielded from government dictation by inter-agency and inter-group tensions. Its own disagreements in turn tend to diffuse its counter-influence in politics. The danger, of course, is a tendency to indecision and drift where national interest may call for clearcut decisions. Only the biggest decisions go up to the Cabinet. There they may still encounter interfactional and inter-Ministerial rivalry, as in the annual contest over the budget. Even then opportunities for noncompliance down the line are considerable. A web it may be, but a web with no spider. What makes the system as workable as it is, no doubt, is a strong *esprit de corps* in the higher ranks of the civil service, and a common social background and university training among leaders in both government and industry.*

Against this background, let us now turn to the Japanese manager in his office.

Postwar Japan has been characterized by the enthusiasm of Japanese management for importing 'modern' technology of production as well as management. This was done mainly from

*William W. Lockwood (ed.), *The State and Economic Enterprise in Japan* (Princeton University Press, 1965) p. 503.

the United States by numerous management missions, a flood of literature, translated and original, and an equally powerful flood of seminars, international conferences, etc. Throughout, the concern was to assimilate, and assimilation has taken place to the extent that today there is a 'modern' (though not necessarily 'western') style of management in Japan.

In the process, Japanese management has become 'professional'. This qualification, though ringing familiar to western ears, should be understood in the Japanese way. Contrary to prewar practice, when managers were promoted on the basis of their kinship to a given family or partisanship to a political regime,* in postwar years management positions have been obtained on the basis of alleged or demonstrated competence. Such competence, however, is not evaluated according to universal 'professional' standards applicable to any individual anywhere, but according to the needs of a given corporation primarily in regard to those who come up from within its own ranks. In general terms it could be said that what is 'professional' about postwar Japanese management is simply the fact that it uses management techniques; there is no 'profession' (at least not yet) in the sense of supplying an individual with credentials which could be meaningful in moving from one company to another. As stated earlier, the industrial identification of a man, be he an employee or a manager, is derived from his work-place. There are two common forms of mobility for managers: *amakudari* and *shukko*.

Amakudari (descending from heaven) is a colloquial expression used when high-ranking government officials, upon (voluntary) retirement from the civil service, move into a directorship position in some large corporation in the industrial line they were active in previously. Thus, some directors of financial institutions come from the Ministry of Finance; in the pharmaceutical industry from the Ministry of Welfare; in the construction industry from the Ministry of Construction, etc. In the private sector former officials do not usually become company presidents, but the Board of Directors is their safe haven and their presence there is the lubricant of effective government-business partnership. The top management of public

*For an excellent analysis of prewar practices and philosophy, see Byron K. Marshall, *Capitalism and Nationalism in Prewar Japan–the Ideology of the Business Elite, 1868–1941* (Stanford University Press, 1967).

corporations and other government-related enterprises is largely composed of these former officials.

Shukko (transfer) is a very common practice whereby a parent company sends some of its executives to a related company for a limited period of say two or three years. This is the way most joint ventures are staffed with managers from the Japanese parent.* The 'transfer' can also be permanent, as in the case of an executive of the parent firm who, upon reaching the mandatory age limit, is promoted to a higher position in a related firm. The purposes behind such a move are varied, but always very specific; there are four possible reasons:

To unload retiring officers, who are not good enough to be kept or would interfere with the promotion scheme at the parent company.
To control the related firm from within, as when a bank sends one of its retiring officers to a major borrower, or when the decision is made to 'rescue' a failing company.
To strengthen ties with a particular industrial grouping, like Mitsubishi or Mitsui, or a smaller more recent group centred upon the personality of its founder, as is found especially in the industrial cluster around a private railway.
To train younger executives by broadening their business experience.

Outside these two cases of mobility, the rule is that managers are promoted from within the company. But what happens when a company is expanding very rapidly from a rather narrow starting point? 'Head-hunting' in Japan comes mainly in two forms:

Recruiting in the market:
It is always possible that an experienced manager wants to quit for honourable reasons. This is rather extraordinary in Japanese companies, but fairly common in foreign ones.
Banks, in particular, sponsor their own placement offices which look for jobs for their retiring employees and managers.
In recent years, several private executive-recruiting agencies have been started; they are, however, mostly active for foreign enterprises and 'hunt' mainly from foreign enterprises.
The public Employment Security Offices sponsor so-called

*See Chapter 7.

Talent Banks specializing in the placement of older and middle-aged employees, including people who exercised some managerial responsibility in smaller firms.

Recruiting through acquaintances:
This is usually a more successful route than the former; it presents the invaluable advantage (in Japan) of involving a sponsor. For example:
An excellent manager in a large corporation, reaching the age of fifty-two or three, cannot be promoted for lack of vacancy on the Board of Directors; his president will be on the look-out for a good assignment for his former subordinate.
There is also a certain unspoken co-operation among Japanese companies that 'tolerate' scouting by up-and-coming companies in dire need of experienced managers, thereby relieving some of the pressure from below within the older established company.

Such a lack of mobility on the labour market is a major handicap to foreign operations in Japan. The problem is easing only very slowly; it constitutes a formidable non-tariff barrier that will protect Japanese industry for several more years to come against the establishment of large hundred per cent-owned foreign establishments as well as takeovers.

Turning now to the management hierarchy, the customary division in the West is: top, middle and lower. These terms are used extensively in Japan, but they do not appear to fit the western structure too exactly. There is a top-management level, where the key figure is the company president; below this level there is the operative management.

Top management

The Japanese Commercial Code, initially a mere translation of the German Code, has three basic requirements governing the management structure of joint-stock corporations (*kabushiki kaisha*):

The general meeting of shareholders (Art. 234); this is considered a mere legal requirement rather than a business matter.
The Board of Directors to be elected by the General Meeting of Shareholders 'at least three in number' (Arts. 254 and 255).

Appointed by the Board from among its members are the 'representative directors' with the power to represent the company legally (Art. 261).
The auditor who cannot be an employee (Art. 276), but is not required to be 'independent' or a professional accountant. Usually the auditorship is a sinecure given to a meritorious retired employee.

In practice, therefore, a Japanese Board of Directors is the final instance of business policy within a corporation. This power is normally concentrated in two or three of the senior directors, who probably are also representative directors; they necessarily include the president who is the chief executive officer of the company. Heading the Board is the Chairman, a title often acquired by the president or given to the out-going president, thus making the role more of an honour than a responsibility. A postwar peculiarity is the fact that several directors are usually full-time operating managers. (Senior managing directors often include division heads, and among the other directors are found managers of major plants or even presidents of major related companies.) With so much of the day-to-day business management represented on the Board, its major function of policy-making is heavily concentrated in the hands of the chief executive officer, the president. In normal circumstances, he may expect the rather passive acquiescence of the Board.

Most corporations have another top-management organ that is not required by law; it is generally called *jomukai* (Executive Committee) or some similar name. If there is any policy problem, it will be discussed in this committee by the same people who meet in the Board, with the exception usually of the Chairman of the Board and a few outside directors. But in the presence of so many operating managers, the Committee will be mostly concerned with routine matters.

Generally speaking, therefore, Japanese corporations at the top are weak in their policy formulation. But this weakness is probably less a matter of management than a feature of the Japanese character that is better at reaction than at action.

The company president

It is thus the president, as chief executive officer, who is expected to provide the kind of leadership that the Japanese industrial organization needs in order to survive both domestic and international competition. In fact the president monopolizes much of this leadership. But leadership in Japanese terms has two basic qualities:

> It is not imposed from the outside; it answers an internal need. The qualification as 'leader' is less a matter of personal talent or merit than acceptance by the organization.
> It supposes that the 'leader' shares in the mutual emotional commitment within the group. The leader-group relationship, therefore, lasts beyond the time and the circumstances of any given task.

Japan's foremost cultural anthropologist has described the matter as follows:

> In the structure of the group, the qualification of the leader rests primarily on his locus within the group, rather than his personal merit; the loyalty of other members towards the leader also derives from their position as subordinate to him. The most significant factor in the exercise of leadership is the personal ties between the leader and his immediate subordinates. Strong, functional personal ties always derive from the informal structure. In a given situation this informal structure may or may not coincide with an institution's formal and visible administrative organization . . . For everyone tends to establish personal ties at a comparatively early stage in his career; and personal ties established in the earlier days tend to supersede those developed at a more advanced stage: the earlier the establishment, the stronger the function. In fact, a man moving to a position of high responsibility tries his best to bring in his *kobun* (followers) as his formal subordinates.*

Not unnaturally, therefore, within the corporation the senior directors usually form an intimate group surrounding the president, while they themselves command similar retinues among junior directors and other managers. As a result, any challenge to the incumbent presidency will come primarily from within the organization. On the one hand the president must hold together his staff and work-force so that the enterprise stays ahead of the neck-breaking speed of the economy by increasing its market

*Chie Nakane, *Japanese Society* (London: Weidenfeld and Nicolson, 1970) pp. 63–4.

share. This is his internal function. On the other hand he must also react flexibly enough to the demands on the organization from lateral commitments: the banks, the industrial group, the trade association, the government, etc. This is his external function.

A president of a well-known corporation sums up the internal function of his office:

> The responsibility as well as the authority of the company president is to move personnel, to place the right man in the right job, to develop the human resources of the company, and to foster the willingness of all employees to participate in the conduct of business.*

It is this internal function that is at the root of the sweeping generalization that Japanese management is paternalistic, if not authoritarian; Japanese scholars, often of Marxist leaning, brand it as feudalistic.

The external function of the company president is much more apparent. Apart from the fact that multiple presidentships are fairly common, a large proportion of the president's time is spent in pursuing public relations activities. He has to meet his counterparts in the industrial group and in the trade and industrial associations; he has to cultivate personal contacts with financial backers, with major clients and, last but not least, with government officials.

The role of the company president, therefore, is essentially a 'social' one from both the internal and external point of view, rather than a direct involvement in the company's real business matters. His leadership rests more on the qualities revolving around human experience and contacts than on technical qualifications. Not surprisingly, Japanese company presidents are usually in their late sixties!

Operative management

Operative management is essentially exercised at two levels: the *bu* (department) and the *ka* (section), a subdivision of the *bu*. Truly functional titles are therefore *bucho* (department head)

*Mr H. Hiyama, President of Marubeni-Iida Co. (Interview in *Nihon Keizai Shimbun*, 9 Feb 1971, p. 21.)

and *kacho* (section chief). Such is the theory; the practice, however, is much more complex. For example the organizational structure of a Japanese enterprise is characterized by what might be called a double multiplicity (which becomes more marked as the enterprise gets larger):

The multiplicity of separate, formally distinct units.
The multiplicity of formal titles.

As a rule, the Japanese organization is a line organization, though the 'line' followed is not exactly the line of authority; it appears to follow rather the 'flow of work' concept. Authority, and therefore responsibility, is diffused throughout the organization. Japanese scholars and managers often contrast the 'top-down' approach of western management to the 'bottom-up' approach of the Japanese. The difference goes back to the independence of the individual versus the interdependence of the member of the group, or to the academic distinction between *Gesellschaft* and *Gemeinschaft.*

In this context, many managerial titles are no more than a mere recognition of status, with little if any definition of the function and responsibility of the positions involved. The danger is that a status-title in an organization that has never fully endorsed the concept of 'staff' as opposed to 'line', unavoidably drifts back to the 'line'. Such a drift is further compounded by the factionalism so prevalent in Japanese organizations and Japanese society.

> Because of the strong collectivity orientation, there is a marked tendency among the personnel of a corporate organization to develop close identity with and loyalty to the immediate formal organizational unit to which they belong. The very close group solidarity tends to give rise to its own sub-goals, which may be in conflict with the goals of the whole organization. This very intense group solidarity encourages each group to protect and promote its own interests against other groups, resulting in strong inter-group rivalry and conflicts of interest. In a collectivity-oriented society such as Japan, with the basic unit of organization being a group, conflicts within a corporate organization often take the form of struggles between groups rather than between individuals. This tendency is further aggravated in Japanese corporations

where the functions and responsibilities of each unit or position are not well defined, thus giving each group more authority within the larger organization.*

It could be agreed, therefore, that Japanese companies are beehives of 'human' activity rather than 'business' activity–in the western sense. What is more, it is often said that the Japanese are hard working.† This is an exaggeration; it would be more correct to say that they keep very busy–busy, that is, with the business of human relations within the frame of the organization, rather than busy performing physical or mental work. It is little wonder that company presidents become so deeply involved in personal matters, having to act as a kind of umpire over the lively factionalism in their organization.

So, just how do decisions emerge from within an organization with so many conflicting human dynamics? Foreign businessmen have rightly observed in their dealings with Japanese companies that decisions are very slow in coming. On the other hand, Japanese businessmen sometimes complain that in their dealings with foreigners, once a decision is taken, nothing happens for a very long time. It is now worth examining the problem of slow decision (Japan) versus slow execution (West).

Slow decision

In a Japanese organization, with its heavy reliance on human considerations, time is required to reach what appears to be a decision; in fact what is arrived at is a consensus for execution. Management is keenly concerned with involving in the decision-making process everybody who will be involved in the execution. This is achieved through repeated formal discussions and formal meetings, which are often aided by the circulation of a document (*ringisho*) stating the matter on hand. Thus when a company is considering the construction of, say, a new plant, nothing much can be expected from a mere decision–that in itself is meaningless unless, or until, everybody concerned has

*M. Yoshino, *Japan's Managerial System–Tradition and Innovation* (Cambridge Mass.: MIT Press, 1968) p. 221.

†The usual proof given is the working hours. All they 'prove', however, is that the Japanese are still working 'longer', not necessarily 'harder'. This in itself is an indication that expectations in regard to the work environment are somehow better satisfied.

been involved. When finally the decision is taken, it is tantamount to the start of work operations.

Slow execution

The western decision-making process largely revolves around the responsibility of the decision-maker. Once the individual who will take this responsibility has been located (he is selected almost automatically by his position on the organization chart) alternative strategies are considered, and what is thought to be the best one is selected (decided). Now starts an often lengthy process leading to execution, as the various levels of the hierarchy are informed about the decision and requested to co-operate and prepare to put it into effect.

Following this schematic contrast, the difference between the Japanese and the western process is not so much a matter of time. Whatever amount of time is required by the Japanese *before* the 'decision' is made, a similar amount is required by westerners *after* the decision is taken. The basic difference between the two approaches is to be found in the style of execution. It is obvious that following a decision by consensus (Japanese-style) the execution of that decision by those involved will be highly motivated in the sense that 'this is *our* decision'. On the other hand, the execution of a decision 'on command' remains just that–motivation being a very secondary implicit element.

However, in view of the factionalism in Japanese companies, it would be quite wrong to see Japanese consensus as a kind of passive acquiescence, or as something that springs forth spontaneously. It is not even decentralized decision-making. The group and departmental efforts are duplicated; authority mostly overlaps; reporting procedures are often confusing; communications end in bottlenecks and specific assignments are often too narrow to be truly challenging, and so on. All these weaknesses result from the lack of western-style 'functionalism'; but such or similar weaknesses are also found where the concept of functionalism supposedly prevails.

The single most important reason why Japanese companies do not stop dead in their tracks is because they have operating managers. Much more than top management *per se* (let us remember that many directors are also managers), they are accountable for the performance of the human organization of which they are a part. But accountable to whom? Essentially, they are accountable to the organization, since management is a function of the *shokuba* (the place of work). Managers, of course, pursue their own career, but it remains understood that this career is with the company.

In the broadest terms, there are five fundamental steps in the career of a Japanese manager:

1 The managerial career begins with college (four years), followed by graduation, followed by selective recruiting. The implications of the school clique are an important consideration for the simple reason that human dynamics work better among people sharing a common educational background. It has to be said, however, that the clique system is not quite as strong as it was. Nepotism has little impact and is generally frowned upon.

2 For the next five to ten years the managerial candidate will work as a general office clerk, rotating jobs in the various sections and plants of the company. In each instance, the technical demands upon him will be great; they are to be answered primarily by on-the-job development and initiative. (These are the young people who surround the senior men who negotiate with foreign business representatives.)

3 After ten or more years of employment in the same company the first threshold is reached, namely promotion to the position of *kacho* (section chief). This is as far as some will ever go, but the practical experience they accumulate as years go by provides the company with essential expertise. For others, it now becomes clear that they are on the way up.

4 For these especially promising executives, the real need now is to widen their 'experience' and not, as might be assumed, to widen their technical qualifications (though they are regular attendants at seminars and other training activities). As numerous surveys have uncovered 'experience' is, in the eyes of their superiors, the major qualification for further promotion. Experience is seen as something that cannot be taught; it is a function of age, and is manifested in what could be generally called human relations. In this context, the manager is expected to develop into a generalist rather than a specialist.

5 After a total of some twenty years of employment another threshold is reached, that of *bucho* (department head). Because of the shortage of vacancies at the top, or because of individual shortcomings, some managers will stay in this position until retiring age (usually fifty-five) at which time they will then be transferred to a related firm or the like. Others, round about the age of fifty-two or three, will be promoted to a directorship, while maintaining their *bucho* position; to them the normal retiring age limit does not apply.

In any consideration of the career of a Japanese manager, however, what must be kept in mind is the fact that group solidarity and factionalism exert strong pressure from below. As with the company president, managers at all levels have to display leadership. They are not supposed to do the work themselves, but they must have it done by their subordinates while at the same time they themselves remain involved in it, which can be difficult.

This system has thrown at Japanese managers what they consider their greatest challenge, the so-called generation gap. They all complain that today's younger generation is rebellious (forgetting that they themselves years back chaffed under their superiors). As with management systems throughout the world, the best cure for subordinates' dissatisfaction is promotion. In recent years of course, due to massive commercial expansion, a great many new promotion openings have been created. Even so Japanese managers today have a serious problem on their hands. The standard solution appears to be as follows: whether he knows exactly what is involved or not, a manager must promote initiative from below by sponsoring the latest managerial technique available, before any other section in the company does!

It is now a hundred years since Japan started to adopt and assimilate aspects of western business management techniques. They were adopted with as much eagerness as was the introduction of western technology. In prewar as well as in postwar Japan, whatever success has taken place could not have been possible without the West's contributions. However, the fundamental question is this: Why has Japan been successful? The answer must surely lie in the human dynamics at work in the industrial enterprise and the economy at large. It would be too western an evaluation to give all the credit for this success to the managers; the credit has to be shared among all the Japanese. Nevertheless, it must be said that Japanese managers have displayed an extraordinary flexibility in leading Japan from an impecunious economy to one of great affluence. So much so that today managers believe they have been singled out as scapegoats for the cost of this affluence–namely pollution. Now a new stage of management development is in the making. On the domestic scene, if the last one hundred years are in any way typical, it appears that management philosophy and practice will continue to change rapidly, without necessarily becoming 'more western' or 'less Japanese'.

However, of far more consequence for the future evolution of Japanese management is the fact that, as Japan increases her foreign direct investments, more and more Japanese managers will become increasingly involved in overseas operations. It is only very recently that Japanese corporations realized (with genuine dismay) that their overseas operations are overwhelmingly staffed by Japanese–an understandable situation so long as *international* operations meant *Japanese* operations overseas. A new and brave 'party line' however is now in the process of formulation, namely management participation rather than management control. It may well be that, after some more traumatic experiences, this approach will be acceptable to both the foreign and Japanese parties. Even so the Japanese side will probably retain the advantage, since its domestic style of management is a question of participation rather than control.

6 Employee and Industrial Relations

JAMES C. ABEGGLEN

INTRODUCTION

The complex interaction of tradition and very rapid change is at once the fascination and the challenge of the study of Japan. No nation in this generation has changed more swiftly; no nation retains its identity more surely. The challenge of analysis and prediction is to separate out those aspects of Japan that will continue essentially unchanged from those that will yield readily to the opportunities and pressures of the moment.

In the economic sector, the dialectic between the stable and the transitory comes into sharp focus in the field of organization, the manner in which people are hired, trained, rewarded or punished, and related to each other in large industrial or financial organizations. Japan has a unique employment system, deriving its strength from its being based firmly on Japan's social system. Yet this employment system is subject to the massive economic changes taking place in Japan as well as to the changes in attitudes and values resulting from industrialization and affluence.

The problem in considering changes in Japan's employment system is that of understanding its bases of strength, reviewing the pressures it is under, and attempting to gauge the effects of the transition-continuity interaction. Japan is clearly in transition, and not for the first time. Yet continuity of values and behaviour remains a central theme. The analysis of Japan's unique employment system, its strengths, weaknesses and the pressures on it for continuity and change provides a test case of the larger issue of continuity and change in Japanese society.

Japan in transition

It is evident that the early years of the 1970s mark a broad-ranging transition period for Japan and its economy. Since the end of the Second World War the nation's unparalleled economic achievements have built the world's most effective industrial complex. Incomes and output are at European levels, an order of magnitude greater than had been thought possible in Asia. Both in trade and in politics the world will be attempting to come to terms with the Japan phenomenon for decades.

Yet this achievement by its magnitude has raised major new issues for Japan, only now becoming clear. They are essentially the issues of defining an international role. In external affairs, the passive policies the Japanese government has been following are inappropriate to its present economic strength, are not responsive to changing world power relations, and are increasingly unsatisfactory to the Japanese public. Relations with the United States, the Soviet Union and the People's Republic of China are undergoing urgent re-examination. Further, the problems involved in massive overseas capital investment and extensive foreign aid programmes, unprecedented in the history of Japan or of any Asian country, are now being addressed.

Within Japan, the long-deferred needs for increased public expenditure have new and higher priorities, as the flow of new investment capital is being diverted into the social overhead sector. Along with this, during a period of slower economic growth, private capital is re-examining the directions of industrial investment over the decade. Further, a new generation of political leaders is just coming on stage, men who will seek to give political focus to the interests of the postwar, urban, industrial Japanese public.

These issues suggest very great changes indeed in Japan over the next several years, changes whose impact on the nation and the world may well be as far reaching as the economic events of the past two decades. But these are changes in public policy and changes in resource allocation. New directions in policy can be undertaken without society necessarily undergoing changes in its basic patterns of behaviour or thinking. To what extent have more basic changes taken place in Japan over this past generation of unprecedented changes in economic circumstance? What changes might be expected in Japanese society;

what new directions are likely in the fundamental patterns of behaviour and interaction?

Continuity in change

As a point of departure in addressing these questions, it needs first to be emphasized that Japan is a non-western society. Its history, geography, religions, language, racial composition and political traditions are Asian, not of the West. It is the only non-western industrialized nation. It is the nation of Asia that has demonstrated that the period of western imperial ascendancy was fated to be brief, first politically and now economically. If this emphasis on Japan's Asian position and unique social traditions appears to emphasise a truism, let it be noted that a good deal of discussion about changes in Japan deplores this emphasis and insists on a considerable similarity between Japanese and western society.

It can be argued that it is the underlying continuity and stability of Japanese society that has made the enormous achievements of the past generation possible. The social changes inherent in the move from per capita output of a little over $100 in 1950 to nearly $2000 in 1970 are enormous. From famine in some Japanese regions at the war's end, rice is now in embarrassing surplus. From nearly half of the work-force in agriculture, the proportion is now only 15 per cent, with Japan one of the most urbanized nations in the world. The death rate has been halved, as life expectancy nears the highest levels in the world, increasing by nearly 20 years in only 20 years. Incomes in current prices have increased more than 45 times in the years since 1947. As a more homely index of social change, the Ministry of Education found it necessary to increase the size of the standard school desk, since Japan's postwar children are larger than earlier generations.

Social change far less dramatic than this has played havoc with the social fabric of nations less homogeneous and less stable than Japan. In Japan's case, these great changes have been joined with a high degree of political stability, very low rates of crime and other social pathologies, and a steadily higher national morale. Some part of this must be owed to good management; some considerable part must reflect the strength of Japanese society and its traditions. Far from being 'a fragile blossom' as one visitor suggested, this is a strong and healthy society. Professor Nakane suggests a key to that strength:

> It is in informal systems rather than in overt cultural elements that persistent factors are to be found. The informal system, the driving force of Japanese activities, is a native Japanese brew, steeped in a unique characteristic of Japanese culture. In the course of modernization Japan imported many western cultural elements, but these were and are always partial and segmentary and are never in the form of an operating system. It is like a language with its basic indigenous structure or grammar which has accumulated a heavy overlay of borrowed vocabulary; while the outlook of Japanese society has suffered drastic changes over the past hundred years, the basic social grammar has hardly been affected.*

The strength of the Japanese economic system similarly has derived from the fact that Japan's industrialization has taken place by the introduction of western technology and methods into a Japanese social context. The result is a unique business system, the most effective approach to economic management the world has yet seen. In the melding of imported techniques to a Japanese context, special business practices have developed, especially in the allocation and use of human resources, in the optimal use of financial resources, and in the inter-relations between government and business, that differ markedly from those in the West.

Japan's employment system

It is the employment system in Japan–the allocation and use of human resources–that is at once the most paradoxical, the most discussed, and the most liable to western ethnocentricity in its evaluation. Paradox arises from the fact that the Japanese employment system has very considerable strengths, yet is commonly seen in the West as inefficient and virtually unworkable. Controversy stems both from arguments over the system's

*Chie Nakane, *Japanese Society* (London: Weidenfeld and Nicolson, 1970) p. 149.

causes and outcomes, and from the view that it must surely change–and in the western fashion.

It seems appropriate, as Japan undergoes still further transitions, to re-examine the Japanese employment system and its effects, and raise again the questions of whether and when the system might change.

The main features of what will be called here Japan's employment system include the following:

1 Recruitment of the employee takes place directly from school. Entrance to the work-force is from the bottom of the age ranking, and not from an open labour market.
2 Recruitment is in terms of personal qualifications, and into the work group. Employees are not hired for specific jobs, nor do they apply for specific jobs. Rather they are hired because of an expectation that additional employees will be required, and on the assumption that skills not provided by general educational background will be provided through company training. Qualifications are intelligence, character and general acceptability as determined by personal history, academic record and company tests and interviews.
3 Employment is for the entire career of the individual. Both employer and employee assume that the employment relationship is permanent, that the company will not discharge or lay off the employee and that the employee will not change to another employer during his career.
4 Compensation depends basically and largely on length of service. Initial compensation is a function of the level of education completed; subsequent increases in compensation are a function of length of service, which in this system correlates directly with age.
5 The trade union bargaining unit includes all company employees, with few, if any, jurisdictional issues. The union contract is generally limited to recognition and to compensation of members, and bargaining is predictably seasonal (the 'spring struggle').

These are the basic features of the Japanese employment system. It has associated aspects that are important and unusual but not critical to the system. There is, for example, a general practice of retirement at the age of fifty-five, ameliorated by the possibility of assignment to subsidiaries and increasingly subject to experiments with a more advanced retirement age. Again an important component of cash compensation is the bonus, negotiated with the union and loosely a function of company profitability, which is paid twice annually and is a considerable increment to the basic wage. Further, a wide variety of allowances is paid to compensate for size of family, hazardous work, posting to undesirable locations, and the like. And a part of the employment pattern is a general tendency to take only brief holidays, rather than following the western pattern of extended vacation. Several of these kinds of unique patterns have important consequences, as, for example, the impact of the bonus payment system on Japan's savings rate. They may be seen, however, as marginal to the basic employment structure.

This structure, emphasizing group membership rather than individual skills, involving employer and employee in a permanent and complex relationship of mutual obligation, and rewarding tenure rather than short-term performance, is consistent with and is based on very fundamental and well-established patterns in Japanese society. It is also a very modern employment system in that it is the result of the restructuring of Japan after the Second World War. It can thus be taken to be the most recent pattern of employment among the developed economies of the world. It is also a paradoxical system–at once rooted in the social traditions of Japan and at the same time the product of recent economic history.

The Japanese employment system as described above is a statement of the ideal. In practice there are, of course, exceptions to each of its essential features. However, this summary fairly states both the norm and the general practice. Conceptually and analytically it is the norm that is critical; the exceptions comprise footnotes to the rule. Among exceptions there is some movement of younger people from small to large companies and considerable movement of workers between smaller firms (although smaller firms follow the system as an 'ideal' within their economic capability). There is some movement of specialists who are in temporary short supply between large companies. Further, large companies have some part of their labour force in the category of 'temporary workers' who are, as the term implies, outside these general rules. As another exception of sorts, female workers generally leave the firm on marriage rather than remaining in the employment system.

Motivation of the labour force

It is surely self-evident that, to be effective, the organization of the work-place in any society must be consistent with the underlying values and patterns of interaction in that society. Thus in a relatively individualistic society, like that of the United States where relationships have a considerable element of contract and where economic relations in particular tend to be depersonalized, it is not surprising that the system of recruitment and compensation in companies conforms to these underlying patterns in the society. If the organization of the work-place were discontinuous from and not congruent with the organization of the family, the school and other primary institutions, the work-place would not function effectively.

By the same token, to the extent that Japanese society is different from that of the West in values and in interaction, it would be expected that the organization of the work-place would differ. Indeed it is reasonable to conclude that the very success of Japanese industry argues for a high degree of organizational congruence with the special features of Japanese culture. The sociological roots of Japan's employment system, and its effectiveness in motivating Japanese employees, are suggested by Nakane after reviewing Japanese family interaction:

> Another group characteristic portrayed in the Japanese household can be seen when a business enterprise is viewed as a social group. In this instance a closed social group has been organized on the basis of the 'life-time employment system' and the work made central to the employees' lives. The new employee is in just about the same position and is, in fact, received by the company in much the same spirit as if he were a newly born family member, a newly adopted son-in-law or a bride come into the husband's household . . .
>
> The relationship between employer and employee is not to be explained in contractual terms. The attitude of the employer is expressed by the spirit of the common saying, 'the enterprise is the people'. This affirms the belief that employer and employee are bound as one by fate in conditions which produce a tie between man and man often as firm and close as that between husband and wife. Such a relationship is manifestly not a purely contractual one between employer and employee; the employee is already a member of his own

family, and all members of his family are naturally included in the larger company 'family'.*

An initial, general view then of the basis for the high morale and motivation that observers commonly credit to the Japanese work-force is that this motivation derives from the fact that the organization of the work-place parallels the organization of Japan's primary institutions. The company is a recipient of the kind of identification and loyalty that is the basis of family organization. It is clear, too, that under these conditions the economic organization must respond reciprocally by concern for the employee's general well-being, his housing, his holidays, and such family events as marriages, births and deaths. Japanese companies do express their interest and concern through appropriate allowances, gifts and company recreation facilities.

It is also clear that, if this is the basis for the relationship, dismissal can be undertaken only in extreme cases. Even lay-offs are rare. When, under pressure of the 1971 turn-down in colour television demand, Hitachi determined that temporary lay-offs were required (and obtained union concurrence), laid-off workers were guaranteed payment of 85 per cent of their previous base wage on the first day of lay-off, 90 per cent the second, and 95 per cent thereafter.

The congruence with the social substrata is the basis for the employment system. This is not to say that the work-place is 'one big, happy family', that all motives are benign, or that ambitious or frustrated men never look longingly over their shoulder at other employers. But consider the effects of the system on job change and on work motivation. A man joins the company fresh from school, and presumably for his career. To be available for employment elsewhere is to be branded in the eyes of most potential employers as one who has been a problem. There must be something wrong or else why is he available? Further, the rather rigid patterns of pay and of retirement allowance as well as the informal work group structure make it exceedingly difficult to fit a new man into an organization except at the bottom of the hierarchy.

In short, from the point of view of the employee his future and his family's future depend on the success of the company that

*Nakane, op. cit., pp. 14–15.

now employs him. If that company prospers and grows, he will be promoted, his bonuses will wax fat, and his family's and his own future are assured. If the company does badly, so does he and so do his dependants. His choices are few, and so his motivation to work hard and do well by the company is correspondingly strong. Under these conditions it is not surprising that there is a high degree of identification with the company and its fortunes. Not only is there a strong social and psychological basis for the identification, but the realities of the career mightily reinforce it.

So, too, for the company. It is no small matter for a Japanese company when an employee announces his decision to leave. By so doing, he is declaring to the community that the company has not taken proper care of him, and is not meeting its obligations to its employees. Most foreign companies in Japan (they are, after all, the organizations that can offer positions to older men without necessarily upsetting their structures) have considerable experience of the very great pressures Japanese companies exert to ensure that no one leaves. The impact on the prestige of a Japanese company of a defecting employee is felt deeply since it affects the company's reputation, its ability to attract recruits and its credibility with its present staff.

It would appear that in a Japanese context the employment system is a powerful mechanism for motivation. It has two faces. It taps first the very basic motives involved in a group-centred, non-contractual, hierarchy-oriented society. And on this base is laid an employment and compensation pattern that reinforces the identification of employer and employee. Personal success and company success become inextricably intermeshed.

Distribution of the labour force

Many western observers suggest that the Japanese employment system contains substantial economic inefficiencies due to the immobility of the labour force that the system imposes. This is a simplistic view; it can more properly be argued that the system makes for an especially efficient allocation of the labour force in terms of economic growth.

Consider the question of labour cost. A well-run economy is that in which the more efficient–and therefore faster-growing–business or industry has steady cost advantage relative to the less efficient company or industry. The Japanese employment system works directly to ensure this outcome.

It has been noted that workers enter the Japanese company directly from school rather than horizontally from an open labour market. It has been further noted that their compensation is a direct function of length of service (i.e. age). Thus labour costs are directly related to the average age of the work-force. It is no accident that Japan is the one country in which standard information on a company includes, along with balance sheet, shareholders and the like, the average age of the work-force, divided usually by male and female employees. This is critical competitive data since it indicates the labour cost levels of the company, and by comparison with other companies, competitive labour costs.

A fast growing company or industry has some competitive advantage that causes its more rapid growth rate. It is in the economic interest of the total economy to support the fast-growth sectors. But fast growth carries with it a requirement that the labour force expand relatively rapidly. Thus the company that is growing rapidly, and for whatever reason gaining competitive advantage, is hiring large numbers of personnel directly from school.

This addition of young workers directly from school lowers the average age of the work-force of the successful and growing company or industry, and so the average cost of labour for the company or industry is reduced. Thus, whatever the factors that were causing the company or industry to gain competitive advantage and grow more rapidly are now very much reinforced by a steady improvement in wage rates compared to a more slowly growing company or industry.

Conversely, a slow-growing company or industry, adding few if any members to its work-force, is subject to a steady increase in its average wage rate as its work-force ages. Whatever caused its slower growth, the result is now reinforced on the negative side by a widening cost disadvantage.

Thus the system of recruitment and pay must be seen as highly efficient in terms of labour cost effectiveness in reinforcing growth. There are still further benefits for the growth sectors. Younger workers hired directly from school are those workers with the most recent technological training. While the work-force of a slow-growing firm experiences a steady obsolescence of its skill levels, the fast-growing firm is steadily improving. In this way new technology is allocated to the various growth sectors.

These benefits are not confined to the lower ranks of the work-force. Since management is not recruited from outside the company, the fast-growing company with a rapidly expanding work-force must place executive authority in the hands of younger, and probably more aggressive, management personnel. Meanwhile, the management of companies in the slow-growth sectors continues to age and presumably becomes less aggressive and risk-taking.

A further factor operates to reinforce the tendency of this system to foster growth in the economy. When the choice of company is a career choice, and essentially irrevocable, a man is likely to spend a lot of time in deciding which company he will join. In fact, he will depend heavily on the advice of senior advisers, especially teachers, friends and family, to ensure that his decision is sound and well based. To the extent that he is perceptive and careful in his decision, he will seek to join a firm and an industry that has the widest choice of the best men in its recruiting, the process again reinforcing the successful firm and working against the interests of the less successful firm.

Mobility from job to job in the firm is possible in the Japanese case both from the fact that the worker has no critical reason to object to reassignment and that management has a considerable incentive to provide training for a new position. From the employee's point of view his tenure is assured and his income based primarily on length of service. A move from one job to another within the firm threatens neither compensation nor employment. For the company the worker is a fixed cost and continued obligation; since employment change is rare, retraining does not run the risk of the worker taking his new skills elsewhere for other employment as it does in the West. Finally, as discussed further below, the union is not a skill union, nor does the union contract specify job content, and thus the labour contract is no obstacle to mobility from one job to another.

Stability of labour relations

The pattern of relations between the company and the trade union that has developed in Japan is an important factor in explaining the economy's competitive strength. Trade unions are a powerful force in Japan, and studies of workers' attitudes indicate that the Japanese employee looks on his union as a critical check against an otherwise excessively powerful management. At the same time, the pattern of labour relations that has developed has avoided any rigidities in work-force management and has worked to minimize the enormous economic costs of strikes that have proved so devastating to the economies of Europe and the United States.

The Japanese labour force is unionized to the same extent as it is in the West. About 30 per cent of the labour force consists of union members, and this proportion has held quite steady for a number of years. The basic element of unionization is the 'enterprise union', which takes in as members all the employees of the company, whatever their particular job. The labour contract deals primarily with union recognition and with compensation; it does not cover such matters as job content, speed of the assembly line and the like as is the case in the West. Negotiation is essentially over compensation. These 'enterprise unions' are generally affiliated to industry-wide federations which are members of one of the several nationwide federations. These federations are essentially politically orientated, the largest being the biggest supporter of Japan's Peking-oriented Socialist Party.

Parallels with the basic employment system of this pattern of union relations are clear, and inevitable. The employment pattern emphasizes company membership rather than occupation or skill identification. No surprise, then, that craft or skill unions are virtually unknown. The bargaining unit takes in all employees of the company, keeping intact even in the context of union relations the concept of company membership and identification. The integrity of the company unit is maintained despite the identification of the union with federations whose activities extend beyond the company. The union serves its purpose as a check on management that otherwise might exploit the work-force.

The stability of labour relations must be seen as a principal source of competitive advantage to Japanese firms in world markets. It makes possible flexible use of the labour force and rapid introduction of new technology while minimizing the costs to the economy of work stoppages. Looking first at the work stoppage issue, without compromising the union as a representative of the worker in disputes with management, the Japanese approach to union–company relations reduces the incidence of strikes, limits their duration and, by their seasonal predictability, very much reduces their competitive costs.

The direct cost of strikes in Japan has, in recent years, been about one-seventieth the cost of strikes in the United States. That is, man-hours lost to strikes, multiplied by cost per man-hour, was seventy times greater in the American case. Note that this is an absolutely minimum estimate of the cost of labour disputes. There is also the cost to the economy of man-hours lost as a result of lay-offs and production stoppages in supplier firms when buyer firms are on strike, and the cost of lack of product.

Further, the costs of strikes in the West are greater than in Japan because of the incidence in the West of strikes in which a few workers in a skill union are able to close down the company's entire production. These considerable effects are not reflected in the simple calculation of man-hours lost due to strikes. Finally the unpredictability of strikes in the West raises considerably their economic cost. Stockpiling of inventories in anticipation of strikes is one example; customers lost to international competitors is another. Consider the cost to Japan, supplying world customers through a ten-thousand-mile pipeline, if assurance of supply to customers was substantially affected by the likelihood of unpredictable supply stoppage.

Japan therefore benefits considerably from its system of labour relations. There are three basic factors for this.

First, the issue of jurisdictional disputes and separate negotiations with several bargaining entities is not relevant in Japan. Management deals with a single bargaining entity, and is not subject to the hazard of a small group in the work-force holding the entire company to ransom to achieve its bargaining objectives. This carries with it the hazard that the single bargaining entity has massive power. Just as one union cannot take advantage of others in negotiations, so management in Japan cannot set one union against another. What limits the potentially enormous power of the single bargaining unit?

Here we must refer again to the system of career employment. If the worker's well-being and that of his family depend very heavily on the well-being of the company as a whole, and if their future and the company's future are rightly interrelated, there is a sharp limit to the extent to which he, or he and his fellows in the union, is prepared to damage the company. Bearing in mind the fact that Japanese companies make heavy use of debt in their financing and thus have a very limited cash position, and noting also that competition for market share in Japan is very strong, it is clear that the consequences of an extended strike for a Japanese company would be devastating and the cost to the worker would be equally disastrous.

Under these conditions it is not surprising that strikes tend to take place during early morning hours, or at lunch hour, at five o'clock, or for a day. This is not to say that these are not meaningful as a threat and as a reminder to management of the union's power. They are a real statement of power relations, but limited in their cost to the company and to the economy.

Note, too, that under the Japanese system of employment there is not the same separation of interest as in the American or European case. In western terms, there are 'parties to the dispute', adversaries whose interests and objectives are quite distinct. But this distinction of parties to the dispute is much less clear when the enterprise union which takes in all of the employees of the company, who expect to spend their careers in the company, deals with the management of that company in a dispute. Their interests are not separate. Thus it is not surprising that a company doing poorly in a given year can ask for understanding in wage negotiations for that year with the promise that the shortfall in wage increase will be made up in a year or two when the company is doing better. The work-force will be there in a year or two, and the promise is a meaningful one.

Finally, the predictability of strikes in Japan needs to be noted to appreciate fully their limited economic cost. A pattern has developed whereby wage disputes, or more precisely the issue of annual increases in compensation for the work-force, come into focus in the spring, the so-called 'spring struggle'. Some 90 per cent of the limited man-hours lost to strikes takes place in April. Thus both the company and its customers can anticipate supply interruptions and adjust inventories accordingly. Again this is an economic advantage difficult to measure but undoubtedly an important factor in minimizing the economic cost of labour disputes.

It should be noted that the unions generally support and are important in reinforcing the present system of employment. A system of compensation based on seniority, and a system of employment tenure, is no less attractive to Japanese unions than to unions elsewhere in the world. Thus the union in Japan, far from being a force for change in employment practices, is, in fact, a significant factor in maintaining the basic characteristics of the employment system.

Because union membership is not differentiated by skills, it is also the case that the union contract is no barrier to job flexibility. In the West the union contract serves to maintain the system of skills existing at a given moment in order to preserve the jobs of union members. This obviously introduces rigidity in work assignment and resistance to technological change. Since union membership in Japan is not differentiated by job, the union contract is no obstacle to work-force mobility from job to job, nor is it a barrier to the introduction of new technology that might change job content.

In summary, labour relations in Japan form a pattern quite different to that in the West. The Japanese pattern of trade union relations is, inevitably, consistent with the overall employment system. The consequences of this pattern are to Japan's very considerable economic advantage.

Introduction of new technology

In 1950 the per capita output of the Japanese economy was at about the level of most of South-East Asia today, a little over $100. In the following two decades output increased almost twenty times to nearly $2000, or the level of Western Europe. This change is both a measure of the magnitude of Japan's economic achievement and also an index of the extent of technological change that has taken place in the Japanese economy. Clearly this enormous economic growth requires huge inputs of technology into the work-place. One measure of the amount of technology introduced is the fact that more than 15,000 contracts were entered into by Japanese companies with western firms during the 1950–70 period for the purchase of western technology.

Each of these technological inputs, whether from foreign or domestic sources, carries with it a change in the nature of the job, some amount of adjustment in the work-place, as the product or the process of production changes to introduce new technology. Since each of these inputs requires job change, this long sustained rate of technological change argues that the Japanese employment system must be highly flexible. Each change in product or process requires work-force adjustment. The skill content of a given job must change; inevitably some jobs are wiped out by new technology; some are downgraded; new skill requirements are introduced; each introduction of technology is a threat to the existing system of work relations. It is not surprising that in the West there is a long history of resistance to new technology; it is fair to say that the rate of technological change experienced by Japan could not be achieved in Great Britain or the United States because of the strain this change would place on employee and trade union relations. How has Japan been able to introduce such rapid technological change without there being a destructive influence on employee relations?

Again, we must refer to the employment system. If employment is 'permanent', then new technology does not threaten the employment of the worker. He will retain his employment in any event, even if the new product or process wipes out his particular job. In fact the new product or process does not even threaten his level of compensation. He is paid basically according to seniority, and therefore the fact that a particular job is displaced technologically is not a threat to income. Thus, new technology is no threat. Indeed if the technology is in fact useful competitively, and thereby improves the position of the company, it is to the worker's advantage that it be introduced since, as the company benefits, so will he in the form of more rapid advancement, larger bonuses, increased job security, and enlarged prestige from company success. In short, new technology in the Japanese system brings with it no negative results; rather, to the extent that it is effective, the introduction of new technology can have only positive benefits.

In the West, the Luddite tradition is never far from the surface. New technologies are a menace. They displace particular jobs, make skills obsolete, and can only be a threat to the work-force. This fact is embodied in the trade union agreements of the West in which job content is specified and job changes require renegotiation of contractual commitments. The Japanese company is freed of these constraints on the introduction of new technology; indeed, the nature of the employment relationship is such that new technology, if it is in fact productive, can only be welcomed by the work-force as a benefit. When the question is argued as to whether the Japanese economy can keep pace with western technological developments, this fact needs to be kept in mind. There is an inherent Japanese advantage, under present conditions, in the race for commercial application of new technology.

It must be said that there is a considerable view both in academic and business discussions that Japanese employment practices are inefficient and need to be changed–'modernized'. While little or no concrete evidence is available to indicate that the system is changing, like any institutional pattern in a rapidly shifting society the employment system developed in Japan has disadvantages and weaknesses.

Lack of labour mobility

The difficulties for the economy that might arise from the reduced labour mobility in this employment system are considerably mitigated by the intrafirm mobility noted earlier. The employment system described here principally characterizes large companies employing thousands of workers. Mobility in the small business sector is more common. This makes small businesses less desirable employers, not only for reasons of prestige but also and more urgently for reasons of lack of job security.

For the individual company, the immobility of the system poses some real problems. There is, first of all, an overstaffing prerequisite because of the difficulty of hiring from outside the company when additional personnel are needed. It is self-evident that in this system a company that expects continued growth must hire from the universities and high schools not the number of men needed at the time of hiring, but rather the number of men that are likely to be needed to fill positions in the future. As a result the large company has a pool of younger, university-graduated staff which tends not to be drawn into meaningful activity for several years after employment.

This real cost disadvantage should not be exaggerated. Since newly hired men are low salaried, the costs involved are not large. Further, the availability of these young men means that Japanese companies are able to do, and commonly do, an amount of staff work in terms of project planning and market research that is prodigious by western standards. Still, it is a real cost disadvantage of the system. This phenomenon also results in a high rate of disaffection among the young workers, who complain about the lack of opportunity and the ponderous nature of the hierarchy.

A further disadvantage of the system in terms of employment costs is the difficulty of removing from the payroll employees of demonstrated incompetence. As an example, the personnel department of a major steel complex identified some fifty employees who, for reason of physical or mental disability, were unable to perform usefully in any job. The suggestion was made to the senior manager of the complex that these people be discharged. The suggestion was rejected on the classic grounds that the company had an obligation to continue the employment of these people, especially in view of Japan's generally poor provisions for social welfare.

It is interesting to speculate on the relative costs to the total economy of welfare programmes provided by private corporations as opposed to those provided by the government. The provisions for housing, retirement and income security by the large Japanese corporations are an alternative to government welfare programmes. One might guess that they are more efficiently provided by the corporation.

These costs to the individual company of 'permanent employment' must, in competitive international terms, be set off against the costs in western employment systems of fairly high turnover of personnel. The frictional costs of repeated recruiting and training of replacement personnel certainly balance, in some degree, the costs of retaining less than competent individuals and of temporary overstaffing.

A more substantial problem arising from the limitations on labour mobility has to do with technology. As the Japanese company seeks to enter a new field in which technical skills are required, which are not available within the company, it clearly encounters a major obstacle from its difficulties in recruiting those new skills. There is some reason to believe this has been a disadvantage to Japanese firms in the computer area, where technology has been changing very rapidly.

Dependence on growth

Can this system of employment survive a long-sustained period of slow economic growth? If the work-force cannot be reduced in size, abrupt downturns in demand can have a devastating effect on costs. If compensation increases steadily with seniority, a continued flatness in demand will result in steady and inexorable cost increases. Given Japan's economic performance, the question has no historical answer. What may be said, however, is that in any economy at any time, barring an improbable and disastrous long-continued depression, some companies and sectors are growing, while others are not. It was noted above that the Japanese employment system works to the considerable competitive advantage of growth companies and industries. It perhaps needs to be more explicitly pointed out that the effects of the system on slow-growth firms and industries are sharply negative. Costs rise steadily, work-force quality erodes, these and other factors limit access to bank and equity funding, and a downward, nearly irreversible spiral sets in.

In terms of an economy that seeks to continue to grow and thereby to continue to elevate the living standards of its people, the consequences of this growth-linked system can only be beneficial. Continued growth, as Japanese policy explicitly recognizes, requires that resources of both capital and labour be steadily shifted and reallocated to higher technology growth sectors. To the extent that the employment system reinforces this policy, the results can only be welcomed, for all the stress that the shift of resources out of a company or industry may occasion.

High fixed costs

A clear consequence of the Japanese employment system is its impact on production and pricing policy. Labour costs become largely a fixed cost. This is in an economy with very high levels of capital investment to meet rapidly increasing demand, and with most of that investment financed by bank borrowings which carry fixed charges. There is then, characteristically, a rather high level of fixed costs for Japanese companies to which is added the labour component. It is true of course that labour is not entirely a variable cost of western companies; not all of the labour force can be discharged on brief notice. The relative difference is very great however.

The results are twofold. First, there is a clear incentive, when faced with reduced demand or lower demand than anticipated, to operate facilities at capacity so long as a price can be obtained that is greater than variable costs. This can be a low price indeed. The western tendency is more likely to be a cutback in output since a more considerable proportion of costs can be reduced. Second, the effects of a demand level that is lower than anticipated can result in enormous swings in profitability and severe difficulties for the less efficient producers in an industry. In this way, as well as in terms of the long-run effects of the employment system on costs, the Japanese economy can be a punishing environment for the inefficient producer.

The problem of mergers

A very considerable disadvantage to the economy of the employment system is its impact on the possibility of effective merger of companies, or the acquisition of one company by another. It is exceedingly difficult, in fact nearly impossible, to combine two large and reasonably healthy Japanese companies. Even when there has been a long history of previous combination, as with Yawata and Fuji Steel, or the three Mitsubishi companies that now comprise Mitsubishi Heavy Industries, combination is not easy to bring about.

The principal reasons have to do with personnel. There is the obvious difficulty of settling on titles and ranks. There is the further difficulty of agreeing on personnel practices. Putting two unions together is a terrible task. More important, the employment system makes it virtually impossible in any reasonable period of time to realize the potential cost benefits of these mergers. Only attrition, a slow process in any event, allows the kind of work-force reduction that is likely to be the principal potential advantage of a merger.

The result is that, while Japan is happily free of the preoccupation regarding sheer company size that handicaps the US economy in particular, it is difficult to take full advantage of the merger potential. Japan's fragmented paper and pulp industry is an example of the problem. Even though the present Oji, Jujo and Honshu paper companies were a single entity before the war, and a merger was seriously discussed a few years ago, the issues of personnel frustrated the merger effort to the competitive disadvantage of Japan's industry.

Consequently, rather than full merger, even when companies are in such difficulties that only a merger will alleviate, a pattern has developed whereby the failing company survives as a legal corporate entity and continues production, but its product line, facilities and sales functions are rationalized with that of a successful firm. This allows for many of the scale and other benefits of combination without requiring formal merger. This pattern has been particularly marked in the auto and agricultural machinery industries and more recently in consumer electronics.

Problems of international management

There is reason to think that the special nature of Japanese employment practices may pose problems for Japanese management as it undertakes directly-owned operations outside Japan. Certainly, the experience of negotiations with Japanese trade unions provides little by way of training for dealing with the unions of Britain and the United States. Then, too, it may well be even more difficult to integrate foreign nationals into executive positions in Japanese companies than has been the case with western firms that have invested heavily abroad.

Something of the nature and extent of these problems might be gained from the experience of foreign firms in the Japanese economy. The problem of recruiting and retaining suitable personnel is almost certainly the greatest difficulty foreign investors have encountered in their Japanese operations. The wholly-owned foreign firm is at an immense disadvantage in obtaining first class personnel; IBM is one of the very few firms in this category which seems to have successfully dealt with the problem; the company is also seen as a highly desirable employer by university graduates. Foreign bank operations and airline offices have been plagued by union problems. Indeed, personnel considerations were not far behind government restrictions in comprising a barrier to direct foreign investment in Japan.

Just as lack of established position and experience in handling personnel issues are problems for the foreign enterprise in

Japan, so they may become problems as Japanese companies undertake direct investment abroad. The issue is one of the future, but the not too distant future.

Changes in Japan's employment system

Is the system of employment practices that has developed in Japan changing? The answer seems to be that it is not changing in any basic or extensive way. The suggestion that change is taking place in this pattern is a recurring one. Often examples are given of individual changes in employment that are taken as evidence that the system is undergoing modification. These seem still to be what they have proved to be in the past, individual cases that offer little by way of evidence of broader shifts.

Certainly, some change has occurred around the margins of the system. There is now a group of western business-school educated younger Japanese who are detached from the system and will contemplate changing employers. There is a larger group in the labour force who, in one way or another, often through employment by the American occupation forces immediately after the war, are outside the system and are prone to change jobs often. These tend to make foreign businessmen in Japan believe that more change is occurring in the total system than is in fact the case.

There are changes going on around the margins of compensation policy. Merit, productivity and rank considerations have some influence on compensation. It is still a modest influence. Retirement practices are under some pressure, with efforts to introduce flexibility into the 'retirement at age fifty-five' rule. The first efforts at introducing pension programmes are under way. However, fifty-five remains the general retirement age, and pensions remain rare and very limited in size.

Clearly, any set of practices in an economy changing as rapidly as Japan's must come under some degree of stress and undergo some modification. It is hardly remarkable that employment practices would be discussed, re-examined, worried over and to some degree altered. Any reasonable view of the past two decades however must conclude that continuity is the predominant fact, and that substantial change, while often heralded, is yet to occur.

Nor is this surprising. The system of employment in Japan is a highly efficient one, and one that is congruent with the main values and behaviour patterns of Japanese society. It is in many ways a more human, less brutal system of employment than the West has developed. It is certainly characterized by less conflict. Both its economic effectiveness and its social value work together to maintain the system.

Will the system change? Of course. As society changes, and it is changing, under the impact of affluence, increased leisure, a much altered pattern of family life and a greatly increased interaction with other nations, so patterns of relations in the work-place will change. Changes in the employment system will arise from these more basic social changes, and will reflect in the future the characteristics of society as a whole.

First published in *Management and Worker: The Japanese Solution* (Tokyo: Sophia/Kodansha, 1973).

7 Joint Ventures

ROBERT J. BALLON

INTRODUCTION

Describing the agonies of European company executives working for joint venture companies in Japan, a German bank director, with many years' experience in Japan, said that there were three main causes why so many European executives end up with ulcers. First is the fact that the Japanese parent company is too market-share conscious, always pressing the joint venture company to gain a bigger share of the market cake, almost regardless of company profitability. Second is the problem of how (and to what degree) to come to terms with Japanese employment practices and the Japanese work philosophy. The third worry is the question of the salary structure with its unique fringe benefits and expense accounts–none of which bears any resemblance to conventional European business practice.

In this chapter, Robert Ballon analyses, step by step, the way to set about establishing a joint venture company. He looks at the common problems involved and brings wide experience and considerable insight to the many human aspects of what is, essentially, a very complicated and delicate business relationship. Of course, it is impossible to describe (or even anticipate) every problem and there will always be something which the foreign parent company finds difficult to understand. The biggest problem of all, as Robert Ballon is at pains to point out, is to find the right partner.

Yet, despite all the drawbacks, joint venture companies have been successfully operating in Japan for over a hundred years. What is more, the hurdles–both physical and psychological–have been systematically lowered, in line with the aspiring internationalization of Japan's economy.

NEGOTIATING THE JOINT VENTURE

Marriage, too, is a joint venture. In western countries, at its best, its basis is love and the long-term fulfilment of two individuals. Marriage guidance counsellors, therefore, stress the need to determine what each partner actually expects from marriage, if a minimum of mutual lasting satisfaction is to be achieved.

In Japan, marriage has been and still is less the union of two individuals than that of two families. This tradition is kept alive by the role of the 'go-between' who is officially in charge of the proceedings and who turns what is, or may become, a 'love marriage' into the socially acceptable 'arranged marriage'. Such marriage counsellors in Japan, therefore, are more concerned about the compatibility of the families than about that of the partners.

The same must be said about a joint venture 'business marriage' between a foreign company and a Japanese company. The language barrier and cultural variants call for adjustments between the partners. But 'business bliss' requires more. To put it in a nutshell, the foreign partner is particularly concerned about law and the way in which the new household (company) will be run. Quite naturally, therefore, he concentrates on the 'marriage contract' and all its legal intricacies. On the other hand, the Japanese partner is concerned about the relationship and its results. To the Japanese a joint venture is a *kogaisha* – a 'child company' – which also implies that 'in-laws' should take joy and pride in the offspring.

Negotiations in business, as elsewhere, aim to reach a meeting of minds. Obviously, the prospective partners will discuss their objectives and reach some mutually satisfactory arrangement. The first stage of any joint venture in Japan is negotiating; if this is not done properly, painful situations may arise at the start of operations which can vitiate the relationship for years to come.

Whichever of the two (or more) prospective partners first took the initiative in founding the joint venture, it should be remembered that this factor will always play a part in the future course of the relationship between the parties. Much negotiating skill will be spent in establishing the equity participation: the fact that there may be no choice but the 50/50 solution is no panacea. Finally, the importance of recording these negotiations cannot be stressed too often.

Proposing the joint venture

Exactly who originated the proposal for a joint venture company is not always clear. Two typical case histories are, first, when the idea grows out of a long-standing trade relationship. Such a natural development, as will be seen later, presents psychological advantages; however, it can easily result in a lack of effort by the partners in properly planning their new form of cooperation. This is often the case where the joint venture is entered into with a former agent.

The second example, which actually occurs more frequently than one would expect, results from a personal relationship, such as the casual meeting of two company presidents who, while 'talking shop', discover some common business interests. Since, in Japan, the company president (*shacho*) has an altogether different function and must possess different human traits from those of his counterpart in the West, a meeting of minds even at this level of the management hierarchy may have very little bearing on further developments.

Between these two extremes there is the full range of business motives, including ulterior motives. In some cases, the initiative is largely left to the Japanese side, with the result that the foreign parent company adopts a rather passive stand in the actual management of the joint venture by not having resident foreign managers and staff and by exercising only limited control over such matters as quality and market distribution.

In recent years, the foreign side, for reasons of its own, has tended to take the initiative in promoting joint ventures, either because it wants to establish a permanent position in the Japanese market, or because this has been a condition for acceding to the desires of the Japanese side. For both partners the joint venture is usually a second best. Surveys conducted by the Ministry of International Trade and Industry (MITI) have revealed that in the majority of cases neither side initially intended to establish a joint venture. Thus, this form of co-operation is often essentially a compromise, frequently glossing over deep-seated incompatibilities.

The 'right' partner

Much concern is always given to finding the 'right' partner. The trouble is that there is usually no clear-cut criterion for determining who is right, except by asking if there is a good chance of reaching a *fundamental* agreement. It is not enough to agree (or give in) on all the detailed provisions of the agreement. As full and complete an understanding as possible should be reached on the motives of each prospective partner before the contract is signed (or for that matter before the Letter of Intent is presented).

Another problem concerns the ulterior motives of each partner, which are of course left unspoken. Such mental reservations damage the joint venture from the start. Trust is not promoted by distrust, neither can trust be engendered by legal documents. To be frank, the very first question which has to be answered is: 'Can a Japanese company be trusted?' The answer is that it can be trusted no more nor less than any company at home. The records clearly indicate that the Japanese is a trustworthy partner; gossip to the contrary should be treated as if you were dealing with a local domestic company. The problem, when it arises goes back to the lack of fundamental understanding; this cannot be assumed to exist merely by virtue of the written agreements between the parties.

What are the ingredients of such an understanding? For the Japanese, it would first involve a long-term proposition and not be the result of some immediate agreement. Major policy changes at the foreign home office, usually decided without prior consultation with the Japanese parent, are quickly interpreted in Japan as a breach of good faith, rightly or wrongly. A few years back, for instance, an injunction was served on a Japanese company which wanted to cancel a management contract when the foreign partner was taken over by a third party.

Secondly, this understanding should be reached at corporate level. Too often it appears to have been obtained only with the foreign negotiator and his immediate superiors at the time. If it is decided to station a resident foreign representative in Japan, this executive should be thoroughly familiar with all the preceding events.

Thirdly, an understanding of the similarities between parents is not enough; it must cover also the dissimilarities, as dissimilarities and not just as points wrapped up in a general compromise. So it is vital that each parent reviews its expectations with the other before any contract is signed.

Joint expectations

It is often supposed that, in view of the capital distribution of the joint venture, conflicting expectations will somehow be resolved in practice. Let us remember that each partner would have preferred to establish its own wholly-owned subsidiary. The Japanese would prefer to acquire the desired technology without foreign equity and management participation, and the foreign side would prefer to establish a wholly-owned subsidiary–if the Japanese government would allow it. On both sides these basic preferences may be short-sighted. Hopefully, the negotiations will show both partners that, especially in the long run, co-operation is not a second best but perhaps a first best.

At the risk of some over-simplification, it could be said that the Japanese side is primarily interested in gaining some *technical* advantage, whereas the foreign side is looking for a *market* advantage. To the foreign parent, the new venture appears to be more of an asset, and to the Japanese parent more of a liability. The extraordinary appetite of Japan for importing technology (product- and process-orientated as well as managerial techniques) is no less well known than her extraordinary capacity for assimilating and developing it further. Since 1950, Japan has entered into over 15,000 technology-import contracts for which she has paid over 2·5 billion US dollars. She willingly pays the price in cash, but balks at the non-cash price–management participation.

So with some reluctance the Japanese parent in the joint venture must now consider contributing capital (mostly borrowed), personnel and local expertise to the joint venture. The foreign parent, meanwhile, has learned about the *affluent*

Japanese. Rather than contribute to enlarging the Japanese pie in return for a windfall profit in the form of royalties, it now expresses the intention of getting its piece of the pie. It will provide capital and technology in return for a certain degree of control, usually in the form of management participation.*

A perfect compromise?

Since the initial desire of both partners was 100 per cent† ownership, the meeting point, strongly endorsed by the Japanese government, is of course the 50/50 joint venture, apparently a perfect compromise. The fact is that a true 50/50 position is a deadlock; to resolve it some special mechanism is necessary–like a third party. In practice, the meaning of the 50/50 relationship is that a veto power is granted to both sides. If veto power is really what the parties want, with proper drafting of the Articles of Incorporation, this can be accomplished under Japan's Commercial Code with *one-third* of the shares. Why then waste so much energy trying to establish control with one-half of the shares?

Another eminently practical aspect of the 50/50 myth is that the daily management of the joint venture and its work-force will be almost 100 per cent Japanese. This is adequate reason to question the concept of management participation itself unless the foreign side is satisfied with the kind of remote control provided by financial reporting, a problem which will be considered later.

But let us return to the negotiations. In a sense, they are a sort of *dry-run* of the coming joint venture. The foreign parent company will probably be represented by some trouble-shooter, a vice-president or the like, planning to clinch the deal in a matter of a week or two. The Japanese, for their part, play the game on their home ground and are ready to give the matter all the time it requires.

*It must be remembered that, according to Japan's Commercial Code, contributions in kind must be evaluated by the courts, a very cumbersome procedure indeed. It is easier to start with a cash contribution, and then have the new company purchase whatever was considered a contribution in kind.

†The 1973 100 per cent liberalization principle applies to take-over bids of existing companies providing the Japanese partner is in agreement. Eds.

The foreign negotiator on the spot

The foreign negotiator soon senses that business in Japan is not a study in black and white, but consists of all shades of grey. After a few days of so-called negotiations, he begins to feel insecure, and as a result clings to the written word of the draft contract he brought with him. Rather than negotiate a business relationship, he tends to negotiate a business contract. This is not the best approach in Japan.

The sophisticated Japanese partner will distinguish two basic approaches to the business contract–American and European. The American approach produces a first-class legal instrument laboriously prepared by the corporate legal counsel who, many thousands of miles away, has tried to provide for as many loopholes as he can imagine. The European approach is to consider the contract as a scheme of grand strategy, carefully figured out in the mind of the negotiator, aimed at getting the best possible deal. Neither of these approaches is Japanese.

The foreign representative usually rediscovers what he was told all along, namely that the Japanese are tough bargainers; the puzzling thing that he probably was not told is that they negotiate from a *low posture*. This attitude is not the result of an inferiority complex; it is a characteristic of Japan's *vertical society*. A man is always inferior or superior to somebody else. This may upset western bargaining tactics that usually are assumed to take place on an equal footing. In Japan, negotiations take place as if the two partners were standing on a stairway at two different levels.

As negotiations drag on day after day, the foreign representative is confronted by a large group of Japanese who keep exchanging remarks (in Japanese), take copious notes (in Japanese), shuttle in and out carrying voluminous memos (in Japanese), endlessly repeat questions already answered, etc. etc. The experience is unnerving.

Then one day, quite unexpectedly, the Japanese declare that they are in agreement. Even complex and delicate matters are now settled so easily. And the Japanese are surprised that everything must be submitted once more to the eagle-eye of the home office overseas. Their feeling about this second review is similar to the western negotiator's own feeling about the Japanese second view–i.e. the one taken by the Japanese government under its validation system. More rounds of negotiations are then called for, both sides implicitly agreeing that they are too far engaged to pull out.

Japanese negotiators in the field

The Japanese will always be deeply concerned with what the new venture will mean to their existing organization and to the close network of relations that characterizes the Japanese business world, with the other members of their industrial group, their financial backers and their counterparts in the industry. All these 'relatives' of the Japanese partner, invisibly present at the negotiations, are taken very seriously indeed. This can be seen in the delays to answers, long silences and interjections from subordinates.

Throughout the discussions there will be a constant desire to probe further into the intentions of the foreign side, not out of distrust, but out of anxiety to adapt themselves more fully, and to be ready to react immediately to the coming 'human' problems that are expected from their direct association with foreign interests. The Japanese side, in fact, is not negotiating a business contract so much as a business relationship, and a lasting one.

Record of the negotiations

The foreign partner tends to believe that the ultimate aim of the negotiations is the proposed new company and consequently focuses his attention on the necessary legal documentation. However, at this stage of the game he should also use his 'legal' mind to keep a well-documented record of the negotiations. Often, years later, this record emerges as a vital contribution in the survival and development of the new company. From the viewpoint of the business 'relationship'–rather than the business 'contract'–these minutes have the great advantage of being more personal and more direct. Maybe, after several years of operations, when the negotiators are no longer available, certain policies will regain their substance through these minutes.

A major hindrance to a long-term smooth relationship will be the quick turnover of foreign executives in the joint venture and at the home office. The record of the negotiations will be of great help to any newcomer not only for his own understanding of what is going on, but also to perpetuate mutual understanding.

ESTABLISHING THE JOINT VENTURE

In Japan negotiations are lengthy because they aim at establishing a new business relationship or giving an old relationship new form. Too often the foreign side would prefer to speed up, if not altogether short-cut, the negotiations–an impossible dream once it is realized that all foreign investment proposals come under governmental scrutiny. Furthermore, the long-term implications should be specifically incorporated into the agreement, since the contract sets a path of development from which it will not be easy to deviate.

Advances into other industries (or perhaps even new product lines) not covered by the original government approval, changes in capital distribution, increases of capital and other important items will again require specific government approval. To rely on further liberalization of investment in order to gain a majority position in the joint venture is probably not wise, since government practice has been, and is likely to remain, to 'liberalize' only for new ventures.

From what has already been said it should be clear that where the foreign side relies on legal documentation, the Japanese side would rather rely on an effective human rapport. Although these two approaches to business are not mutually exclusive, nonetheless there is a clear difference in emphasis. This point can be illustrated by a simple comparison of the numbers of practising lawyers in Japan and in other countries. In round figures, per 100,000 people, the United States has 150 lawyers, Switzerland 42, West Germany 33, and Japan 8. Different social dynamics are at work, not in the sense that Japan has almost no disputes compared to other industrial countries, but that litigation is handled in a different way. The fact is that the Japanese rely less on the legal profession and the courts; even when the courts are called upon, they are valued more for their help in reaching a compromise than in issuing a judgement. (See Chapter 3.)

The contract

Can one expect the Japanese to abide by the contract? The answer is not less and not more than westerners. However, the true binding force that the West expects from the contractual relationship, Japan expects to come from the human relationship, the gentlemen's agreement. Some disturbing stories of Japanese default can easily be gathered from any group of foreign businessmen; similar stories about western businesses are available from Japanese businessmen.

Let us turn to the contract. On the Japanese side, legal counsel will mostly be informal, provided from within the organization or industrial group. Basically, it amounts to a personal guarantee of the partner's intentions. Usually, it is the foreign side that brings in formal legal counsel.

Occasionally the foreign investor expects that all aspects of a joint venture can be set out in a single document. This approach is not consistent with Japanese law and practice; in fact, the foreign party can better secure his position by working out a variety of documents as described below:

The Articles of Incorporation, which must be reviewed by government agencies and registered in the corporate registry, form the basic corporate document for establishing the new company. Its general requirements are set out in the Commercial Code, which can also be relied upon to enforce its terms. Of special importance is the wording of the purposes of the new company, since later changes will require amendment of the Articles of Incorporation and government approval.

Technological agreements, (technical assistance, patent and know-how, licences, distribution contracts, etc.), because of their technical nature, should be drafted separately. These are contractual documents and are enforceable as such: they must be specifically approved by government authorities who may require specific revisions of certain provisions.

Joint venture partners often make a separate agreement dealing specifically with *major policy decisions*. In short, such an agreement specifies certain decisions concerning the operation of the joint venture company that cannot be made without the express approval of both partners. This, too, should be shown to government authorities and will be an enforceable contractual obligation.

It must be emphasized that all these documents should be tightly interrelated and should be presented to the various government authorities as a complete package. Piecemeal submission is dangerous since one matter might be approved and another rejected.

Government scrutiny

It is sometimes said that the Japanese partner is able to agree to anything knowing full well that the government, at the time of validation, will secure his interests. Such cases exist. But basically the reverse is true. The Japanese side, in fact, has to sell the whole idea to the government, acting not only as promoter of the national interest but also as arbiter for the industry concerned.

The application for validation is another of the necessary legal documents for the establishment of the joint venture. The application must include an explanatory statement describing the proposed business of the joint venture and showing how it will benefit the Japanese economy (without having an exceptionally detrimental effect on Japanese industry). The drafting of the application itself has special importance in that the activities of the joint venture will be limited to those matters stated in the application. If the company later wants to engage in new activities, these will require approval through yet another application.

Before the application is submitted, an informal sounding of the government's position is regarded as important, and is very necessary. The prospective Japanese partner and/or the representative of the foreign side will have verbally informed the appropriate ministry departments about the specifics of the plan, so as to try and find out what the official reaction will be. What, to the foreigner, appears as sheer bureaucratic arbitrariness, is, for the Japanese, business participation between government and industry. It is good to remember in this instance that Japan's leading bureaucrats are top-flight intellectuals: the best graduates of the best universities still aspire to this career. At this stage, however, the informal approach will not necessarily result in positive support but it may indicate what hope for approval exists without substantial revision.

Approval procedure

Formal approval procedure consists in presenting the complete set of legal documents, together with the validation application and the explanatory statement, to the Bank of Japan (BOJ). From here the documents will be channelled for study to the various agencies; they end up at the Foreign Investment Council for formal approval. This approval is then transmitted to the BOJ which will inform the applicant of the result.

Whatever the type of approval expected according to official capital liberalization policy, automatic or case by case, an application must be filed. In other words, 'automatic' approval cannot be assumed. The role of the BOJ is essentially to act as a window. It forwards original applications to the appropriate ministries, with copies to other agencies that may have an interest in the project, and transmits the results to the applicant.

These ministries might include, for example, the Ministry of Health and Welfare for pharmaceuticals, International Trade and Industry for heavy industry, oil, computers, etc. As mentioned above, one of the bureaux within the ministry will usually have been sounded out informally before the application is submitted. In some instances, a bureau official may phone the foreign representative asking for elucidation of unclear points or to ascertain the interpretation of specific statements. The file is usually passed on within a month.

The Foreign Investment Council, composed of representatives of the various ministries, sits once a month and passes on validation for projects not in the automatic approval categories. Automatic approvals are expedited by a sub-committee of the Council which sits every week. A refusal is rarely conveyed to the applicants; procedures simply get bogged down until satisfactory changes are made, or the request is abandoned by the interested parties.

Even when official approval is received, there remains one more government hurdle. All international contracts, including the joint venture contract, must be filed within thirty days of their execution with the Fair Trade Commission (FTC) which judges their appropriateness from the angle of anti-monopoly legislation. This legal requirement has only been enforced since 1968; it is now standard procedure. The FTC does not issue an 'approval', but simply instructs the parties to delete or amend offending provisions. If the FTC's guidance is not heeded, it may turn to the courts for legal sanctions.

The Board of Directors

The joint venture agreement and the Articles of Incorporation determine the proportionate representation of both parents on the new Board as well as the extent of their ultimate authority over the joint venture. This is the problem of corporate control. Even if the agreement of the Japanese partner can be obtained for foreign control, the government is very likely to object to a greater degree of foreign control than is warranted by the ownership of capital stock.

On this Board, a minimum of three directors is required by the Commercial Code (Art. 255); usually the number is six to seven. In Japanese corporations the highest position, Chairman of the Board (*kaicho*), is generally occupied by a former president who has little *de facto* responsibility. In a joint venture, the title of chairman may well go to the president of the foreign parent company who will be listed as a non-active director. It is advisable, at some later date, to replace him by a Japanese national, who then may be extremely helpful in government relations as well as for more delicate personnel problems.

The president (*shacho*) of the joint venture company should be Japanese. (Quite a number of joint ventures have a non-Japanese as president, thereby compounding, at the very top of the company, all the problems encountered by the foreign representative.) At the start of operations, this position is often filled by the president of the Japanese parent company; later he should be replaced by a senior executive of the Japanese side. The president, as chief executive officer, will be one of the two or three 'representative directors' appointed by the Board from among its members to represent legally the corporation (Commercial Code, Art. 261).

The other Japanese directors, in all probability, will be

full-time operating executives in the joint venture, with the possible addition of the top financial officer of the Japanese parent. It is to be expected, therefore, that Board meetings will readily turn into discussions at the level of the operative rather than the corporate policy.

The international executive

On the foreign side, it is fairly common to have several non-active directors, usually executives at the home office, besides the foreign resident representative, who should also be one of the 'representative directors'. His function is most challenging in that he is expected to be the only true international executive in the entire group.

All that has been written about the international executive applies to Japan, and even more so to a joint venture in Japan. More specifically, the following appear to be the main problem areas:

It has often been noted, in Japan as elsewhere, that the *resident foreign representative* is called upon to assume a much wider scope of authority and responsibility than would be normal at the home office. This scope is probably even wider in Japan, as very often the home office will be in no position–notwithstanding claims to the contrary–to evaluate properly what is going on in the joint venture, be this the result of language and cultural barriers or of the very different tempo of economic growth.

Since *continuity of personnel* is important in Japan, it should be matched on the foreign side as far as possible. Ideally, therefore, the foreign resident should also have been a negotiator of the joint venture; his successor's first task should be to familiarize himself with past events.

Given the *traditional respect for age* still prevailing in Japan, if there is a choice preference should be given to a senior foreign representative–perhaps a man in his forties. Should he be able to speak Japanese? Theoretically, yes; but in practice open-mindedness will be his most valuable asset.

MANAGING THE JOINT VENTURE

A new legal entity has now been established, the joint venture company. If the foreign share is over 20 per cent of the capital, MITI surveys will include it among the 'foreign-capital affiliated enterprises' worth some special consideration. What is it like to have a company in Japan?

From the mere legal viewpoint, the joint venture could have been incorporated either as a *kabushiki kaisha* (joint stock company) or a *yugen kaisha* (limited liability company). But the Japanese side insisted on the first form, largely because it has greater prestige in Japanese society, and is considered to represent a more explicit commitment than the *yugen kaisha*. What is this commitment? The answer calls for an explanation of the management of a corporation in Japan.

Kabushiki kaisha, or KK as it is usually abbreviated, is a literal translation of the western legal term 'joint stock company'. But the term stands for quite different economic and sociological values. The clearest evidence is given by the debt–equity ratio of Japanese corporations which averages 80/20. Such heavy reliance on debt would in the West spell bankruptcy; in Japan it means growth. It does not necessarily mean bank control, but very simply *interdependence* of all business institutions, including in the last resort the Bank of Japan. In other words, whereas equity capital in the West is the largest portion of a company's capitalization and stands for the *individuality* of the corporation–thus individualizing the business risk–in Japan, debt capital stands for *interdependence*, thus spreading the risk and stimulating growth on a collective basis.

Interdependence

Outside this network of mutual obligations there is little hope for success, even in the case of an international joint venture company. Since this is the way the Japanese partner and the Japanese managers look at business, even in the day-to-day management of the joint venture, the foreign side should be prepared for interdependence rather than independence of operations.

The first manifestation of this interdependence is that the

Japanese parent will consider the joint venture as a *child company*, added to the cluster of companies that form a typical Japanese industrial group. The tendency is then to manage and evaluate the new company in terms of its contribution to the group. Though this is rarely to the liking of the foreign parent, it may well be the secret of long-term success, but at the cost of some short-term sacrifices.

It will take time for the joint venture to reach 'adulthood'; in fact, maturity cannot be reached as long as the practice of personnel transfers from the Japanese parent company persists. But even when adulthood is reached, it will be less as an independent company than as a responsible member of the industrial family. Its individuality is not denied, but its strength is derived from participation in the group. Unless this fact is recognized by the foreign side, the company will remain unfulfilled, to the frustration of its own work-force which will feel outside the mainstream of business activities. The absence of participation in trade associations and management organizations, the lack of managers who enjoy social standing in the industry, failure to cultivate contacts with the banks and the government agencies, etc.–all these have a demoralizing impact.

Personnel problems

One of the striking features of business participation is the common practice of transferring personnel from the parent to the child company. Given the lack of labour mobility among corporations, this is a necessary outlet for taking care of surplus and aged employees. One of the biggest hurdles facing new businesses in Japan is the recruitment of trained and senior staff, since, traditionally, Japanese companies take their new staff direct from school and university and train them from the start. The initial staffing, therefore, has to be by transfer from the Japanese parent company or from within its group.

Qualified staff as a rule will be transferred on a temporary basis, say, for two to three years; the foreign partner, who discussed staffing policies during negotiations, should insist that at least some of the managers of the joint venture be transferred permanently from the beginning.

Since the joint venture approach is usually a second-best

alternative for the Japanese partner, the danger exists that he will not necessarily volunteer his best people. There will also be some managers, close to retirement age (in their early fifties), not really needed by the parent company, and available for a higher position in the joint venture. This is a standard form of recognition in Japan for many years of loyal service.

Manufacturing

A manufacturing joint venture company often appears much easier to handle than a marketing tie-up. The main reason, perhaps, is that manufacturing requires fewer value judgements than marketing. As noted earlier, the Japanese are eager to acquire foreign technology and to apply to it their own ingenuity, especially for further development. It has often been said that Japanese Research and Development puts the stress on D rather than on R. Such statements are based on two dangerous clichés:

(*a*) 'The success of Japanese development in R & D is due to their talent as copiers.' In recent years, it has become increasingly obvious that 'development' implies much more than 'copy'.

(*b*) 'The weakness of Japanese research in R & D is due to an innate creative poverty.' Again, in view of recent happenings, it would be safer to assume that the Japanese simply felt that it was cheaper to 'buy' new technology than to 'create' it. It seems that national pride does not deter the Japanese from assimilating and thriving on western technology.

The foreign partner probably will have little difficulty in negotiating favourable terms for transferring his technology, always bearing in mind that in the validation process government authorities have been known to reduce royalties and contract duration. He would also be advised to negotiate cross-licensing rather than straight licensing, knowing the Japanese propensity to improve on his technology. Without such cross-licensing it soon becomes difficult to determine the original foreign contribution.

Once the contractual arrangements for the transfer of technology have been established, the entire manufacturing process is left largely to the Japanese side. Though the Japanese are very eager to learn *all* about the new techniques, the transfer may well be hindered if the technician also acts as manager. Proprietary protection should not be sought through so-called 'technical assistance'.

Personnel problems in a manufacturing joint venture are easily complicated by the presence of a blue collar work-force. Initially the work-force may have been provided *en bloc* by the Japanese partner. Such transfers, however, should be permanent. Again, this point should have been carefully discussed at the time of negotiations so that agreed principles can be invoked. The idea here is that when faced with some labour problem, the joint venture company should not have to call directly on the Japanese parent company, but be in a position to invoke its own principles of personnel administration as established at the time of the negotiations.

Manufacturing will almost always bring the foreign partner into direct contact with the widespread practice of subcontracting. In Japan, this is a close business relationship. Much of the business participation dynamics, described earlier, enters into play. In the eyes of the foreign manager, too much will be decided on a subjective basis, apparently to the detriment of economic rationalization. This attitude proves that the foreign manager does not yet appreciate the multiple ramifications of business participation in Japan.

Marketing

Most joint venture companies in Japan are in the marketing field. Marketing, as experience shows, is a business activity where the relationship with the Japanese partner comes under greater strain.

The problem comes to a head over the question of adopting more rational marketing procedures, by shorter distribution channels or even direct sales. Agreed, notwithstanding the strong conservatism in the Japanese distribution system, it is always possible to shortcircuit it. Some successful cases, always the same, are quoted. But this is at a cost, and a heavy cost–a point not so often made.

Though rapid changes are apparent, Japanese corporations are still reluctant to streamline distribution for two main reasons, both related to cost.

Wholesalers (primary, secondary, if not also tertiary) are actually a sales-force that the manufacturer or importer would otherwise have to carry on his own payroll permanently; sales representatives, too, are hired for life.

Wholesalers also perform a financial function when, in most cases, financial transactions are settled by promissory notes. If concentrated in the hands of the manufacturer or importer, this financial burden would soon become intolerable.

Furthermore, distributors also are members of the industrial family, and should not be bypassed simply because of economics. Some foreign interests have earned the reputation of being ruthless–paying a price out of all proportion to the gains by summarily eliminating the intermediary. (See Chapter 9.)

Japan's distribution system is under pressure from at least two sides: the manufacturer wants more direct access to the consumer, and the consumer questions the costs of too complex a distribution system. The government is also in the picture with substantial outlays aimed at an overall revamping of the system. One particular aspect of this growing government participation is the increasing influence of the Fair Trade Commission (FTC) on domestic business, especially marketing. The primary function of the FTC is to *regulate* business and trade practices; it is reinforced nowadays by the beginnings of consumerism. Its guidelines have started to spell out in increasing detail the basic principles of marketing in Japan. Since these guidelines are new on the scene, the Japanese partner himself is not always adequately aware of their impact; they are necessary homework for the foreign marketer.

Managing a sales-force in Japan has some peculiar aspects, mostly sociological. A straight commission system is out of the question since the salesman is also a 'permanent' employee. Incentive payments vary in importance in relation to regular pay. Nevertheless, such incentives are usually more group-orientated than individual-orientated. To single out a successful salesman may actually embarrass him, and thus reduce his performance, while jeopardizing motivation among his colleagues.

Advertising

Finally, but by no means least in this analysis of marketing in Japan, is the question of advertising–the cost of which is often of staggering dimensions. Again, it is interesting to watch foreigners compare the cost of advertising and forget that Japan's national dailies have a circulation of several millions and that television peak viewing time involves up to forty million viewers. Costs are calculated accordingly. Savings are then attempted by using advertising campaigns that have been successful in other countries. The risk is rarely worth the saving. Many foreign managers have fallen for the temptation of evaluating Japanese copy on the basis of a translation in their own language. This mistake will be more costly than the fee of a professional copywriter. (See Chapter 10.)

CONTROLLING THROUGH FINANCIAL REPORTING

Although legal instruments are meaningful in the case of a business problem, they are not of much direct help in the control of day-to-day business operations. For this type of control, one must turn mainly to financial reporting. What the foreign manager needs here is not only an overview of historical costs, but an insight on today's operations; both are difficult to obtain in Japan. Since the Japanese use the same arabic numerals and since it is easily assumed that accounting terms, once translated, are clear, the foreigner feels that the financial report is his only true and valid 'working' document. This impression is further reinforced by the home office clamouring for monthly financial reports and other financial studies.

Accounting and auditing procedures in Japan are changing fast. The trend is towards complete adoption of the American-inspired Generally Accepted Accounting Standards. Amendments of the Commercial Code, tax laws and Security Exchange law are under way and are strongly endorsed by the Ministry of Finance. The small number of professionals in the field remains a major bottleneck; Japan has only about 4000 certified public accountants of whom two-thirds are active in industry. This number is much smaller than those of other advanced industrial countries. In Japan accounting has yet to achieve the professional status it enjoys in the West.

Accounting departments in Japanese corporations are staffed from within the organization; the accountants are people with a great deal of experience but too little formal training. The joint venture company has little hope of recruiting from the open market; it may well have to rely exclusively on transfers from the Japanese partner's staff.

Auditing

Luckily, the auditing function may fare better. The Commercial Code so far has been satisfied with one or two so-called statutory auditors. By tradition, these posts are sinecures. However, an external auditor must be called in if the company is publicly listed. In this instance, great strides have been made recently by the newly recognized auditing corporations of Japan, which are similar to western auditing partnerships. It will be no problem, therefore, for the joint venture to be audited by a foreign-based or Japan-based auditing organization. Audited international reports usually give two sets of figures; one set follows the Generally Accepted Accounting Standards, the other the requirements of the Commercial Code and the tax authorities. Often there are major discrepancies between the two. The former set would not be valid in Japan; the latter would not be acceptable internationally. The reconciliation of two such different sets of figures cannot be done only on paper; it is a matter of developing an understanding of the differences, a major headache for the foreign manager.

The Commercial Code

The term 'financial statements', used without qualification, will not be understood by the Japanese businessman in the sense of statements prepared for investors and externally audited. He has in mind the traditional statements required by the Commercial Code; these are much less informative and are not really reliable from the investor's viewpoint. After some perfunctory examination by the statutory auditor and approval by the shareholders, these statements are only a 'first' set of net-income figures. On this basis, tax returns must be prepared. Since some allowances and reserves for tax purposes are not authorized by the Commercial Code, but are specifically required to be entered in the business accounts, these are now incorporated in the first set and in due course will be approved again by shareholders. Thus they constitute a second set of net-income figures, from which taxable income will be derived at various levels, all local taxes being computed mainly on the basis of the national corporate tax.

If the corporation is publicly listed, it must prepare a third set of figures in accordance with the Security Exchange Act. This was enacted under American influence in 1948 and is thus little in accordance with the reporting standards of the Commercial Code which is of French origin. At present, the main weakness of Security Exchange financial statements is that they are not consolidated; this is not yet recognized by tax authorities.

The foreign partner is legitimately bewildered. But so is the Japanese partner who is required to prepare yet another set of figures, this time for international purposes. The simplest method is to agree on external auditing by auditors familiar with both systems of reporting.

This shared bewilderment may develop into near panic when the foreign home office demands financial data which will satisfy management information needs, especially in a format determined by international needs. Such procedures will include monthly reports, periodical budgets and other financial information of varying contents and frequency.

Divulging data

But it should be clearly stated that, under normal circumstances, the Japanese side is not against divulging financial data; the problem is that it cannot do it in the form prescribed without a change in outlook. Foreign reporting requires a high degree of discernment, whereas in Japan independent judgement–in the sense of a given individual taking full responsibility for some action–is not a part of the business tradition and it is not supported by what the West would call recognized professional standards. Furthermore, human elements in business are still paramount in Japan, as manifested in trade practices that work havoc with accounting procedures: monthly billing, collection by the sales staff of monies which are due, lump-sum payments on fixed dates, customers' open accounts, inspection receipts, payment in cash rather than by cheque and so on, as well as the universal reliance on promissory notes and the multiplicity of bank accounts.

Conclusion

In the field of international business, the Japanese challenge has grown considerably, and every indication is that the challenge will continue growing. The challenge is not just to enter and survive in Japan's domestic market, but also to be *with* Japan in its world markets and technological advance. Some ten or fifteen years back, in order to survive as international businesses, European companies had little choice but to establish themselves in the US market. Today, the same must be said about Japan. But, whereas the US market and business practices were fundamentally similar, in Japan history and culture (not to speak of a very different pace of growth) constitute a further problem.

It is often assumed, somewhat naïvely, that the main obstacle to entering and operating in Japan is her protectionist government. Even without the Ministry of International Trade and Industry and the rest of the protectionist apparatus, the challenge would still remain formidable. The same problem could be expressed in a different perspective. The foreign company looking to establish itself in Japan might feel that it could best do so by being allowed to open a wholly-owned subsidiary, in other words to be allowed its own way. Even so, it would still operate in the Japanese environment and be managed largely by Japanese, a situation not so different from that of a joint venture company.

In conclusion, it may be helpful to stress again two important points:

The joint venture company must be a *new* company. Holding companies are prohibited by law; acquisitions are generally opposed by the government, if not also by the public; mergers with foreign interests are resented.

Because government validation is granted on the basis of what is clearly spelt out, and not beyond, there is no *piecemeal* approach to joint venturing in Japan.

8 Trading Companies

INTRODUCTION

The subject of trading houses, both Japanese and European, is so vast and complex that there are no short cuts to a full appreciation of the subject; there is certainly little room for generalizations. Yet for the potential exporter to Japan trading houses offer one of the most economical and streamlined marketing systems that exist in the business world today.

Against the mixed handful of European companies there are, in Japan, in excess of 5000 listed trading companies, although a mere ten of them dominate the whole trading house economy. More importantly, the major Japanese companies are prime movers not only of goods but of the entire economic superstructure of Japan. The configuration of these Japanese companies is kaleidoscopic; their interests and organizations affect every walk of life; their ability to evaluate, plan, execute and finance is, to say the least, stunning; their role in Japan's future development will be seen to be far greater than we have been able to appreciate hitherto.

In contrast, the European companies appear diminutive. Their turnover, compared to the Japanese giants such as Mitsubishi and Mitsui, is little more than a hundredth. But to stop there is to grossly misread the appropriate roles. Size and strength are certainly business criteria but so is success; helping to support the European companies' success is a great deal of history, experience, acumen and access; and in the East access, or 'connections', is a trader's most important qualification. Whatever trading route one may finally take, the business of trading houses is the business of entrepreneurs. Every good businessman, whatever his dealings, is an entrepreneur at heart. Hence the structure of this chapter. The main contributions come from the field, from men who have been and still are closely involved in trading house business. At the risk of appearing repetitious we have approached the subject from a variety of personal viewpoints believing this to be the best way of appreciating its many subtleties and configurations. In so doing, we have preferred to interpret concepts rather than simply relate facts and statistical data.

NEW DIMENSIONS IN TRADING AIMS

Charles Smith

The economic landscape of Japan has a reputation for being intriguingly, and sometimes disturbingly, different from that of the West. Institutions with familiar names turn out to function in unexpected ways–so western businessmen often find–while business operations which would be simple and straightforward in the United States or Europe turn out to be slow and complex (or, quite possibly, vice versa). If this is a fair generalization, and it would probably be accepted even by many Japanese, it is particularly true that Japanese trading companies are a new kind of institution operating under an old, established name. For the typical trading house in Japan bears very little resemblance to any foreign counterpart and plays a role within the Japanese business world which is not precisely duplicated by any single organization familiar elsewhere.

The leading trading companies are both bigger and far more diverse than the outsider would imagine and their operations are far more central to the economic process in Japan than those of a mere import–export agency could ever hope to be. Because of their strength and size Japanese trading companies have a good deal to offer to would-be or potential exporters to the Japanese market. But there may also be pitfalls for those who do not understand the complexities of the system.

When the first trading companies started to do business in the 1870s they were little more than 'commission houses', handling textile exports for Japanese domestic manufacturers and importing machinery and consumer goods. Their operations followed similar lines to those of famous European models such as

Jardine Matheson & Company. However, with the arrival of the twentieth century and the expansion of Japan's overseas interests, the trading houses also began to diversify.

Nowadays, the ten largest trading companies handle an estimated 50 per cent of Japan's exports and about 60 per cent of its imports. A 'first-class' firm (meaning in practice one of the first four or five) may expect to maintain over 100 overseas offices with 800 and 1000 Japanese staff members posted abroad and another 2000 or so locally employed overseas staff.

The two largest trading companies, Mitsubishi and Mitsui, each handle between 9 and 10 per cent of Japan's exports and between 12 and 14 per cent of its imports (precise estimates differ according to sources). The next four, Marubeni, C. Itoh, Nissho-Iwai and Sumitomo, are collectively responsible for at least another 20 per cent of exports and 23 per cent of imports.

Worldwide investments

But it would be wrong to imply that the role of trading companies in Japan's present-day economy consists of nothing more than the exports and imports of a few giant concerns. For a start, even the big Japanese trading houses are at least as heavily involved in domestic trade as in international business. In the second place, there are an estimated 5000 trading companies in Japan, many of them highly specialized, even though by far the largest share of total business is done by the first ten to fourteen.

Finally, the trading companies are becoming ever more involved in activities other than trade. The renaming of the former Mitsubishi Trading Company as Mitsubishi Corporation (and similar re-christenings of other leading companies) symbolized this change of function. The reason for the change and its impact on other branches of industry and commerce have been of profound significance for the overall development of Japan's economy.

In the 1960s, the trading companies began to move into new territory and, with their overseas contacts and experience, they were spectacularly successful. The early 1960s, for example, saw the negotiation of the first major long-term import contracts for iron ore between Japan and producing countries such as Australia, India and Brazil. The trading companies not only negotiated the contracts but also financed the Japanese share of the capital when such contracts involved international joint ventures.

Still within the field of foreign trade, but no longer directly involving Japan, the trading companies became active in handling commerce between third countries. This process has now reached the point where a major trading house such as Marubeni Corporation attributes seven per cent of its turnover to third-country trade. The trading companies are also emerging ever more significantly as intermediaries within Japan's complex system of industrial financing. Because of their international standing and impeccable credit ratings the bigger companies are able to borrow, either from leading Japanese banks or on international capital markets, and re-lend to smaller manufacturing concerns which would not be able to go directly to 'first-class' lenders.

Key role in the 1970s

But the key to the trading companies' role in the 1970s lies in their function as collectors and exploiters of business and economic intelligence. All the larger trading concerns have been taking an increasing interest recently in the planning of industrial projects which require the resources of not just one industry, but of a whole group of related or even totally independent industries. They are to the fore in the planning of the new fuel and food 'combinats' in which a series of importing, processing and distributing operations is combined according to a single master plan and often on a single site. They have also been instrumental in the planning and execution of some of the new town projects which form an important part of Japan's regional development strategy.

The trading companies' role in these projects may extend to the drafting of plans for industrial development, negotiations with the industries and companies involved and the selection of materials and equipment for urban and municipal services. In carrying out the planning and implementation of such projects a big trading company will make use of information and material gathered from many different sectors of Japanese industry and from many of its overseas offices.

Structure and implications

Faced with the complexity of the system and with the enormous number of companies involved, it is not surprising that some western exporters to Japan feel baffled about how to use trading companies. There is the question of whether a specialized product is likely to be more effectively handled by one of the giants of the industry or by a smaller concern which is itself highly specialized (there are trading companies in Japan whose entire business consists of importing and distributing, say, high-quality writing paper). There may also be doubts as to whether a Japanese trading company is, in principle, likely to be more helpful to a western exporter than one of the western concerns which are very active in the Japanese market.

These are questions to which no rule of thumb answer is available; there are just too many companies and too many different products in Japan's international trade today for there to be a single clearly marked route to success. But one general concept may prove useful in finding a way through the undergrowth, especially as it is one which Japanese businessmen themselves are usually only too ready to explain to foreigners. This is the view of Japanese industry as a series of conglomerate groups in which manufacturing companies from different industries, not to speak of banks, are related to one another by more or less concrete ties.

The conglomerate system extends to trading companies too–indeed such concerns as Mitsubishi, Mitsui and Sumitomo play a central role in the affairs of the groups whose names they bear. Thus the exporter who approaches a trading company needs to remember that, when he signs his agency agreement–or commits himself to whatever arrangement he may have in mind–he will be establishing contact not only with the company he has singled out as a partner but also, indirectly, with the numerous concerns to which that company may be related.

To appreciate the significance of these ties it is necessary to examine, in a little more detail, the position a major trading company holds within an industrial group. The first and most important point is that the relationship is not an exclusive one. Nowadays, even the most 'clannish' of Japanese trading companies do a substantial proportion of their business with companies outside the group and only about 25 per cent with related companies. The same relative diversity applies to the provision of working capital for trading company operations. Like most other sections of Japanese business, trading companies rely heavily on long-term bank credit in relation to the size of their equities (one leading company has borrowed funds of yen 1,200,000 million in relation to a capital of yen 40,000 million).

Considering the extent of their needs it is not surprising that all the major concerns spread their borrowing among several major banks, giving only marginal preference to the bank which happens to be a member of their own industrial group. Yet while in formal business terms the trading companies may only be loosely tied to their fellow conglomerate members, for practical purposes the relationship is often very close. It is established practice for group cohesion to be maintained by the transfer of senior executives from one company to another within a group and for presidents and senior executives of a group to meet at fixed intervals to discuss strategy and long-term business policy. At meetings of this kind the officials of the trading company in a group have a peculiarly important role to play. They represent the organising 'brain' of the group, in contrast with its financial core, or its executive arms in the different sectors of industry.

Links and connections

The development of ever more subtle and far-reaching links between different sectors of Japanese industry is something which an exporter ignores at his peril. This is particularly true now that trading companies are building their own bridges to the retail trade sector, including the new chain stores which are starting to revolutionize the Japanese distribution system. However, there is still another kind of link which needs to be borne in mind by the exporter: this is the relationship between the trading companies themselves. At the moment the fourteen biggest trading companies are members of a 'Trading Firms' Presidents Club' which meets three or four times a year to discuss issues affecting Japan's foreign trade as a whole as well as domestic economic problems. The Club is eminent and weighty enough in terms of the share of Japanese trade controlled by its members to exercise a perceptible influence on national economic policy. Of more restricted scope, but of considerable relevance to Japan's foreign trade partners, is a sub-committee of the 'Presidents Club' which discusses joint ventures between the major companies.

It would be misleading to suggest that the trading companies see only the foreign exporters' point of view when formulating their own business policy. After all, they have their domestic trade to consider and their links, sometimes of overriding importance, with Japanese manufacturers. But it would be no exaggeration to say that trading firms, as a group, are committed to freedom and responsibility in international trade and to the maximization of Japan's involvement in international business. They therefore possess both the motive and the capability to help would-be exporters to Japan.

ANATOMY OF A JAPANESE TRADING COMPANY

Michael Isherwood

It has been said many times that Japan presents the foreign businessman with a situation that is considerably different from that of his normal experience in other countries. Perhaps the principal feature is the traditional separation of manufacture and commerce. In the West it is usual for a company to combine both these elements–it manufactures a product and sells it–often developing sophisticated marketing techniques peculiar to its product field. But in Japan, the majority of industrial producers concern themselves solely with manufacturing techniques, leaving the selling of their product, and indeed the purchase of their materials, to a trading company.

Over the years, Japanese trading companies have developed an expertise in all matters relating to commerce: marketing, distribution, import and export, banking, insurance, ocean, air and inland transportation, and research into foreign markets and techniques. They have set out to provide the most comprehensive service possible for their manufacturers–resulting in mutual loyalty and a close interdependence. Sometimes a trading company is spawned by one of the big industrial groups to service its own needs; sometimes it collects together a group of companies simply through introductions and the existence of mutual interests.

The 'group' concept

The Japanese business world is dominated by the concept of groups–informal groups where tradition and loyalty are the key factors rather than joint ownership. A peculiarity of the Japanese economic system is the much greater reliance on borrowed money rather than share equity. This makes ownership less important than the channels through which working capital is borrowed. The longer the relationship between two companies, the stronger the bond of obligation. And it is the trading company that acts as the link. It co-ordinates the business between members, selling their products, buying their materials, helping to sort out problems. Above all, it is the means of contact with the 'outside'–it negotiates on behalf of group interests with other groups. The trading company uses its influence with banks when development capital is required; it arranges distribution, retail outlets, short-term/long-term transportation, time charters etc. the purchase of raw materials and machinery; it looks for other outlets and for other partners that will bring mutual benefit.

The long-term effect of this trading company 'specialization' is the concentration of the major part of Japan's commerce in the hands of a few giant general trading companies, known in Japan as *sogo shosha*.

The 'big ten'

The economic scene, as noted previously, is dominated by about ten mammoth organizations. Between them, their annual sales amount to 11 per cent of the sales of all industries, or almost five and a half times the National Budget. However, it may come as a surprise to many to learn that only one of the 'big ten' makes more than 1 per cent overall profit on total turnover; most only make around a half per cent. It follows that their services come extremely cheap.

The major trading companies also have very close relationships with the government and are called upon to provide a great deal of business intelligence when matters of national policy are considered. As the main co-ordinators and organizers of business in Japan, they are quick to respond to changes in national economic thinking and to take the lead in new directions. From this point of view they could best be described as the country's 'vanguards of development'.

Why a trading company?

As an exporter interested in the Japanese market, how then should you view the trading company? Is it interested in your business and can it help you?

There is no easy, clear-cut answer to these questions. It depends on you, the product, and the timing of your approach.

Perhaps the first advantage the trading company offers is an office in your own country staffed by experienced businessmen who are likely to know a good deal about your particular business. This allows you the convenience of meeting them face to face. Whether they are interested depends on the nature of the business, its scale and potential, whether they can 'connect' it in Japan, and whether they feel they can do business with you as a person.

If the Japanese side is interested, perhaps the greatest advantage it can offer you is 'connections'. Your company and its product will be introduced to the Japanese market through the principal commercial channels and linked to the high prestige that the trading company's name bears. Through its communications system and its business contacts the Japanese trading company will be able to approach a manufacturer, a distributor or a retailer in Japan with whom it will start negotiations on your behalf. Information can be exchanged and a relationship built up without the attendant and very considerable problems of language and differing business practices which you would face if you tried to go it alone.

Costs

The *Keidanren* (Federation of Economic Organizations) recently estimated that US companies have to spend about three times as much in developing a market for their products in Japan as they do for their domestic market. The same would probably hold true for a European company wanting to handle its own marketing operation in Japan.

The complexities of introducing a consumer product are many. Basically, you will be dealing with a large number of retailers through a large number of wholesalers in an atmosphere of keen competition and where a high level of service is demanded. The product has to be established (*a*) in the mind of the consumer (an introduction through the mass media could cost between $500,000 and $700,000 in the first year), and (*b*) with the wholesalers and retailers through incentives such as rebates, discounts and the reservation of shelf space. To succeed in the latter you will have to organize and maintain an efficient sales-force. For single or small-scale items, the cost can be prohibitive.

The big trading companies could help reduce these costs substantially either by introducing you to a manufacturer and tying your product to his or by making use of the trading company's own distribution channels.

When you visit Japan to see the situation at first hand and to meet the companies you are doing business with, it will be the trading company that will act on your behalf–arranging your itinerary, meeting you at the airport, booking your hotel, making appointments and so on.

In other words, in the interests of the 'group' of companies it represents, it is introducing you and acting as a kind of chaperon and guarantor of your company.

Understanding the 'connections'

The complex network of 'connections' in Japan has sometimes been likened to the English 'old boy network'. But one major difference is that the Japanese do not lean on privilege and class as the English do. Connections in Japan are invariably group-orientated and are built up through close experience based upon mutually successful business transactions.

The Japanese are always on guard against the heavy-footed foreigner who tramples on these sensitive relationships in ignorance of their existence. It is essential that new ventures, even purely domestic ones between Japanese partners, are introduced with the utmost regard for existing relationships and without unduly upsetting the delicate balance of the system. This is reflected in whether or not government approval is given and is a reason, albeit a secondary one, why Japan resisted foreign investment for so long. Japan's planned economic growth is likely to make it increasingly difficult for western enterprises acting independently to gain a foothold.

Japanese companies selling abroad

The method of selling Japanese goods abroad follows a fairly traditional formula. A manufacturer in Japan asks his trading company what the prospects are for selling his goods in a certain area. The head office of the trading company asks its branches in the area to investigate the market. Research is done very thoroughly and information passed back. Eventually, when the prospects seem favourable, a local distributor will be selected and approached and asked if he has an interest in an agency agreement. The local branch office will build up a relationship with him, will oversee the business in its early stages and help solve any difficulties and at a later stage, when the business is established and going well, will gradually withdraw from the day-to-day operation. It does much the same in reverse for the foreign exporter who wants to sell in Japan and, indeed, will do the same thing between third countries. For example, the organization is quite capable of arranging the sale of European machinery in the United States.

Importance of imports

It would be wrong to assume that the Japanese trading companies are principally concerned with finding export markets for Japanese manufacturers. As the statistics show, they are bigger importers than exporters although, to be accurate, the bulk of their import business is in raw materials such as oil and metal ores. But the importation of machinery and in particular sophisticated consumer goods is something the trading companies are today very much interested in and eager to expand.

With a standard of living rising faster than that of any other country in the world and a population of 108 million people whose per capita income now exceeds that of Britain and Italy, there exists a huge new consumer market hungry for prestige luxury goods and the pursuit of the good life. With a European standard of living, the Japanese people are acutely conscious of their remoteness from the other centres of sophisticated living and they crave European and American luxuries and life-styles.

Housing in Japan is still cramped and poor by western standards. Most houses still lack modern sewage disposal (in 1970 only 21 per cent of houses had a modern sewage system), electric power is mostly run in overhead cables, the quality of water supply varies considerably and most roads remain unmetalled (in 1969 only 10·8 per cent of Japanese roads were metalled). The Japanese are now demanding better and more spacious living accommodation, and this gives rise to opportunities for the import of techniques and goods in which European countries have good experience to offer: system-built housing, construction equipment, public service equipment, home heating systems, modern plumbing, bathroom and kitchen equipment, and western furniture and furnishings.

Western foods are also much in demand, as are fashion wear, fabrics, sport and leisure goods. Foreign consumer goods are seen as prestige symbols, and items which already enjoy popularity and a reputation for high quality in their own countries stand a good chance of succeeding in the Japanese market.

Retail outlets

However, wholesale and distribution systems in Japan are simply not capable of dealing with the expansion now demanded. Apart from the big department stores, Japan is still a country of small shopkeepers. By comparison with most western countries the number of retail outlets is enormous–1·4 million, over half of which deal in food.

The big trading companies have been quick to grasp the opportunity. Utilizing their vast resources of knowledge and their networks of international connections, they have stepped in as advisers and organizers of new systems of distribution and marketing. They have allied themselves to existing department stores and to the emerging chain stores and have provided both capital and know-how to aid rapid expansion. Through their overseas offices they are actively seeking new sources of consumer goods for these outlets.

Major developers

The trading companies are in a unique position to organize and co-ordinate a whole range of industries in support of major ventures. With the use of the huge financial resources to which they have access, and their accumulated expertise, they are rapidly taking the lead in many new development spheres. Recently, they have been instrumental in the search for new energy resources and have played a central role in organising the rapidly developing natural gas industry. They have invested in and organized large-scale mining developments in Australia and Africa to supply Japan's industries with raw materials. And they have taken on large-scale developments at home such as the relocation of industries, the construction of new towns, the reorganization of distribution involving investment in such sectors as land, warehousing, cold storage facilities, road, rail and sea transport, and in the knowledge and communications industries.

International collaboration

Today, more than ever before, the Japanese trading companies are seeking closer participation with western companies in joint ventures. They have often been accused in the past of lacking marketing expertise in the newer and more complex technical products. They have not been equipped for the direct marketing of sophisticated consumer goods. Television receivers and motor cars require a very specialized knowledge and an expensive back-up operation for servicing and repair.

In such sectors the trading companies are now looking for opportunities for collaboration with foreign companies, for example in the establishment of joint manufacturing, assembly and servicing facilities. They need the knowledge of specialized marketing techniques and they need access to the overall sales networks so as to avoid unfair competition and to bring about orderly marketing. They can contribute their own specialized services, investment capital and sources of products.

EUROPEAN TRADING COMPANIES

Gil Holdsworth

Generally speaking, the Japanese trading company does exactly what the name implies; that is, trades–but its role is much broader than this because the relationship between industry and the Japanese trading companies is very close. Moreover, they fill the gap represented by the absence in Japan of merchant bankers. (Merchant banking operations are currently carried on through three separate channels: banks, security houses and trading companies.)

Thus, all large industrial groups or companies have their own subsidiary or affiliated trading company; in some cases, the trading company dominates the group of which it is a member, influencing product policy in the factories, acting as bankers, financing factory equipment, arranging finance for the group's customers and, in many cases, operating a vast overseas network of sales offices to handle not only the parent group's products, but also a wide range of products from other sectors of Japanese industry.

European trading companies in Japan cannot be compared with Japanese trading companies in these respects. Even the largest European trading company in Japan has a turnover of not more than a hundredth of the Mitsubishi Corporation because, apart from other considerations, government legislation does not at present permit European trading companies to participate in certain activities. For instance, European trading companies have very limited scope within the retail trade,* and they may not engage in real estate trading; and again, whilst Japanese companies combine with foreign companies to develop overseas supply sources for raw materials for Japan, it is difficult for a European trading company to become involved in such an activity by itself.

Most European trading companies in Japan have developed from the traditional 'import, export and shipping agent' base which is a common pattern found throughout the Middle and

*Traditionally, foreign trading companies were only permitted to set up a maximum of 11 retail stores in which their equities did not exceed 50 per cent. This policy is to be liberalised to allow 100 per cent foreign equity.

Far East. Many of them have old-established connections with other territories, and a number of those now trading in Japan had their original roots in China.

While the Japanese companies primarily perform a service for Japan, the European companies are in Japan primarily to serve western commerce and industry–although, of course, in so doing they do bring considerable business and commercial assistance to Japanese industry.

The activities of the European trading companies can be listed as follows:

1 Consumer products: the importation and distribution of foods and liquors, textiles, leisure and sporting items.
2 Machinery: the importation and distribution of all kinds of machinery including business machines.
3 Transportation: acting as agents for foreign liner and tramp shipping companies; shipping brokers; air cargo and passenger agents; surveyors and insurance representatives.
4 Exporters: acting as exporters of Japanese products to overseas markets.
5 Manufacturers: either as partners in joint ventures or as licensees of overseas companies.
6 Consultants: acting as advisers/consultants to foreign companies who may wish to participate in Japan either through direct export, licensing, joint venture or wholly owned subsidiary.
7 Retail: on a small scale.
8 Raw materials: this activity is almost entirely covered by Japanese trading companies but because of overseas connections some European trading companies are active in the importation of timber and fuels.

Distribution

From the end of the war until 1960 European companies played only a minor role in product distribution in Japan. The European trading company could not fulfil a marketing function because of the 'false' state of the market due to quotas, and the company itself was unlikely to 'own' much quota.

With the liberalization of imports the role of the European trading company has changed. In consumer goods requiring national distribution the agent has found that in order to survive he must play a far bigger role in marketing and distribution than heretofore. The European houses, such as Amram, Caldbecks, Dodwell, Jardines and Soficomex who are agents for foreign liquors, find themselves competing not only with the Japanese trading giants and specialist traders but also with the Japanese brewers and distillers who themselves have acquired agencies for foreign liquors. This trend is not so evident in food, but in this case foreign manufacturers whose products are suitable for wide distribution in Japan have the possibility of combining with a Japanese food manufacturer either through a joint venture or through licensing. Lieberman Waelchi and Siber Hegner are very prominent in the importation and distribution of watches. In some fields the European company can work together with a Japanese trading company, and in some products, for example business machines, the Japanese trading company will be an important customer.

Machinery

In machinery several European trading houses have found it necessary to manufacture in Japan in order to be either competitive or in a position to ensure speedier delivery. A notable example of this is Gadelius, a Swedish company, which has extensive manufacturing/fabricating facilities in Japan. Cornes & Co. have a joint venture with Gestetner in Japan for the fabrication of duplicators. Dodwell have arranged for the local fabrication of ship's heating coils for their principals, Charlton Weddle, and they have also arranged for the manufacture of tank cleaning systems for another principal. Companies who enter this field must have qualified engineers on their staff, and they must be in a position to perform after-sales service either through their own organization or by arrangement with their principals through contractors. Kjellbergs are important distributors of machinery.

Transportation

In transportation the European companies represent European or other foreign companies. Swire Mackinnon is a combined venture mainly designed to service Overseas Containers Ltd, and Eurobridge is a joint venture formed by Dodwell and Royal

Interocean Lines. Both Swire and Dodwell–through their joint venture with Kamigumi who are a large Japanese forwarder–are engaged in the air cargo business.

Two-way trade

Many European trading companies including Amram, Dodwell, Kjellberg, Lieberman Waelchli, Siber Hegner and Swires export Japanese products to European and other foreign markets. Most trading companies are devotees of two-way trade as they fully appreciate that trade cannot be one-sided.

Consultancy

Some European trading companies have set up consultancy units and provide the following services:

Conduct market research.
Assist in locating licensees and potential joint venture partners and in making appropriate applications to the authorities.
Advise on traditional Japanese business practices.
Act on behalf of the foreign partner in licensing arrangements and in joint ventures.

Cornes, Correns, Dodwell and Siber Hegner are involved in one or more of these activities. European trading companies play an active role in lumber imports. Jardines have a sales joint venture company with Macmillan Bodell, and the East Asiatic Co. import from their overseas branches.

Financing

The larger European trading companies naturally have a considerable financial stake in the Japanese market. They cannot–nor would they wish to–match the financial commitments of the Japanese general trading company which has access to certain credit lines not available to the foreign trading company. Many would be reluctant to adopt completely the financial gearing practices of the Japanese company. Nevertheless, in the business in which it is engaged the European trading company will be involved to the extent of financing debtors and stocks, and will invest for the purpose of promoting its business.

The European trading company owes its origin and prime financial support to a European parent company. It may be a branch of that parent, a branch of another overseas subsidiary or, as in the case of Siber Hegner and Gadelius, a *kabushiki kaisha* or KK as it is called (literally a 'joint-stock' company). It will normally be European managed and employ many European management practices. These are the features which distinguish it from a Japanese trading company; moreover, it will normally have strong business ties with its country of origin even though it may not be actively trading there. It will also have good contacts in other markets (Cornes, Swires and Jardines in Japan are members of large trading groups; Dodwell are members of the Inchcape Group and Siber Hegner have associates in many parts of the world).

Independence

The European trading company does not have the local group connections which all Japanese trading companies have and is, therefore, free to sell its products widely in Japan. The European trading company can serve a European exporter in representing him from an independent base in Japan, using local market knowledge to seek opportunities and pick the best trading partner. While it does not have the close connections, particularly with the various government departments and banks, enjoyed by the Japanese trading company, the European trading company does possess a greater degree of flexibility than its Japanese counterpart, committed as the latter may be to its own segment of the highly competitive Japanese economy. By contrast, the European trading company can maintain close relations with all the Japanese trading companies and bring into the pattern the Japanese partner appropriate to a particular sale.

The European trading company adopts many of the personnel practices of the Japanese company, although it cannot offer the same proportion of top jobs to local personnel because many foreign principals look for the European presence.

Future role

How will the European trading company fare in the future? Will there still be a place and a role for the European trading company in the Japan of the future? The answer is undoubtedly 'yes', but as Japanese trading companies are changing to correspond with changing business conditions in Japan, so will European trading companies need to plot changes in their practices and structure.

European trading companies will find it necessary and desirable to become more deeply involved in distribution by acquiring licences, participating in joint ventures and even taking on such ancillary functions as packaging, bottling, fabricating, etc. In many spheres they will welcome a Japanese partner to enable them to become more involved in business activities which they have ignored until now (probably for good reasons). They will give even greater opportunities for advancement to their local staff whilst at the same time preserving their unique European image. The European trading company will continue to specialize in activities best suited to it and is likely to avoid activities which call for mass distribution (except in collaboration with a Japanese company). The European trading company is likely to make even more use of its overseas contacts by entering into 'off-shore' arrangements with Japanese companies.

In short, despite meeting severe competition, European trading companies will adapt themselves to the new conditions and survive and grow. Their activities will generally be complementary to those of the Japanese trading giants. Although small by Japanese standards, the European trading companies in Japan are not small by European standards–four of the groups have staffs in Japan of over a thousand each, and turnovers in the neighbourhood of $100 million which would put them fairly high in the list of companies in *The Times 1000.*

'THE *SOGO SHOSHA* IS THE NATION'

Sadao Oba

Yoshie Hotta, a Japanese novelist and world traveller, who has written a novel based on Japanese business communities abroad, has come to the conclusion that a '*sogo shosha* is the nation'. His reason is that the Japanese general trading companies (the *sogo shosha*) now fill a very vital and powerful role in the growing and expanding Japanese economy.

The source of the power of these general trading companies originates from their dominant position in Japan, and one can no longer speak about Japan's economy without mentioning the *sogo shosha*.

The rise of the *sogo shosha*

There are several factors which have contributed to the powerful position the general trading companies now hold. First, they have taken positive and vigorous advantage of the rapid expansion of world trade and the internationalization of Japan's economy.

Secondly, they have brought their 'organizer function' into full play. They organize their resources, money, man-power and technical know-how into new emerging industries such as oceanology, space, housing, leisure and research. In order to develop these industries, the general trading companies act as a go-between, linking the manufacturers of the different products with the banks, insurance companies and so on within their group. They gather information from all over the world, and furnish key managers for newly-established specialized companies. There is a belief in Japanese industry that if a general trading company participates in a project it is bound to be successful.

Foreign participation

Foreign companies wishing to participate in these fast-growing industries in Japan can do so with the help of the organizers–the general trading companies–as recent developments show. C. Itoh & Co., for example, reached an agreement with Holiday Inns (the biggest hotel chain in the world) to establish a Holiday Inns chain in Japan. It is reported that Holiday Inns chose a trading company as their partner in Japan because this was the best way to secure the land and to supply the materials and equipment for the hotels. Mitsui & Co. is launching a joint venture with an American company to manufacture disposable medical equipment in Japan. Mitsubishi Corporation are co-operating with Kentucky Fried Chicken for a restaurant chain.

Third country trade

Thirdly, the sphere of activities of general trading companies is not limited to Japan but covers the whole world; they export US grain to Yugoslavia, British machinery to South-East Asia and German chemicals to Latin-America. They are also actively engaged in the exploitation of natural resources (iron ore, copper, coking coal, petroleum, timber, etc.), in farming, fishing and manufacturing, and in developing hotels and tourist resorts. Mitsui & Co. have joined in The International Agrobusiness Corporation of Iran whose shares are subscribed by Iranian, American and Japanese interests. This newly-formed company will cultivate wheat, sorghum, grass and sugar beet on 17,000 hectares of Iranian land. These efforts by trading companies are undoubtedly bearing fruit; in the last few years, the share of off-shore business (trade not related with Japan or third country trade) in their total turnover has increased from 2–3 per cent to 5–6 per cent. In a few years, it will undoubtedly reach 10 per cent.

As a result, some foreign governments which are watching the remarkable activities of Japanese trading companies with great interest are hoping to develop similar general trading companies in their own countries in order to increase exports. The Williams Report, for instance, recommends development of Japanese-style general trading companies in the United States. The President of Mexico, during his stay in Japan in March 1972, requested Mitsui and Marubeni to establish a trading company in his country. The two companies accepted his proposal and reached a basic agreement to establish a joint venture trading company with shares divided between the Mexican Mining Promotion Bureau, Mitsui & Co. and the Marubeni Corporation. In the early stages, this trading company will handle mainly zinc and lead and the semi-finished products produced by the enterprises related to the Mining Promotion Bureau. The trading company will also import the machinery, equipment and materials for those enterprises. At a later stage, the company will diversify the current commodities and products.

Financing power

Fourthly, the financing power of the general trading companies has expanded rapidly and is now very great. In this world of economic growth, money follows if a project is feasible. General trading companies have originated many new methods of raising the funds urgently needed for the economic rehabilitation of Japan, for export financing and for economic development, or the exploration of natural resources in overseas countries. In this respect the trading company is often compared with the merchant bank. Both have similar historical backgrounds. Old *zaibatsu* families began as financing houses or entrepreneurs and in the process of their development they established a trading company as an independent branch. Merchant banks started as merchants and gradually transformed themselves into 'wholesalers of banking', yet they are still involved in commodities. Trading companies also provide credit for manufacturers, wholesalers or customers. They finance big projects. They hold stocks of smaller companies which are under the wing of the trading companies. Sometimes they act as go-between in collaborative ventures and mergers of smaller firms.

Communications network

Fifthly, the general trading companies have established throughout the world a most up-to-date and well-organized communications network. Some companies have acquired OCR (Optical Character Recognition) equipment which reads telex characters and makes tapes instantly and automatically. This enables them to take immediate measures following any new developments such as monetary realignment.

As international operators, a facility with languages is an important part of the trading company communications network. Many companies, therefore, encourage their staff to learn foreign languages, pay for their tuition and send them to foreign universities.

Finally, as each trading company becomes more multinational, so the group as a whole becomes more multinational.

Complementary relationships

The relationships between Japanese trading companies and the European trading companies are complementary. For European trading companies the most practical way to succeed in the Japanese market is to utilize the financial and marketing capability of their Japanese counterparts which have established distribution channels for nearly every commodity and product throughout Japan.

There are already, in fact, many cases of co-operation. For example, Scotch whisky, French wine and Spanish sherry are exported by European trading companies, imported into Japan and distributed by Japanese trading companies. In the case of products, patents or know-how and the finance related to the new industries mentioned above, European trading companies will find more business opportunities through co-operation with Japanese trading companies who are the core of the organizational network of these new industries in Japan.

The cost

Quite often, European manufacturers or trading companies who are newcomers to the Japanese market hesitate to utilize Japanese trading companies in order to save commissions or other expenses involved. This is a false economy because of the complicated distribution system in Japan. Neglect of the special characteristics of marketing in Japan can very easily lead a foreign company to failure and so exemplify the proverb, 'Penny wise and pound foolish'. (See Chapter 9 for an in-depth analysis.)

SOME GUIDELINES FOR USING TRADING COMPANIES

1 First, identify your own needs. Will the trading company be buying as a principal or as an agent? If the trading company is buying as a principal, you will probably be working through more than one company.

2 If the trading company is acting as an agent, what functions do you expect it to undertake? Having carried out some market research, you will know:

The normal pattern of distribution for your product.
The type of customer.
Whether it is necessary to carry stocks in Japan.
Whether after-sales service will be required and what form it should take.

3 You will have to decide whether it would be helpful for your product to be marketed alongside similar products.

4 You will determine whether you will wish to exercise any control over marketing aspects such as distribution policy and advertising. You should also consider the following:

5 The trading company's group. All the larger trading companies are members of a group which will include a bank. What advantages is the group likely to bring to your product?

6 Finance. Unless you are familiar with the financial structure of Japanese companies you may be surprised by this, and you should not reject a company merely because its financial structure does not measure up to western standards.

7 The trading company's philosophy. Does your product generally fit in with the company's own explicit development pattern? For instance, some Japanese trading companies have stated they are interested in promoting the leisure industry; others are connected with the promotion of supermarkets, and yet others are interested in computers.

8 Does the company have qualified staff to handle your product?

9 Seek the advice of a trade organization such as the local Japanese Chamber of Commerce, JETRO, or the commercial section of the Japanese Embassy, or your own local embassy in Tokyo. Alternatively, approach the local office of one of the trading companies and ask them frankly about their ability to market your goods.

10 From the analyses of European and Japanese trading houses developed in this chapter it will be obvious that there are many elements which are unique to one group or the other. The

following points may be of assistance to the businessman looking specifically at a Japanese trading house.

(*a*) You have the choice of a small trading company that specializes in your particular field or the wider connections of one of the big trading companies.

(*b*) The local offices are usually listed in trade directories. Make a positive approach bearing in mind that you have to establish an initial connection with someone in the organization. Don't just write a letter–the Japanese are not the best of correspondents.

Present them with general information about your company and particular information about the product–illustration, specification and prices. Remember they have to transmit the information to Japan.

(*c*) Take the initiative in the first stages of the relationship. Follow up your enquiry by telephone or letter asking for the reaction from Japan. If reaction is slow in coming, ask what the problem is.

At this stage you need to know whether they are going to take up your product or not. If they find little interest at the Japan end, they may be slow in letting you know and you may waste valuable time.

(*d*) If the reaction is negative try another trading company. But tell the first one what you are going to do. Say frankly that, as they seem unable to take up your product, you intend taking it to another trading company.

(*e*) Early on you will no doubt grow increasingly interested in planning your first trip to Japan. There is no golden rule about timing but there is a golden rule about objectives. Go first to discover Japan–as a country and as a market, and make acquaintances. Assuming you are on the way to doing business through a trading house, don't rush out to see what the trading house is doing for you and how it is organizing your affairs. In Japan, above all, questioning the sincerity and integrity of a business deal when commitment has already been made will only serve to undermine the relationship. If you make your general interest in Japan clear to the trading house it will usually be only too pleased to help you plan and execute an itinerary. (See Appendix 1 for list of Japanese and European trading companies.)

The Alpha & Omega Trading House of Japan

The major European and Japanese trading houses are certainly not averse to advertising their services and aspects of their excellence. In fact, many of these advertisements go into considerable detail and are most informative. Below, we have drawn up an advertisement for our own 'Alpha & Omega Trading House'–compiled from ads placed in West European newspapers by some of the bigger trading companies. None of the wording is ours–only the message: that through the trading companies potential exporters to Japan have one of the most sophisticated and thorough marketing channels available.

THE ALPHA & OMEGA TRADING HOUSE OF JAPAN

World-wide trade, for all your needs, 1440 minutes every day, through our 116 offices and affiliates in 72 countries

Import–export (over 10,000 items). Triangular trade: we sell American steel to Italy African marine products to Europe Brazilian raw cotton to South-East Asia

And not only trade
Investments, development of natural resources, co-operative ventures

Join us and we link you immediately to our trade, banking, industry and business connections round the world

We specialize in *everything* – particularly marketing and financing for
metals, machinery, ships and transportation
textiles, foods, chemicals
petroleum and other fuels
timber and
general merchandise

Through us, you will be linked with the world's leading trading centres by leased channel, telex and telegraph, and OUR OWN ON-LINE, REAL-TIME INFORMATION SYSTEM WE ARE THE WORLD'S JACK OF ALL TRADES

THROUGH US, YOUR ENTRY INTO JAPAN

or any other country

WILL BE MADE EASIER AND MORE PROFITABLE

9 Distribution and Marketing

YOSHIHIRO TAJIMA

INTRODUCTION

In recent years, foreign companies and their governments, looking for a marketing foothold in Japan, have paid increasingly greater attention to Japan's existing distribution structure. Such companies clearly understand that the success of their business with Japan largely depends on how they dovetail their conventional marketing strategy into Japan's conventional market situations.

Many foreigners are bewildered by the complexity and awkwardness of the Japanese distribution system. Some, perhaps out of desperation or sheer ignorance, even try to force their own well-tried marketing know-how on to Japan, while neglecting the indigenous Japanese systems. Except for Coca-Cola, they are mostly unsuccessful.

There are others who tend to drop into the existing system with nonchalant indifference, and do not attempt to exploit it. Only a few companies study the character of Japan's distribution structure in any depth–showing some sophistication and making some effort to seek ways to apply it to meet their marketing objectives.

Without such effort and planning, Japan's marketing structure will certainly remain a non-tariff barrier for a great many foreign products.

THE JAPANESE DISTRIBUTION SYSTEM

In many cases, criticisms about non-tariff barriers revolve around the very high retail price of imported goods, which is quite simply the result of Japan's traditional multi-stage distribution arrangements in wholesaling (the triple-layered structure of primary, secondary and tertiary wholesalers). Quite naturally, foreign companies fear that the high retail price of their products in Japan will restrict the sales volume.

This is true, as many foreign exporters discovered during the period of the floating and revaluation of the yen. And even though import prices dropped as a result of the bilateral rearrangement of the foreign exchange rate, at first the price advantage of imported goods was mostly absorbed by wholesalers. Since then, and as a result of 'administrative guidance' (government regulations), the price advantage of imported goods has gradually begun to be transmitted through to the retail level with sales volumes expanding accordingly.

Thus the critical point of Japan's marketing structure is at the wholesale level. But this still leaves foreign enterprises the freedom to select appropriate wholesalers as part of their distribution channel, or to bypass them. Some people make the criticism that the Japanese government even forces large retailers such as department stores and supermarkets to purchase through wholesalers, and not directly from the manufacturers. This is not true. Any retailer is completely free to use wholesalers as he sees fit.

To sum up: from a production point of view the Japanese economy is highly modernized, and in this sense Japan belongs to the Far West. But in the area of marketing Japan belongs very much in the Far East, even though she has an increasing number of western marketing elements such as department stores, supermarkets, shopping centres, advertising agencies, mass media, and so on.

Structural analysis

The basic distribution pattern is essentially the same as anywhere else in the world; however, there are two important characteristics of the Japanese system that should be noted:

First, compared with the American and European systems, there is far greater intervention on the part of wholesalers into the distribution, not only of consumer goods, but also capital, industrial and institutional goods.

The main reason for this is historical. For nearly three centuries, until the Meiji Restoration of 1868, the Japanese economy was dominated by wholesalers. During that time, the scattered tiny handicrafts manufacturers were completely dependent on the wholesalers both for finance and the sale of their products. Shipping and other forms of transportation were also monopolized by the wholesaling fraternity. All retail stores and even pedlars were under their control since they were organized (by the wholesalers) into merchant guilds, merchandise categories and regions.

Many of today's department stores, big trading companies, city and local banks, and even some of the huge business groups known as the *zaibatsu* have their origins in the wholesaling business.

Another reason for the wholesalers' 'supervision' of the economy today lies in the very rapid industrialization of Japan during the last hundred years. Manufacturers concentrated on production, leaving sales and distribution in the hands of wholesalers. This is true even of capital and industrial goods manufacturers.

Secondly, the distribution pattern differs considerably from industry to industry. Attempts to make broad generalizations, therefore, are rather pointless.

For example, major electrical appliances such as TV sets, refrigerators, washing machines and record players are distributed from manufacturers to retail outlets through wholesalers. But most of the wholesalers are regional sales companies owned by the manufacturers. Traditional wholesale merchants are not given any scope at all in the distribution of goods in this sector.

Institutional outlets, such as hotels, restaurants, night clubs, cabarets and so on, are supplied with alcoholic drinks mainly by retailers–not wholesalers. The point here is that the law (at least until 1971) grouped these outlets in the 'consumer' category, and required that they be supplied by retailers, not by wholesalers.

Another example of the idiosyncrasies of Japan's distribution system is in the field of ethical drugs, where doctors play a very important role. Doctors, in fact, are permitted to administer drugs directly to patients without them having to go to a drug store with a prescription. As a result, the distribution of prescription drugs is made directly to doctors and hospitals through wholesalers and not to drug stores.

Marketing institutions

Wholesaling and retailing, therefore, are the two essential arms of the marketing structure and both perform a distributive function. In a wider marketing context one would include advertising, market research, transportation and so on; these are omitted in this discussion to avoid confusion of the central issue.

According to the 1972 Census data, the total number of distributive establishments in Japan numbered 2,238,218 (excluding Okinawa Prefecture), which showed an increase of 3·9 per cent over 1970. Of these, 259,863 were classed as wholesale establishments, 1,494,643 were retail stores, and the rest (483,712) were food and beverage establishments.

These totals are greater (proportionately) than those for America, where in 1967, according to the *Statistical Abstract of the United States,* the total number of distributive establishments, including food and beverage establishments, amounted to approximately 2,074,000.

The huge figures pertaining to Japan clearly indicate the essentially small-scale operation of her distributive system. Wholesale establishments, for example, employing four or less regular workers, account for some 43 per cent of all wholesale operations. In retailing, the smallest stores employing two or less regular workers account for 52 per cent–over half the total. As the statistical definition of 'regular worker' includes shop owners or family members working for the store, many of the smallest stores can be said to have no paid employees as such.

The number of food and beverage establishments in 1972 increased by 13·6 per cent over 1970–an interesting pointer to fundamental changes in the eating and drinking habits of the average Japanese.

WHOLESALING

Structure

According to Japanese statistical data, wholesalers are divided into regular wholesalers and agent wholesalers.

Agent wholesalers, who represent sellers or buyers, do not keep stock and take brokerage. Although they continue to play a significant role in the fields of assembly and dispatch of farm and marine products, their number is rapidly diminishing and most of them are small concerns. Regular wholesalers include traditional merchant wholesalers, sales companies owned by manufacturers, manufacturers' sales branches, the central warehouses of chain stores and retailers, co-operatives and, of course, trading companies.

Even though the statistical breakdown of these categories is not available, it can be safely assumed that the traditional merchant wholesalers are by far the largest group.

Wholesalers can be classified according to function and status in many ways. Classification into primary wholesalers and secondary wholesalers (and sometimes tertiary wholesalers) is most commonly used.

Primary wholesalers purchase directly from manufacturers and sell to larger retailers and secondary wholesalers. Small retailers are usually served by secondary wholesalers.

According to a MITI analysis of 1968, even in industrial marketing the number of secondary wholesalers exceeded that of primary wholesalers.

Recent trends

Traditional wholesalers are today experiencing growing difficulties. Their traditional labour intensive operations are now becoming prohibitive due to labour shortages and rapid wage increases. Keen competition among them also weakens their financial basis. Finally, the growth of large retail outlets, such as department stores and supermarkets, threatens their very *raison d'être*.

Increasingly, manufacturers are expanding their activities to include the distribution network; they are doing this by setting up subsidiaries, taking over wholesale functions and acquiring existing wholesalers.

As the import of consumer goods continues to increase, the so-called general trading companies are organizing and expanding their domestic distribution networks. Some current trading company 'schemes' include the financing of department stores and supermarkets, organizing merchant wholesalers as their distributors, and participating in shopping centre projects.

In industries such as steel, aluminium, sheet glass, cement and other building materials, modernization of physical distribution is urgently required. Huge investment in land, warehouses, machines and facilities is necessary. This very fact implies a still further increase in the power of the general trading companies with their huge financial reserves and, at the same time, the continued undermining of the merchant wholesalers whose financial resources bear no comparison.

RETAILING

Major types

Retailers in Japan can be classified into four major categories: neighbourhood (or local) stores, speciality stores, department stores and supermarkets.

Neighbourhood stores include food and drink stores, the number of which, in 1972, was about 711,000 and accounted for a little less than 50 per cent of all retail stores. Most retail stores, in fact, dealing in a limited line of merchandise and serving local residents, are considered part of the 'neighbourhood store' category.

Speciality stores handle mainly high-price merchandise, such as jewellery, fashion items, imported watches, imported furniture and so on. The number of these stores is not clear, but is obviously growing–reflecting higher income levels and the consumer's preference for quality goods.

Traditionally, department stores have been the only major retailers in Japan–at least until the appearance of the supermarkets. But in order that smaller retailers might be protected, department store activities such as store hours, sales promotions and expansion programmes have been tightly restricted by the Department Store Law. Although they have already lost their 'king of retailing' status, department stores today account for almost 10 per cent of total retail sales. In 1970 there were 260 stores. In non-food items, especially luxury and fashion goods, they still have an overwhelming power.

Supermarkets began appearing in the late 1950s. They first operated as discount stores, concentrating on processed foods, clothing, non-prescription drugs, cosmetics and toiletries. Through aggressive chain expansion, diversification and cost-saving systems they have achieved a surprising growth. Their share of total retail sales is now comparable to the department store achievement. (In 1970 supermarkets accounted for 9 per cent of the retail trade, with 9403 operating units.)

Big retailers

It is now becoming rather difficult to distinguish department stores from supermarkets. Many department stores have supermarket chains as subsidiaries, and leading supermarkets own shopping centres and handle a similar wide assortment of goods to the department stores.

The main points of strategy common to both supermarkets and department stores are:

Expansion of chain operation.
Expansion of operating scale.
Construction of shopping centres.
Organization or acquisition of other department stores and supermarkets.
Diversification to non-retailing business.
Affiliation with foreign retail enterprises.
Vertical expansion to wholesaling and manufacturing.

Thus the polarization in retailing becomes increasingly apparent. The bigger retailers will become bigger, the smaller ones smaller.

Other trends in retailing

Voluntary groups of smaller retail stores, both retailer-owned and wholesaler-sponsored, are slowly increasing in number. Franchised organizations seem to be more promising, especially in the food business, and particularly convenience and take-away foods.

Consumer co-operatives, including farmers' co-operatives, in retail business are not highly developed in Japan. But the recent inflation will most certainly accelerate their growth.

MARKETING SYSTEMS: TWO EXAMPLES

The beer industry

An examination of the beer industry provides an opportunity of discussing three key marketing questions:

(*a*) How the tightly controlled production structure of this industry affects the marketing system.
(*b*) How government and the law affect the marketing system.
(*c*) How the industry's institutional outlets are served.

In 1971 Japan's beer production ranked fifth in the world, and beer occupied over 60 per cent of the total consumption of alcoholic drinks.

This industry is monopolised by four brewers, amongst whom competition is very keen indeed. And, as economic theory suggests, price competition is normally rather rare within an industry controlled by so few. The major tools of non-price competition are brand promotion through massive advertising and the control of distribution channels.

Beer wholesalers, for example, are divided into two groups. One group, composed of about 800 comparatively small wholesalers, handles only beer. The other group handles all kinds of alcoholic beverages including beer; the total membership of this group amounts to about 1200 which normally operate on a larger scale than the first group.

Brewers select their distributors from amongst this total of 2000 wholesalers and make an exclusive contract with them. Very few beer wholesalers are big enough to dictate their own terms. Thus the brewers can control wholesalers by selection and by exclusive contracts. Similar to the beer industry, with power and market share limited to a few major producers and a comparable type of distribution control, is the electric appliance industry, the automobile industry, the sheet glass industry and the steel industry.

The law states that wholesalers and retailers have to be licensed to handle alcoholic drinks. Institutional retail outlets do not require a licence since their legal status is that of a consumer. According to the legal definition involved, those who sell alcoholic drinks to consumers are retailers. Therefore, institutional outlets have traditionally been served by those holding a retail licence. Although retail and wholesale licences were integrated in 1971, very few wholesalers as such made any determined effort to break into the institutional market for alcoholic drinks. Most wholesalers have no desire to compete with their retail customers.

The price structure in this industry is also rather different. In most other industries wholesalers make their profit by adding to the manufacturer's shipping price; but in beer the brewer's shipping price is the retailer's purchase price. Beer wholesalers make their profit directly from the brewers, who pay to each wholesaler according to the volume moved through his hands. Normally 8 per cent of a wholesaler's sales is returned as margin or commission, with some extra as rebate for promotion. From this 8 per cent and extra rebate, wholesalers pay their expenses and also their own promotional rebate to retailers.

The pharmaceutical industry

Analysis of the pharmaceutical industry sheds light on the following three issues:

(*a*) The relationship between Japan's medical system and the marketing of pharmaceutical and other medical products.
(*b*) The different market segments for these products.
(*c*) How government and the law affect distribution in the pharmaceutical industry.

Drugs are divided roughly into two groups: ethical or prescription drugs dispensed by doctors, and proprietary or non-prescription drugs, such as analgesics and vitamins, bought for self-treatment by patients. Ethical drugs, incidentally, account for about 75 per cent of all drug production. As a general rule in western countries, both prescription and non-prescription drugs are distributed through drug stores. But in Japan, as mentioned earlier, medical doctors can dispense medicines directly to patients in their surgeries and hospitals. Medical doctors and hospitals, therefore, are the most important outlets for ethical drugs.

Although some pharmaceutical manufacturers supply their clients directly, most drugs are distributed through pharmaceutical wholesalers. Some wholesalers specialize in supplying non-prescription drugs to drug stores, while others supply only prescription drugs to medical establishments. However, the majority of Japan's thousand pharmaceutical wholesale companies handle both products.

Unlike the beer industry, there is no monopoly situation in the manufacture of drugs so it is difficult for any one manufacturer to dominate wholesalers and arrange exclusive agreements. Even so, large manufacturers of competitive products can exert strong influence over wholesalers to give preferential treatment to their products. The most important ways of bringing this influence to bear are through rebates or other forms of financial assistance.

It is a fact that pharmaceutical wholesalers make very frequent visits to their clients. One survey showed that about 70 per cent of the total volume distributed was delivered daily, and that the rest was delivered every two to four days.

The wholesale price of all medicines covered by health insurance is decided by the Ministry of Public Welfare and registered in the 'Pharmaceutical Price Standards'. It is interesting to note here that there is much cut-throat price competition at the wholesale stage and that the actual wholesale price level is often lower than the Standard. Just about everybody in Japan today is covered by some form of health insurance, while the number of medicines covered by these insurances (registered in the 'Pharmaceutical Price Standards') is increasing. One obvious result is that prescription drugs are growing faster than non-prescription drugs.

Proprietary or non-prescription drugs, which account for about 25 per cent of the pharmaceutical market, are sold at drug stores. The Pharmaceutical Affairs Law provides that a new drug store cannot be opened within a given distance from an existing drug store. The actual distance is decided by prefectural ordinance in each prefecture. In Tokyo, the distance is 240 metres in residential areas, and 120 metres in commercial areas. This so-called 'distance regulation' helps to protect existing drug stores by discouraging new arrivals or the expansion of chains.

Japan's Anti-Trust Law provides that the resale price of

proprietary brands, cosmetics, toothpaste, soap and detergent can be maintained by contracts between retailers and manufacturers. Resale Price Maintenance also serves to protect drug stores from unnecessary price competition.

This form of government protection given to elements within the industry has received wide criticism and is now tending to be withdrawn or relaxed. The comparatively slower growth of non-prescription drugs, therefore, and government policy towards the industry, suggest that drug stores should reconsider their marketing posture if they are to remain profitable in the long term.

SOME CONCLUSIONS

The Japanese market, with a population of over 108 million and a rising income level, has great potential.

The Japanese government's aggressive liberalization programme in recent years has produced favourable results. With a few exceptions, such as leather, leather goods and some agricultural products, most products can be freely imported. Quotas of restricted items are also expanding. Tariff barriers have become lower than ever before. With regard to foreign capital investment in Japan, the former 50/50 restriction has now been replaced by hundred per cent capital liberalization.

However non-tariff barriers, including the language handicap, the difficulty of acquiring information regarding legal and governmental regulations, and traditional trade customs peculiar to each industry and market, are serious problems.

In the case of finished goods, competition should be the first consideration. Clearly, those products which cannot be found in Japan, or have no direct obvious competition, stand the greatest chance of success.

Any technology which will complement and enhance Japan's new industrial structure will most certainly do well. For example, Japan needs technology and know-how in the fields of water purification, clean air and noise prevention. Japan also needs labour-saving machines and equipment, medical equipment and hospital supplies. These are just a few examples.

Consumer goods have similar market potential. Due to the rapid improvement in income levels, the Japanese consumer is looking for high quality goods, more westernized goods, more contemporary and more individualized goods. Well-known brands will obviously stand a better chance of getting placed in the market more rapidly.

Here again it is inadvisable to try to introduce a whole range of products all at one time. It is better to make a very careful study of the market requirements and approach cautiously.

Choice of market

The more expensive your product is, the more you should concentrate on the big cities and limit your retail outlets. If you do this, your market development energies will be more efficiently employed and the marketing structure required for your product will be simpler.

As your products begin to gain market acceptance, you can analyze your marketing territory or expand your retail outlets and in this way bring about successful market penetration.

Market segmentation

Consider the beer industry once again. To achieve success like this industry you have to decide which market is to be served first, home or institutional consumption.

In the home consumption market, brand promotion through massive advertising, especially on TV, is indispensable. The long-range investment plan for advertising, independent of any short-term profit or loss calculation, may decide market acceptance. But since television coverage on any scale is prohibitive, a market well worth investing in is undoubtedly the 'gift market'.

Japan has two major gift seasons, in June and December. Gifts are exchanged between family members and intimate friends at Christmas and New Year; but even more gifts are presented by companies to important customers, by subordinates to their employers, by patients to doctors, and so on, in order to express the sender's gratitude for patronage or help. Since gifts tend to be purchased at and delivered by the big, prestige department stores, you can concentrate your marketing budget for limited periods on selected department stores, and on in-store promotions instead of costly TV commercials.

The quality image of many European products will undoubtedly boost interest and sales. The fact that more and more

Japanese people are visiting Europe is also a favourable factor. Should you decide to go into the gifts market, negotiate directly with the department stores or with wholesalers who have strong business connections with them.

Selecting a distribution method

Basically, there are three alternatives open to you. The first is to distribute through a partner–manufacturer. The second is to distribute through a powerful wholesaler or trading company, using him as your sole agent. Finally, you could set up your own distribution network.

Distribution through a partner–manufacturer is certainly worth considering. Your partner should be selected from among those companies which have a strong distribution network. But remember that the size of a company is no yardstick for the quality of its distribution facilities.

If you decide to distribute via a wholesaler as the sole agent, consider the following:

His status in the wholesale society (another wholesaler will not want to act as secondary wholesaler if he actually enjoys the same status as your principal wholesaler).
His customers and his influence on them.
The quality of his management and his employees.

The most aggressive exporting companies may well decide to set up their own distribution network–a decision which will require even more planning, forethought and follow-through.

A final reminder: never force your wholesaler to accept the business methods of your own country, but at the same time do not fully adapt to conventional Japanese trading practice. And remember, the real key to your success in Japan (once you have grasped the strategy) is the man you send out to represent you. This person does not need to understand the Japanese language, but he does need to understand Japanese people.

10 The Role and Application of Advertising

INTRODUCTION

In Europe and America, advertising takes on the appearance of an exact science and is closely related to marketing strategy and market rationalization. At the basis of this scientific, empirical approach is the call for a logical product 'concept' and implementation. Because of the continuing refinements in research data collection and interpretation, it would seem that we are now well on the way to 'programming' our advertising in order to achieve an increasingly higher recall and commitment response from the consumer public. This response is invariably engendered and promoted from an *individual* and *intellectual* platform. Whatever indirect or direct emotional subterfuge and folksiness may be built into the ad., and whatever forms of 'family' or 'social' or 'community' appeal may be marketed, the real goal for the western advertiser is the *individual* end-user, whose judgement will be conditioned by all the logical processes he is accustomed to using. Quite a complex and sophisticated strategy and, obviously, ideally suited to the West.

However, as George Fields points out in the second part of this chapter, there is a very obvious chasm between this western and the Japanese approach to advertising, a difference which is essentially culture-orientated. The word *haragei,* stomach art, observes Mr Fields, is still commonly used within the context of business negotiations. It implies the existence and value of simple but highly refined 'body language', or what is sometimes known as non-verbal communication. From this standpoint, therefore, the West's insistence on logic and synthesis is virtually irrelevant. The nuances inherent within the framework of interrelationships and mores in Japan, the fact that the group and group well-being is considered and *is* more important than the individual, together with the extraordinary subtlety of the Japanese language itself, evidently demand their own unique advertising formula. It is also worth remembering that Japan's own indigenous advertising framework works exceedingly well among the Japanese, even though Japan is one of the few countries in the world where commercials for two competitive brands of soft drinks run back to back–with no redress to either advertiser.

ADVERTISING IN JAPAN: BACKGROUND TO THE MARKET'S IDIOSYNCRASIES

David Gribbin

Having been asked to describe, for the benefit of western executives, the part played by advertising in the Japanese marketing process, I find myself thinking of the Buddhist parable concerning a man wounded by a poisoned arrow.

According to the parable the man refuses to have the arrow removed or his wound dressed until his anxious comrades have informed him, in the minutest detail, of the identity of the archer, his caste, the name of the arrowmaker, the kind of feather on the arrow flight, and so on. As the Buddha observes, the unfortunate warrior would have succumbed to the poison long before even a fraction of his queries could be answered.

For would-be marketers in Japan, as well as seekers after Nirvana, the parable has a point. The executive who delays his company's entry into Japan until he feels confident that he understands it fully will find that more often than not, by the time he can get a complete picture of his opportunity in this highly competitive market, a competitor will have seized that opportunity.

So, before considering the part played by advertising in the Japanese market, it might be appropriate to make a few general comments on the forces which determine how the Japanese evaluate both their own and imported goods and services.

Japanese companies advertising in multinational media such as *Fortune* or *Newsweek* almost invariably run corporate advertisements. And, since corporate advertising is often referred to in disparaging terms by sophisticated western advertisers and their advertising agencies, a western executive may have already formed, or half-formed, a view that Japanese advertising has yet to become as sophisticated as American or European advertising.

The truth is that in the United States and in Europe advertising is designed to encourage consumers to believe the myth that they are individuals living in an individualistic society far removed from the ultra-conformist societies of the Far East and the far left. This has given rise to an interesting Orwellian situation in which the degree of simulated folksiness and 'character' in western advertisements rises in direct proportion to the way in which the goods and services being advertised become ever more indistinguishable from competitive goods and services at the same price. Commercial film-makers comb the casting directories, even the streets, for people endowed with crumpled faces, curious accents, and the ability to chomp with rustic abandon on the latest sodium-glutamated facsimile of a Boston baked bean or a Cornish pasty.

Group activity

The Japanese, on the other hand, are keenly aware of being members of groups. Indeed, group activity is the keynote of Japanese life and harmonious group relations are highly valued (and bought at the expense of individual wishes) in every group–ranging from the nuclear family group to the largest group in the world, the Japanese nation, all of whose members are shareholders in the enterprise known as Japan Inc.

The concept of status-role (*bun*) within a group has been, and remains, a potent force in every situation, including the buying situation. The nation's best-loved drama concerns the tragedy which befell a feudal lord (*daimyo*) who failed to play his status-role adequately. As a consumer, a Japanese man, woman or child will react favourably or otherwise to a product or service according to the way in which it can be seen to accord with and enhance his self-image and his position among his fellows in the group. The price which a Japanese is willing to pay for something is very largely determined by this consideration.

Status

Personal possessions and status-role have always been closely interrelated in Japan. However, Japanese companies never make explicit references to the profit motive; instead, they make public announcements concerning their determination to 'make a better life for all peoples of the world'. It is perhaps no coincidence that the founder of Matsushita Electric, a highly successful company famous for its management skills and high profitability, should also be the founder and publisher of *PHP* (standing for Peace, Happiness and Prosperity)–a monthly magazine which is something of a miracle in publishing circles because it manages to combine a lofty moral tone with a huge circulation.

Similarly, it is status, not cash, which makes Japanese graduates compete so fiercely for the privilege of becoming members of the large and powerful Japanese corporations. Once recruited (during the student riots a few years ago the ringleaders were said to be in great demand because of their proven qualities of leadership), they commit themselves completely to the corporate 'family' and strive to increase both their company's market share and their own status as a big company employee or *salaryman*–the two objectives being virtually synonymous.

Market share

Following this observation about competition and market share the western reader will naturally conclude that advertising is closely linked to it, since in the West advertising is seen as a most important factor in the struggle to outsell the competition. Paradoxically, market share is far more important to a Japanese company than it is to a western one and advertising is far from being the magic ingredient which it so often becomes in the eyes of western marketers. Japanese corporations are, in our terms, far more reliant upon borrowed capital and, since their ability to borrow from the banks depends to a large extent upon their market share, they are reluctant to delegate control over such a crucial issue to anything so intangible as advertising.

Of course huge sums are invested in advertising, particularly in the fields of cosmetics, foods and liquor. Without exception though, the market leaders in all these fields in the Japanese market are companies known for the sophistication and penetration of their distribution systems and for the readiness with which they embrace the latest technology and respond to changes in taste and fashion. The 'real' qualities of the product are felt to be extremely important. Most important of all, Japanese companies compete both in Japan and elsewhere in the world on *price*.

The paramount importance of the selling price means that Japanese companies make every effort to increase efficiency so as to be ready to take maximum advantage of the economies of scale which come as a result of a large, well-drilled, and enthusiastic sales-force willing to devote seven days a week to the job. Even more than the Americans, Japanese businessmen think big. They also think small. Matsushita, for example, is the largest single advertiser in Japan and has built up the most efficient accounting system in Japanese industry to keep track of where the money is going. Perhaps as a result of being aware of the constant presence of the accountant, Matsushita managers are known for their flexibility and willingness to spend a little more time and trouble so as to obtain maximum return on every yen invested in advertising. Strangely enough, Matsushita advertising campaigns frequently win awards, whereas one would expect that the highly-pressurized executives who approve the advertising would tend to settle for the 'play-it-safe' advertisements on which so many huge corporations seem impelled to waste their money.

Imported concepts

In this alien economy, where market share is more important than profitability, where status is more important than salary, and where innovation is never allowed to interfere with the prime aim of producing the highest possible quality for the lowest possible price, what kind of advertising industry exists and what can the foreign marketer do to evaluate it?

First of all, it is important to remember that mass production and mass marketing were imported to Japan from the West. And, like everything else imported into Japan by the Japanese, both of these have been subtly modified so as to conform to the peculiar needs of the Japanese and their highly individual market.

The 1950s saw a large-scale expansion overseas by rich American corporations eager to make sizeable direct investment in foreign markets at relatively low cost. To service this business and in the long term to protect the account in the United States, the large American advertising agencies followed the banner of Kelloggs, Chrysler and Coca-Cola around the world.

In Japan, it has only recently become possible for wholly-owned foreign advertising agencies to establish themselves and this is why it has been the usual pattern for foreign agencies to open joint venture agencies in association with Japanese agencies.

The international agencies

For a foreign advertiser in Japan, there is obviously a lot to be said for giving his account to the same agency which handles the business in the rest of the world. Communication problems are likely to be fewer and campaigns prepared back home–approved by top management there–can readily be adapted for the Japanese market, often by simply translating copy or dubbing a voice-over into Japanese.

J. Walter Thompson, McCanns, Grey, Botsford Ketchum, Young and Rubicam are all in Japan, together with many other agencies whose representation is often no more than a loose arrangement whereby both parties can write 'Tokyo' and 'Los Angeles' into their respective lists of 'associate offices'.

Unlike the situation in, say, the United Kingdom, where American agencies have a dominant share of the market, Dentsu, which has no tie-up with a foreign agency, is very much the market leader in the agency field in Japan. Indeed, if foreign and joint venture agencies are judged by Japanese standards, namely by their market share, it must be said that foreign agencies have yet to make a significant impression in Japan. The reason for this lies partly in the amazing capacity of the Japanese to emulate foreign practices. The huge Japanese agencies have been very much shaped by Madison Avenue advertising philosophy.

In Japan there are also scores of small units calling themselves production companies, advertising agencies, even advertising laboratories. These are the Japanese equivalents of the hot shops which were so fashionable in the West a few years ago.

The difference is that these units manage to coexist with the agencies' in-house creative departments in a uniquely Japanese way, demonstrating that even a highly charged business like advertising can be successfully organized to conform to the Japanese passion for order and group solidarity.

The large agencies

The large Japanese agencies, including Dentsu, often act as media brokers, placing advertisements created by the hot shops and by the clients' in-house creative departments. Between 1955 and 1969, total advertising expenditure in Japan increased more than tenfold–from yen 60·9 billion to yen 628·7 billion.* As a result, competition to secure space and time in Japanese media is extremely keen. Naturally, media costs are correspondingly high, between two and four times higher than in the United Kingdom, for example. What is more, media costs are inflated because Japanese advertisers, particularly in areas like cosmetics and pharmaceuticals, invest on a very large scale. In Tokyo there are five commercial television channels, all in colour. Major Japanese advertisers usually use all of them several times on the same evening. Thus, for the majority of foreign marketers, the existence of a domestic producer with an iron grip on the market, or the mass-market at least, usually means that the only viable opening is at the top end of the market.

Since it is most unlikely that you will go it alone in Japan, you will almost certainly decide to try to find a Japanese distributor and/or manufacturer. Although some will agree to handle almost anything, the more professional will first attempt to determine whether or not there is a market for your product and how well it can be positioned with regard to the vital status-role factor and other unique-to-the-market considerations. Once a product has been so positioned, the advertising approach has largely been decided as well, although certain danger areas lie between this point and the realization of your goal.

Faced with the heavy cost of advertising in Japan, your financial people will almost certainly be on the look-out for ways both to achieve maximum impact and to save money, and one may be led to hope that advertising prepared for use in other markets can be adapted for Japan.

*Source: *Dentsu Advertising Annual, 1969.*

However, apart from the fact that the savings involved tend to be cut severely once all hidden costs–like expensive retouching and size-changes to suit local media needs–have been accounted for, there is another, more important, reason why pressures to adapt existing campaigns should be resisted.

The fact is, everything which the Japanese have imported themselves, from *ch'an* Buddhism to Cadillacs, has been subtly changed to suit local taste. (*zen* Buddhism is very different from *ch'an* Buddhism, and Cadillacs in Japan acquired lace curtains for the rear window in response to the Japanese company presidents' desire to enjoy the privacy which is, in Japan, a perquisite of high rank.)

'Foreign' status

So far as your product is concerned, the main advantage which it has of course is that it is foreign, an import. From this fact alone it enjoys considerable status-giving qualities and therefore considerable sales potential. However, it is unfortunately true that the Japanese consumer will be less able to identify with 'real' foreignness than he would with a foreign product which has been skilfully 'Japanized'.

Two examples of this, both in the liquor market where foreignness is a major asset and competition is ruthlessly keen, concern Harveys' sherry and Cockburns' port.

Harveys, as market leaders in the United Kingdom, were positioned in Japan as being the *ichi-ban* (number one) producers–as blenders and bottlers–of superb Spanish sherries brought to perfection for the discerning English market.

The successful policy of grouping advertising expenditure in key periods rather than dribbling away the same amount of money on an 'invisible' series of tiny black-and-white advertisements all the year round was also followed. The advertising agency involved also took great care to associate the product with auspicious events in the Japanese calendar, such as Adults Day when younger people, the target audience, reach their majority. However, the basic international advertising platform for British 'Cream' sherry was left unchanged.

Cockburns' port, on the other hand, posed different problems since port is far less well known in Japan than sherry. In response to the fact that wine in general is rapidly becoming an in-drink in Japan, it was decided, in collaboration with the distributors, to position Cockburns' port as a drink selected by the younger internationally-minded executive who has assimilated western life-styles.

These are two examples of successful 'Japanizing' involving the contribution of top-class Japanese creative people. Other ventures are sometimes less successful. For example, advertisements for confectionery, clothes, coffee and other products frequently involve the use of western 'models' who are induced to produce the most ludicrous caricatures of *gaijin* (foreigners) as the Japanese imagine them. This unhappy situation is compounded by the fact that many of the 'models' are recruited, like Andy Warhol film actors, straight off the street. My own wife, for instance, was once approached in a supermarket and asked if she would like to be a model.

Media space

As has already been mentioned, there is fierce competition for prime media space and time and the foreign advertiser, faced with the need to obtain maximum results for minimum investment, is in competition for this with domestic advertisers who may be outspending him by hundreds or even thousands to one in the media.

In my experience, the most effective solution to this problem, and the related one of obtaining the best creative work possible, lies in an *à la carte* approach to the suppliers concerned. This implies that the distributor, who will almost certainly be representing a large number of clients, should be encouraged to exercise his considerable influence with the big agencies and the media, in order to ensure that good positions and times are obtained.

At the same time, a concerted effort should be made to persuade the big agency to make its services available on a fee basis, leaving you and your distributor free to go to a specialist outside source, with the agency acting as middleman, so as to obtain the best creative work.

Conclusion

By far the most important factor when it comes to evaluating creative work is the supplier's ability, whether it is an agency, hot shop, or in-house creative department employed by your distributor, to produce ads for prestige products *in Japanese*; if *you* like the concept or the copy, that is a bonus, not an essential requirement, since the advertisement is, after all, designed to sell your product to the Japanese, not to you.

ADVERTISING AND THE SPECIFICS OF CULTURAL IDENTITY

George Fields

Enter the western businessman (who has come to Japan to straighten things out with his branch) into his suite at the Land of the Cherry Blossom Hotel. He is used to spending millions–dollars not yen–in advertising back home. 'Saturation advertising', as he calls it. He believes absolutely in the power of TV advertising, as he should. So naturally he turns on the TV in his hotel room. But what's this? The advertising is lousy. Nothing but scenarios, slapsticks, all mood stuff with the product tacked on to the end. No wonder the branch is not doing well. Thinks: 'It's about time we introduced some marketing know-how around here.'

Enter the Japanese businessman (who now has to think of himself as being part of a multinational company, which isn't always very easy) into his twin bedroom in the Washington Astoria Hotel, in the United States of America. He has done very well in his own country with regard to television advertising, so naturally he turns on his TV set. But my goodness, how irritating these American commercials are! Just incessant talk. Still, that's the way things are with foreigners. Thinks: 'Obviously we must adapt ourselves to their ways.'

WESTERN AND JAPANESE REACTIONS TO EACH OTHER'S COMMERCIALS

The anecdotes above probably typify the chasm that exists between the western and the Japanese approach to advertising–a difference which is essentially culture orientated. This much we have learned from our experience of servicing equal numbers of Japanese and western clients in the perplexing and not always exact area of advertising research.

Although oversimplification is dangerous, we have found that the communication processes are indeed very different between the cultures. This point is very well illustrated by the following two case studies.

The first, in the field of educational psychology, tested the learning efficiency between matched samples of American and Japanese students. The first test took the form of a lecture in which an identical subject was presented to the students in their own language. Subsequently, both groups were tested on their level of comprehension and the American group was found to have a higher comprehension level than that of the Japanese. Surprising? But does it prove that English is more efficient in communicating ideas? Not necessarily so.

In the next experiment, the matched groups were handed an editorial-type statement to *read*, for a fixed period of time. A similar comprehension test followed. The Japanese level of comprehension was found to be higher than that of the American.

Reactions to perceived differences

The effective communication process is indeed different. In some ways, the Japanese businessman has been smarter than his western colleague in that he has accepted that the ways of the foreigners are incomprehensible and therefore he tends to entrust the direction of his advertising to the local 'expert'. There are, of course, dangers in this, in that it has a hit-or-miss element since the Japanese executive has no fixed judgement criteria; thus, he has no real basis for fully evaluating the effectiveness of his company's advertising.

Yet the western advertising man tends to err in the other direction. He tends to *impose* his western criteria on an alien culture and expect it to work. There is a touch of cultural arrogance in this–'Don't give me that rubbish about Japanese being different–it worked in Sweden, in Venezuela, and even in the Philippines'.

Still, we must acknowledge the fact that many Japanese advertisers have been very successful in communicating to the consumer *in their own way*.

Reasons for the differences

Why should there be this difference between two sets of human beings who, after all, share basically the same needs and desires? When one thinks of the cultural differences the whole situation is not nearly as strange as it may seem.

The western foundation of 'intellectual' communications could be said to have been established by the Greeks and is essentially a culture of 'debate'. The western businessman states his position at a meeting–the thesis–and this is probably taken up by a counter point of view–the antithesis. After further debate, the meeting is expected to arrive at some sort of decision and resolution–the synthesis. it is essentially an aural system of communication.

The Japanese, on the other hand, have no such tradition of verbal debate. Jack Sewald in his very perceptive book, *Japanese In Action* (purportedly for students in semantics), gives a very vivid illustration. In the highly structured Japanese society of the *samurai*, the farmer, the artisan, the merchant, in that order of social ranking–free and direct verbal communication could be quite risky. The *samurai* had absolute rights over the rest of the community, described as *kirisute gomen*, literally, 'I can chop your head off and you have no recourse to the courts'. The *samurai*, on the whole, did not abuse this right, because society somehow evolves a way of preserving itself from destruction. The fact remains that such a right existed and thus there emerged a very cautious form of verbal response within the community generally. Obviously, one should not offend by giving the wrong answer. But it came about that if you could not be certain of the *right* answer it was better for everybody if you answered in a way that could be either 'yes' or 'no'.

Stomach versus head and heart culture

The Japanese still use the word *haragei*, stomach art, for business negotiations. This, of course, is oversimplification on their part and what is really meant are highly developed and subtle sets of body language–otherwise known as 'non-verbal' communication. I prefer to call it 'stomach culture', implying that the whole essence of being is 'head and heart culture'. The westerner communicates with his head–logic and heart–emotion. (Typically, when a westerner commits suicide–the destruction of the total being–he either shoots his brains out or stabs his heart *à la Juliette*. The Japanese commits *harakiri* and disembowels himself.) Incidentally, the Japanese are one of the largest consumers of stomach remedies and the smallest consumers of analgesics among the advanced industrialized nations.

Comparative TV commercial results

Not long ago, my organization developed a unique set of data drawn from the tested results of some 150 thirty-second food commercials which were organized under identical, controlled conditions, using exactly the same methodology in both Japan and the United States. (The averages derived from these tests were based on the reactions of approximately 38,000 female consumers.)

The differences appear highly significant and help to explain the bewilderment of the two businessmen noted in the opening paragraph. First of all, to understand the significance of the results, one should appreciate the fact that a TV commercial sets out to achieve a number of objectives:

1 It must generate **interest**, in that people will watch it, and it must **involve** the viewer
2 It must **communicate**. The viewer must **comprehend** the product benefits and **retain** both this and the brand name after a lapse of time
3 Most importantly, it must **generate desire for the product** and specifically shift the consumer from the competitive brand to your own.

The research technique applied cannot be examined here in detail except to say that, basically, two techniques were used. First, there was verbal playback, i.e. the respondent either picked an adjective from a list or told us what she understood and remembered, *in her own words*; secondly, there was non-verbal playback, i.e. the respondent picked a brand of her choice before *and* after exposure to the commercial. The following summarizes the differences between Japan and the United States.

Measurement	*Differences*
Interest (non-verbal)	Japan–*higher*
Involvement (verbal)	US–*considerably higher*
Brand recall (neutral)	US/Japan–*identical*
Comprehension and sales message recall (verbal)	US–*outstandingly higher*
Effectiveness (non-verbal) (i.e. desire for a shift towards the advertised brand)	US/Japan–*identical*

Results through different routes

If we agree that the ultimate objective of a commercial is to be 'effective', then it seems that perhaps intuitively the creative talents in the two countries have arrived at the same end via different routes–the Japanese largely through non-verbal communication and the United States largely through verbal communication.

Irritants

One final example seems to be in order to drive the point home. When testing commercials which have been adapted directly from the United States, we have generally found that, when aurally tested, the Japanese absorption of the number of sales messages is very much lower than the American capacity. For the Japanese, the irritation of being 'talked at' presumably raises a psychological barrier to shut out the sales message. Dismaying as it may be for the manufacturer who feels he has a lot to tell the consumer about the product, it is sometimes more effective when the sales message content is reduced. On the other hand, the westerner is irritated when his visual enjoyment is interrupted by writing appearing on the screen. Referring back to the example of the faster comprehension of the written word by the Japanese, the same degree of irritation does not exist for them. In fact, it is a standard part of the Japanese TV programme for the sponsor's abbreviated message to wiggle across the screen. (It is not surprising that the Japanese are adept at reading the subtitles on the screen for a western movie.) The difference simply arises from the fact that Chinese characters are instantly recognized by the shape–visually perceived–while western writing is based on phonetic spelling–aurally perceived.

Concept and execution

The scientific approach has revolutionized marketing efficiency throughout the world–the 'marketing concept' being one of the most important aspects. From this followed the 'product concept' and 'advertising concept' in rapid succession. It is now almost standard in the West to think of advertising in terms of 'concept' and 'execution' and again it is standard to give more weight to the 'concept': if the concept is 'right' and the execution 'wrong', the argument says, there is 'no problem' since it is always possible to improve the execution. However, the reverse does not work, i.e. if the concept is 'wrong' and the execution 'superb', nothing can be done, since the concept is an absolute and can only be either 'right' or 'wrong'.

Developing a concept in Japan

Empirically, by and large, the scientific approach has worked in the West with some notable success stories. The trouble with this approach in Japan is, first, a practical one. Most Japanese marketing terms are simply derived from the English, e.g. 'marketing' being *makechingu*. However, it is only a very erudite westerner who can explain the meaning of concept. This has not been too important in that, marketing being a pragmatic system of approach, we have developed an understanding in practical terms, through actual cases. Thus, without actually defining 'concept', the researchers have had quite a few instances of success in *testing* concepts. However, when a term is of foreign origin, quite naturally there is a tendency to want it defined in dictionary terms or at least explained fairly concisely. It did not matter too much in the case of the term 'marketing' for this is an operational term. However, 'concept' is an abstract and how do you explain something to somebody in an alien culture which is difficult to define in one's own culture? In lecturing to Japanese audiences, in Japanese, I have had more trouble with this term than any other.

Execution as part of the concept

The scientific approach probably works in the West because the process is logically derived within the western system and understood. But what if the 'execution' is part of the concept? Nonsense? Not at all. Take *kabuki*, the Japanese highly stylized theatrical form, or better still, take the even more stylized *noh* drama. In both of these dramatic frameworks it is the form that matters because the form itself presents its own intrinsic values. Take *haiku*–the evocative Japanese poetry form which has a mere seventeen syllables. In actual words very little can be said and yet the atmosphere it evokes is more than words. In *haiku*, what is left out may be so much more important! Not surprisingly, therefore, a Japanese advertising man will frequently begin his thinking with a largely visual idea–an approach which may strike the western advertising man schooled in the best way, *in western terms*, as placing the cart before the horse.

Finally, borrowing some of David Ogilvy's precepts, here are some personal observations:

Testimonials–There is probably more of this type of advertising than any other. The form can be very successful in the West provided the personality being projected is consistent with the product's characteristics. Japan is no different in this respect. The difference is that there is less of the 'straight sell' and more reliance is placed on the mood generated by the personality.

Problem solution or product demonstration–Basic principles are the same but whereas it is best to be logical and direct in the West, the Japanese *tend* to go about it in a more roundabout way and are almost coy about it. (However, there are outstanding exceptions.)

Purely visual 'mood' commercials–Predominantly a Japanese phenomenon and the chief source of the western advertiser's complaints–'half the time you don't know what is being advertised'! The aural side depends on highly effective use of music to generate the mood.

Slice of life–As far as this writer is concerned, no known example of success.

Burr of singularity–To project a unique personality to the product via the commercial seems a principle that applies equally to the West as well as to Japan and the latter seems particularly adept at symbolizing the product.

Fact versus emotion –Without a doubt the latter predominates in Japan.

The environment and TV advertising

Finally, a brief word on the environment in which TV commercials are shown. Although on a cost per thousand basis TV is less expensive than in the United States, the clutter (commercials bunching up) or the noise level (the sheer number of commercials to which the consumer is exposed) is much higher in Japan. This may be another reason why interest or mood-provoking commercials *seem* to have a higher rate of success than the hard sell. There is no doubt that it is much harder to get your message heard, to be noticed, in Japan.

For some time now, the major Japanese networks have enjoyed a seller's market, particularly for prime evening time, and the advertiser has less control than his western counterparts for 'slotting'. Thus, it happens that two competitive brands of soft drink commercials can run back to back, with presumably no redress to either advertiser. Advertising life in Japan is not entirely easy for those schooled in western advertising codes.

A PROFILE OF THE JAPANESE CONSUMER

George Fields

When talking about the consumer, one is always tempted to do so in terms of the 'average' consumer. Every country has its housewife/husband/family stereotype, but the usefulness of this 'average' concept depends on the particular characteristics of the society in question. Within a heterogeneous society, such as that of the United States of America, the concept appears almost meaningless; likewise, if there is a great deal of social inequality and wealth is concentrated amongst a tiny minority the concept has little relevance in marketing terms.

Japan is neither. It is both a racially and culturally homogeneous society and its wealth is fairly well distributed. Not surprisingly, therefore, the western marketer who goes to Japan is often guilty of sweeping generalizations concerning the Japanese; so it is essential to appreciate from the outset that the image of the so-called 'average' consumer is open to wide interpretation on several levels.

Generalizing from statistics

Where the product's future is directly related to socio-cultural factors, statistics on average behaviour patterns can be seriously misleading. For example, the proportion of the weekly budget spent on rice has declined significantly while consumption of western-type foods has increased noticeably. Since the end of the war the influence of the school meal in which, for institutional reasons, the children were provided with bread rather than rice, has been profound. In one study, we found that, in some cases, the housewife was preparing two types of meals for the same family meal sitting–the traditional Japanese dishes (i.e. rice-centred rather than bread-centred) and western-type food, the former for her husband and herself and the latter for the children.

Given this frame of reference, one might assume that the Japanese were ready to take to western breakfast cereals–almost in their stride. Yet for one major manufacturer who invested a considerable amount of money in advertising and promoting a premier breakfast cereal, his product ended up being positioned as a minor snack.

'Westernization', Japanese-style

On the other hand, visit a Japanese home yourself at breakfast time and you could well find the housewife serving western-style package soups. Hindsight rationalizations are always easy but the soup was more acceptable than cereal simply because it was an extension of the conventional Japanese breakfast which invariably includes *salty* bean paste soup. To many Japanese, the idea of eating cereal with sugar and milk first thing in the morning was equivalent to confronting the westerner with bean paste soup. Clearly, what the children were demanding was a bread-centred breakfast–not necessarily a *real* western breakfast.

This brings us into the realm of *qualitative* information input as opposed to quantitative input and in this context we should know that westernization proceeds along Japanese lines, i.e. Japan is seldom able to break away completely from habits and tastes established over centuries. A Japanese housewife, for example, who tells you that her family prefers western meals is, more often than not, referring to a meal that is far removed from the English, American, or French original.

So we continue to fail

A more recent example of the marketing failure of a western food product (developed again from a statistical rationalization) may prove the point even more convincingly. It is a fact that the purchase of shop-baked cakes in Japan accounts for quite a respectable percentage of the food market trade; the trend is clearly towards western cakes made from pastry and away from traditional Japanese cakes made from kneaded rice and sweet bean paste. it is also a fact, however, that the Japanese housewife does not bake cakes of any kind in her own home. The tiny minority who do have western-style ovens may well have experimented with cake-making. However, the marketing rationalization of the product in question established the fact that the Japanese housewife does make instant puddings from prepared packet mixtures, which is a new culinary trend. Thus, it was argued, if the *means* were available, surely a substantial market would automatically develop for cake mixes as had been the case in numerous western markets. And suppose, also, one could develop a cake that could be made to an acceptable quality level in the automatic rice cooker–an item that exists in practically every Japanese kitchen? Bingo! Here, surely, was the basis for creating a new mass market for cake mixes.

Unfortunately, the 'rice cooker cake' was a technical concept, not a marketing concept. Let us look more closely at the reasons why the whole marketing programme failed. First, the rice cooker is in use most of the day–cooking rice; secondly, unlike the oven, the rice cooker was designed solely for the one purpose–given the Japanese penchant to put things into neat conceptual pockets–i.e. to cook rice; so it may have been too much of a mental switch to consider using the cooker for preparing a completely different type of food. Thirdly, to ask a Japanese housewife to bake a cake in her rice cooker is like asking an English housewife to make coffee in her tea-pot: cooking rice like making tea is a ritual and any 'contamination' of the cooking vessel is instinctively shunned.

This case study simply suggests that available 'facts' must, in turn, be interpreted in relation to the social, economic and cultural environment of the consumer.

Keeper of the purse

While it is logical to start the observation of a typical day at the beginning–the morning, for the purposes of this study let us consider the housewife and her activities at the end of the afternoon, since it is at this time she normally records the day's expenditures. This exercise can be seen as a summary of the day's activities; it also epitomizes the essential role of the Japanese housewife in the home. In addition, therefore, to the supremely important task of bringing up the children and planning for their education, the Japanese housewife is also the keeper of the purse.

As the chief accountant for all domestic expenses, there will no doubt be times when she budgets for a deficit–a practice possible because of the twice yearly bonus system (which is not without some important implications for the marketer, as will be touched upon later). Of the total budget she spends about a third on food, which is a steadily declining proportion. In addition to this there are other important account classifications, such as 'recreational activities' and 'social expenses', each of which currently accounts for about 8 per cent of the budget, but both are clearly increasing in importance. All these expenses considered, it is important to remember that the average Japanese household budget is currently able to achieve a saving of 20 per cent out of disposable income (the highest saving rate of any consumer in the world), compared with 8–9 per cent in the UK and the USA. This propensity to save, incidentally, continues to increase.

In the home/out of the home

This budgeting expertise suggests that the housewife is a meticulous planner when it comes to shopping. She is in the sense that she has made up her mind beforehand on approximately how much she intends to spend on food and other items on any particular day. However, in the sense that she generally does not plan ahead on the actual food items she is going to buy during the day nor does she stock up to any extent, one could argue that her shopping 'plan' is far from meticulous. Herein lies a fundamental difference between the daily life-style of the Japanese and western housewife. Relatively speaking, the Japanese housewife spends less time in the kitchen than her western counterpart but more time out shopping. The importance placed on shopping by the Japanese housewife has profound repercussions on the entire distribution system of consumer goods–a system described as an 'Alice in Wonderland' situation by some western marketers, who also place much of the blame for their lack of success in breaking into the market on this one factor.

The small purchaser

The chaotic distribution situation that still exists in Japan, at least from the western eye, is a subject on its own. (See Chapter 9.) The Japanese housewife, of course, is keenly aware of (and annoyed by) the inflationary price spiral which, to a large extent, is a result of the distribution system. However, consider the following:

1 The Japanese housewife likes to shop daily–this is part of her way of life.

2 Typically, there is always a shop around the corner, say, within five minutes' walking distance.

3 Thus, she does her shopping-round on foot. Even if she had a car, and could drive it, the chances are that there would be nowhere to park it.

4 Since daily shopping is best justified and is most satisfying when one is buying a fresh food bargain, her shopping pattern revolves around *fresh* food first.

5 The fresh food prices can vary enormously from day to day. It stands to reason, therefore, that the actual meal is planned after the purchase, not before.

6 She only buys enough food for the day's meal. Meat is sold in

slices of 100 gms. The quantity can be fractional to meet the requirements of any meal or just one person.

7 She returns home with the goods that will fit into her small shopping basket, and which are preferably not too heavy to carry. (Beers, soft drinks and rice–all heavy items–are invariably home delivered.)

To cater for this demand to shop daily, in small quantities, and centred around 'fresh' perishable items, there are about a million-and-a-half retail outlets throughout Japan; of these about half a million handle food, and of these outlets some 180,000 handle fresh perishable foods only. In other words, there is a food outlet for every 66 homes and 235 persons, and a store for every 20 homes and 70 persons.

Small families to feed

It is worth while remembering that the size of the average family in 1970 was only 3·5 persons which means that, to a large extent, the old family structure of grandparents to grandchildren living under the same roof has disappeared. It also means that a large proportion of families has only one child and at most two. Today, Japan has one of the lowest population growths in the world and some demographers even predict a decline in population from around the year 2000. (The fragmentation into small family units has greatly increased the demand for housing and land which went up an average of 30 per cent in 1972.)

Space, therefore, is at an all-time high premium in Japan. The space occupied per person is five-and-a-half *tatami** mats, or less than 100 sq. ft. Thus a family of four, for example, would occupy a dwelling no larger than 400 sq. ft.

Within such a home, the area occupied by the kitchen would most likely cover between two and six *tatami* mats. The standard kitchen is generally equipped with a small two-burner calor gas unit and an assortment of small electric food processers (e.g. electric rice cooker, frying pan). Thus, since the typical kitchen is very small, there is nowhere for the housewife to store the food, even if she wanted to.

*The standard *tatami* mat measures 6 × 3 ft and is the traditional unit of measurement for all forms of accommodation.

Leisure as a new factor

So far we have only considered the housewife as a consumer in terms of her daily life-style; the male consumer, who has relatively little say in the disposal of the daily budget, has, alas, been ignored. On the question of budgeting for leisure, however, it is a different matter.

Leisure time spending is now the fastest growing sector in the Japanese market and within it, like any other market in the world, the increasingly affluent youth segment is the most attractive.

However, increased leisure time and the frequently asked question of what to do with it may be at the basis of a profound social revolution in Japan. Incredible as it may appear, as recently as 1972 a survey taken by Japan's Ministry of Labour showed that only a minority of salaried workers took up their full entitlement of annual leave. Most people still work on Saturdays in Japan, but there has been a concerted effort from some government quarters to *make* people take more time off. Yet the question still has to be asked, what is the housewife to do with her husband lolling about in 400 sq. ft. of confined space, (the entire area of the home), not just one day a week, but two days a week?

Gifts

Unlike leisure spending on a mass scale, gift giving has been an established custom in Japan for centuries. Commercially speaking, the twice yearly bonus system* (in June and December) has a great impact on the gifts budget. Gifts are given not only to clients, but also to superiors at work or suppliers in order to cement or confirm a relationship. The department stores, which account for 10 per cent of gross retail sales throughout Japan, handle most of the 'gift' sales because of the prestige associated with their name and because the consumer is buying the wrapping, in that he must project the image of quality and superiority on to everything he gives–appropriate to the status of the recipient. Daily utility items, for example, are attractively gift-wrapped for the occasion; one of our surveys showed that

*The equivalent of approximately four months' pay is given in a lump sum.

many homes never buy toilet soap since they always get enough given to them during the two gift seasons to last the whole year.

Even more important for the western marketer, on these two occasions the consumer buys things for himself that he would not normally buy, e.g. Scotch whisky, imported confectionery or prestige brand cosmetics.

Conclusion

The foregoing observations are simply a series of impressions on the theme of the Japanese consumer's life-style. It is undoubtedly tempting for the visiting marketer to latch on to the obvious similarities he sees in the market place since these give him some sense of security; even so, all too often the marketer's confusion and frustration over what he sees is often expressed thus: 'Don't give me that damned rubbish about the Japanese being different . . . they are all people'. Certainly, the Japanese are the same as anybody else in the sense that they love their children, enjoy their food, and try to provide for comfort in their old age. Stay at any first-class hotel in Tokyo and you will see the same things as you would see in any big city the world over–office buildings, men in business suits, girls in mini skirts, and people drinking coffee and eating western convenience foods. At this level of abstraction, i.e. the *visible culture*–the Japanese are indeed no different from anybody else among advanced industrial societies. However, unless you belong to the lucky few who are gifted with supernatural intuition or luck, then it will certainly pay you to take heed of Japan's invisible culture, which is the world of values, attitudes and motivations. The information input you demand must be qualitative as well as quantitative.

THE CASE OF MATSUSHITA ELECTRIC

Fumio Yamamoto

Perhaps the most fundamental point to remember about the business of advertising in Japan is that, although the Japanese are an intensely practical people, their reaction to advertising is far from practical. It is worth remembering, in fact, that the traditional reverence felt by Orientals for the written word is still very much in evidence in present-day Japan. This attitude of mind also applies to advertising. Not surprisingly, therefore, and in sharp contrast to westerners, the Japanese are inclined to forget that advertising messages are designed to *sell*, so they take what they read and see at face value.

In the same way, testimonials by famous people (which are approached with a good deal of scepticism by a western audience) often carry considerable weight in Japan, especially when the person in question is recognized as a *sensei* – an authority in his field. The judgement of or the lead given by such a *sensei* has a unique pull in Japan which is not easy for the foreigner to appreciate.

Consumerism is now an established feature of the Japanese scene and is likely to expand rapidly. Even so, there has been no significant erosion of the consumer's natural instinct to accept advertising at face value.

The West's logical approach

The creators of advertisements in the West often resort to logic, or, at least, what looks and sounds like logic, in an effort to convince a fundamentally sceptical audience. On the other hand, since their audience is naturally sympathetic, Japanese admen are not very concerned with logic; the Japanese have always responded more readily to the emotions and intuitive feelings rather than to logic and deductive thinking.

Although the West's preoccupation with logic in advertising is beginning to influence Japan (particularly in the field of property, where the high price of land restricts the audience to an élite), the greater part of Japanese advertising is conducted on a lower plane, and aims for a 'gut-reaction'. So, Japanese advertisements are repetitive, they make frequent use of jingles and, as has been said above, often involve testimonials. Nescafé, for example, recently organized a large number of print advertisements and commercials involving well-known Japanese actors and musicians. *Ajinomoto* (a powder used by Japanese housewives to bring out the flavour of food in cooking) hired Andy Williams to record a song about its product. The opinion of the westerner is often highly respected in Japan.

Youth market

Nearly half of Japan's population of over 108 million is under 35. Thus the youth market, where a high proportion of the total disposable income is concentrated, is a key market for many Japanese advertisers; it is also a sector in which foreign advertisers trying to establish themselves in Japan are likely to find that they face the strongest competition from domestic brands. As in other countries, young people in Japan put a high value on styles and fashions. But because life moves so fast in Japan fashions come and go very quickly indeed. So quickly, in fact, that a foreign advertising agency might well have difficulty in keeping pace. (This difficulty would be overcome to a certain extent if a foreign agency were to employ Japanese executive and creative personnel and allow them a completely free hand: it is my experience, however, that such freedom is rarely given.)

Visual impact

It is part of the Japanese tradition to respond to the visual impact; Japanese advertisers today appeal to such traditional responses and know that what their advertisements look like is at least as important as what they say. They play on the senses rather than on the intellect.

There is a very appropriate example of this practice in the field of television. Some years ago now, in the domestic advertising division in Matsushita, we were faced with the task of advertising a new range of black-and-white National television sets.

When we analysed the product, we found that it was of high quality yet there was no single feature which could be claimed to set it apart from competitive products. Clearly, we had to come up with some way of making television (which was then relatively new) appear desirable to the consumer; if we did our job well enough, he would buy National. We finally decided to concentrate our campaign on a district called Saga in the western part of Kyoto. Here, there were many old, narrow streets, temples and bamboo groves; the place was a nostalgic symbol of the very heart of Japan. We made sure that the filming schedule would capture conditions at their most effective–an early autumn morning with dreamy mists, a golden summer evening, a blue spring day with the green burgeoning.

We ran our Saga campaign for five years, at a cost of yen 2000 million, without a single major modification. The campaign was a significant success; two million sets were sold and National achieved the position of market leadership it still enjoys.

This experience is a useful example on two counts. First, it underlines the effectiveness of an advertising campaign appealing almost exclusively to the emotions. Secondly, it shows that an advertiser cannot hope for success in the highly competitive mass market in Japan unless he is ready to invest very considerable sums of money in advertising.

Kuchikomi

Advertising in Japan could be said to be a case of all or nothing. For although a small advertising budget in the mass market is almost certainly money wasted, yet, curiously enough, one can be successful without any advertising at all! Johnnie Walker Black Label is an excellent illustration of a product achieving a position of market leadership *without advertising*.* Johnnie Walker's distributors relied on one of the unique features of Japan–the effectiveness of *kuchikomi*, word-of-mouth communication. Personal recommendation the world over plays an important role for a consumer in deciding between a choice of products; but nowhere in the world is it as influential and decisive as in Japan.

The Japanese put great emphasis on status, and are ready to spend heavily so that they can be seen to be living up to the life-style expected. If others in the same status group were known to prefer Johnnie Walker Black, there was no practical alternative. This keen regard for status also makes it easy for the Japanese to identify with authority figures. President Kennedy, for instance, was deeply admired in Japan: I myself, a seasoned campaigner, converted to Jack Daniels Bourbon solely on the basis of the tip (from the head of a well-known Japanese advertising agency) that it was the brand that Kennedy preferred! The power of *kuchikomi* is also in evidence in the high repute enjoyed by English tweed and English clothes in general in Japan.

*The 30-year import control on whisky and the controlled distribution of this particular brand inevitably contributed to its prestige and success. Eds.

National's philosophy

In National we are, of course, fully aware of the vital effect in Japan of word-of-mouth communication. But we do not stop there. In fact, we are one of the top-level spenders on advertising in Japan. The prime objective of an advertising campaign in National is to win the consumer's goodwill towards an individual product rather than to strengthen our brand image. We think that the latter derives from and is nurtured by the individual consumer's goodwill towards the individual product.

There are three basic strands in National's overall advertising policy:

1 To take the lead in the youth market by establishing a high technology image for Matsushita Electric.

2 To ensure that our innovative R&D programme can be seen to be innovative in the advertisements. If a product has unique features, 'clever' advertising gimmicks are not allowed to obscure the real product benefit. (The Saga campaign was put out on a purely emotional platform precisely because there was nothing innovative about the product.)

3 To ensure that, in all our advertising, there should be clearly evident the feeling of freshness and creativity and the quality of being 'slightly ahead of our times' which is part of the character of Matsushita Electric.

Some case studies

Let me try and show how we translated these policies into practice. First, an example from the youth market. We introduced midnight disc-jockey show commercials for a cassette tape-recorder and, rather than attempt to write the commercials ourselves, we let the DJs ad lib their own material after explaining the features of the product to them. In fact, one of these commercials won the performer's gold prize award and the topicality award of the All Japan Commercial Council in 1972.

A further example. High fidelity equipment is one of the most important advanced technology areas in the consumer field, and, in Japan as in the West, consumers traditionally looked to small, specialist manufacturers for hi-fi components. So we found that consumers did not expect advanced hi-fi components from a producer of our size and nature when we introduced, in 1966, a range of advanced loudspeakers with the brand name of Technics. To overcome these prejudices and to establish the advanced technology of these products, we ran a series of advertisements in specialist media and, in 1971, we opened a Technics showroom on the Ginza–Tokyo's busiest and smartest shopping area. Today, the Technics range is widely known in Japan; its image is equal to that of the specialist manufacturers, in terms of both sound quality and design.

A final example from the other end of the scale. We felt that a new kind of radio with a more feminine appeal would fill a gap in the man-dominated transistor radio market. We tested 45 mock-ups and tried 350 pet names, and our new products specialists finally came up with a completely new medium-wave radio. We called it Toot-a-Loop: it comes in a bright primary colour range and can be worn like a bracelet round the wrist. Rather than conventional advertising, we chose a mixture of PR activities, tie-ups with the mass media and demonstrations by Toot-a-Loop girls. The outcome was that we exceeded our target by about 400 per cent.

11 Six Case Studies

GENE GREGORY

INTRODUCTION

Believing that the opportunity to learn from other people's successes (or failures) can often be worth while and sometimes far more meaningful than the know-how transmitted by academics and consultants, we have compiled six in-depth case studies drawn from European companies who have made a success of the Japanese market. The companies represented are Dimplex–for oil-filled radiators, Olivetti–for office machinery, Pez–for confectionery, Philips–for household products, Uclaf–for pharmaceuticals, and Triumph–for women's clothing. It should be recognized from the outset that the selection we have made is quite arbitrary and does not attempt to reflect any statistical criteria concerning market sector, profitability, seniority or nationality. In the event, all the companies represented are in manufactured goods. The decision to concentrate on this area was taken because of the enormously wide potential for so many producers. Nevertheless, the philosophy, know-how and business strategies that are discussed in this chapter we hope will have far wider appeal. Readers will note, incidentally, that the countries represented are Germany, France, Britain, Italy, Holland and Austria–from the very large (in economic status) to the rather small. At the end of the chapter we have added a supplement on the British electronics company, Sinclair, which, although barely established in the market, can be justifiably considered as one of the most spectacular selling success stories in recent times.

If there are any particularly striking underlying themes to be drawn from this analysis they are these: Japan, while being one of the most idiosyncratic countries in the world, is also one of the most professional. Thus, it is not a market where half-measures can be applied; lack of conviction and application is ruthlessly eliminated. In doing what is natural to Japan which, in terms of understanding this new market, is the beginning of the beginning, you will discover that your philosophy behind your marketing strategy and the strategy itself is quite unlike that of any other world market. This does not mean, however, that what works elsewhere will not work even better in Japan. But remember that the adage applies specifically to product and not promotion.

Japanese society is also one of the most competitive in the world and competitive, often ruthlessly, within itself. On the other hand, the striking cohesiveness and interdependence of society as a whole suggest a fundamental contradiction–one of the many that need to be considered and accepted as you discover Japan. Emerging from this interaction is a highly developed sense of values and an enormous emphasis on relationships. So much so, that your business might well succeed or fail on the basis of the quality of your relationship with your Japanese associates.

DIMPLEX

(OIL-FILLED RADIATORS)

Today's analysis of Japan reveals a rapidly growing market with many unsatisfied demand sectors rather than a solid monolith of consumer preference for local products.

Few cases provide better illustration of this situation than the story of Dimplex Limited, the Southampton-based manufacturer of electric heating appliances who claims 31 per cent of oil-filled electric radiators' sales in Japan. At a time when the popular thing to do seemed to be to complain about the inaccessibility of the Japanese consumer to European manufacturers, a series of events conspired to 'pull' Dimplex into this 'most difficult of markets'. And once opportunity had knocked, Dimplex set about developing the Japanese market into what is now its largest single export market.

Raw winters

From all the conventional wisdom on the subject, one would have thought that among the first items a major Japanese electric appliance manufacturer would include in its product range would be a good electric heater. Latent demand would seem almost as obvious, even to the casual observer, as the Tokyo Tower on a smog-free day. Japanese winters are known to be cold and raw and in the northern parts of Honshu and in Hokkaido they are certainly longer than a Tokyo winter. Japanese houses, with the exception of those built of more sturdy construction in more recent years, are notoriously draughty. Equally important, because of a preponderance of wooden buildings and as a result of Tokyo having been burnt to the ground twice, most Japanese have an obsessive fear of fire, which puts kerosene, oil, and gas heaters at a decided disadvantage with consumers. And, even before pollution control became a prime concern, in small Japanese dwellings the fumes of fuel-burning heaters were so offensive that any alternative form of heating was welcomed.

But despite these 'compelling demand' factors, Japanese manufacturers failed to respond. Perhaps the reason is that the development of the Japanese electrical appliance industry after the war was predominantly orientated toward the American electrical industry, which supplied much of the know-how for production of consumer durables–and domestic heaters are not an important item on the lists of major American appliance makers.

Whatever the reason, the gap was there, and it was filled by Dimplex. How this came about is a tale that owes its auspicious beginning to serendipity, in large part, and its happy ending–with Dimplex winning Britain's 1973 Queen's Award for Export Achievement–mainly to effective market development strategies.

The opportunity

Opportunity came to Dimplex, out of the blue, not long after the end of the last war, by way of a circular letter from Suita Trading Company Ltd of Kyoto. In 1948, with the Japanese electrical industry still struggling to rise from the ashes of destruction, Suita Trading was founded by a Kyoto family which had emerged from the war with its centuries-old (est. 1625) jewellery and fine-art goods business in shambles and hardly susceptible to revival in a Japan that had little need for such luxuries. At the outset, its main business was the export of decorations for Christmas and Easter, but in the 1950s, the company expanded to the import of quality electrical appliances for Japan's department store trade. Thus it was that, in 1953, Mitsukoshi Department Store, one of Japan's leading emporia, approached Suita Trading to supply quality electrical appliances for one of its first British Fairs after the war.

Suita's canvass of the British industry was generally successful, but among those manufacturers participating in the Fair none responded to the opportunity for market entry with greater enthusiasm than Dimplex. For its part, Suita Trading, recognizing the inherent suitability of Dimplex heaters for Japanese homes, set out to make this line the leader among the quality appliances it offered to department stores. And department stores, Dimplex soon discovered, provided the best distribution channel to that sector of the market where effective demand for quality imported products, such as they were at the time, was concentrated.

Stores as the outlet

It is certainly very true today that large department stores often are the most suitable outlets for imported consumer products in Japan, especially those branded higher-quality products selling in the upper ranges of the price spectrum. Department stores not only handle a much larger percentage of the overall retail trade in Japan than in most other countries, but they have a reputation for quality, reliability and service. Hence, since they tend to set fashions, once a product gains acceptance and is featured by department stores, it obtains an immediate promotional impetus that rapidly fixes the image of the product and establishes it in the galaxy of Japanese consumer demand. Through their advertising and point-of-sale promotional efforts department stores offer a most effective and selective channel for direct communication with consumers.

As a result, floor space and promotional efforts of these vast emporia are in high demand and command high premiums. Many manufacturers pay a kind of rent for the space allotted to counters featuring their products. Decorations are made at their expense, and the counters are manned by the manufacturer's personnel. Inventory, in these instances, is usually consigned by the manufacturer, entirely at his risk.

Close relationship

For these reasons Japanese department stores rarely import directly, and as a matter of policy they tend to limit their sources of supply. But this policy is further buttressed by the social or human aspects of Japanese business. Once an importer or wholesaler has established himself as a supplier to the department store trade, he has established much more than a functional business relationship. A close personal relationship, a relationship of trust and association, develops which is much more important than product speciality or other aspects of business.

The Suita family has had that kind of relationship with major department stores for at least two generations. The relationship, developed by the father of the three Suita boys who now run the business, was passed on as part of the family heritage. And where it once served to supply quality jewellery and Japanese art goods before the war it proved an equally useful channel for electrical appliances in the early postwar years and, more recently, for a wide range of the finest of European products–from neo-impressionist paintings to Meissen ware, St Louis crystal glassware, Wedgwood china and Italian interior decorations.

But this relationship has another dimension that is strictly business, and helps further to explain its durability. As Osao Suita, Suita Trading's Managing Director, puts it: 'An order from a department store is not an order in the strict sense of the word. Nor, in our case, is it essentially a consignment order. The department store buys, but it is a sale with a difference. At any time, for any reason whatsoever, it may return the merchandise to the supplier. This means that the supplier retains the primary risk, even though the merchandise has been technically sold'.

But whatever the character of the transaction, whether it is a direct sale or a consignment, Japanese department stores buy in exceptionally small lots. They maintain virtually no inventory of their own, and often order on a day-to-day basis. 'Our customers call us in the morning', Suita explains, 'and expect to have delivery in the afternoon. Orders may be for one or two pieces of a certain item, or for a few dozen products that move rather rapidly'.

Reciprocity

Reciprocity is also a part of this relationship, and one which neither department stores nor their suppliers talk much about. At the semi-annual gift-giving season, for instance, suppliers to the department stores may receive informal, but very firm, requests to buy gift tickets and various merchandise. All this takes place in a very matter-of-fact way and as a matter of course. And, in return, when a department store is looking for a new product or new source of supply, it will first call on its various established suppliers to determine if they can fill its requirements.

This explains how, in 1953, Dimplex came to Mitsukoshi through Suita Trading, and why Mitsukoshi remained the sole outlet for Dimplex heaters until 1958, when Suita added Takashimaya, Matsuya and Daimaru department store chains as franchised Dimplex distributors.

It was true, of course, that there were import quotas for electric appliances and imported heaters were too expensive for most Japanese consumers. But Suita purposely followed a shortage strategy, giving the impression that supply was limited, to keep demand higher than supply. This added to the prestige of the product, kept inventories to a minimum and assured sales at premium prices.

Consumer magazine

But, in 1968, two factors conspired to cause a ground-swell of demand that Suita was quick to exploit. Sharp annual wage increases and large semi-annual bonuses began to augment consumer purchasing power, bringing Dimplex heaters within the reach of a much larger buying public. And, quite fortuitously, it was just at this time that an article appeared in *Kurashi no Techo*, Japan's leading consumer magazine, highly recommending Dimplex heaters for their safety, cleanliness, mild temperature, automatic controls, trouble-free operations and overall durability.

Largely as a result of this article, which Suita is still using as one of its main pieces of promotional literature six years later, sales jumped over five times in 1969, and almost tripled in 1970 and 1971. Suita could have sold even more during these years, when Dimplex had the market pretty much to itself, but the factories in England just could not keep up with escalating demand.

During this period, Suita broadened its distribution base, including 185 department stores in its sales network. Careful consideration was also given to the idea of expanding sales through appliance shops, but Suita decided against it. The reasoning is instructive.

Department stores reach the main market for Dimplex heaters, Suita's management decided, even in an affluent Japan where potential demand has expanded far beyond the luxury market. And the costs of developing a marketing network, which would entail using intermediary wholesalers or extending credit to a large number of retailers, rendered the additional sales to be achieved through those channels of marginal interest, and possibly even self-defeating. By confining sales to the relatively few department store outlets, Suita is able to avoid product discounting, risks entailed in extensive financing and complications inherent in the use of intermediary sales channels. Suita sells directly to the department stores, with no credit risk, and a co-operative, direct-to-the-customer, nationwide service system which is partially supported by department stores in the country.

Common mistakes

European manufacturers, Osao Suita contends, often fail to appreciate the importance of department stores as a distribution channel for their products in the Japanese market. They are apt to think in terms of multi-channelled strategies that have little direct application in Japan. It is inconceivable, he recognizes, that Dimplex, for example, could hold 31 per cent of any European market by selling exclusively through department stores. But, as the experience of Dimplex suggests, this is not at all unusual in Japan.

Another mistake European manufacturers often make in

approaching the Japanese market, notes Suita, is failing to distinguish between different types of trading companies. They see the big *shosha*, or general trading houses, and assume that all others are simply smaller species of the same genus. But, Suita points out, this is not at all the case.

The general trading firms, with their large organization and resources, are business organizing and financial institutions, highly diversified in their activities–not unlike the conglomerates of recent American vintage. But the smaller trading companies, unlike the giants, live solely on their marketing acumen. And these smaller, more specialized trading companies often offer the right mix of marketing skills, relationships, organization and resources needed to develop the Japanese market for European manufactured products.

Advantages of Suita

More than 110 European manufacturers who use Suita Trading as their distributor in Japan have made this distinction and have achieved varying degrees of success in penetrating the Japanese market through this channel. Among the broad mix of services and facilities which Suita and other smaller trading companies offer are:

Specialized expertise in the marketing of high quality products and a keen knowledge of their particular market.

Longstanding relationships with department stores, which provide immediate access to the right retail outlets needed to reach the discriminating Japanese consumer.

Heavy investment in distinctive product promotions.

Maintenance of adequate inventories–assuring Japanese department stores of a back-up inventory of products necessary to meet the needs of the market and maximize turnover.

In the case of Dimplex, Suita also maintains the parts supply and after-sales service organization which is the *sine qua non* of customer confidence and market development for imported electric appliances. Fortunately, Dimplex radiators require very little service. But when service is needed it is provided anywhere in Japan on a 24-hour notice basis by a well organized team of twenty highly mobile servicing experts.

These are the qualities most foreign manufacturers are looking for when in search of a distributor in Japan. Since the most crucial decision in the development of the Japanese market via the distributorship route is, quite obviously, the choice of a distributor, Suita serves not only as an indicator of directions to be taken, but a model for the choice of the vehicle most suited for the voyage. Most certainly, if success be a standard, Dimplex's experience charts the course for specialized European manufacturers of quality products who are seeking successful entry to and development of the burgeoning Japanese market.

Export Director Mr R. H. Hudson sums up: 'Our close co-operation with STC has enabled us to understand each other's problems and to act in the best interests of all concerned. The overall marketing strategy is decided jointly, so that the Dimplex/STC operation is dovetailed to the needs of the market.'

OLIVETTI

(OFFICE MACHINERY)

Two decades ago, Olivetti in Japan was just another European manufacturer of typewriters, calculating and bookkeeping machines, represented by a Japanese wholesaler of office machinery. Today, the Olivetti Corporation of Japan supplies 25 per cent of the typewriter market and 38 per cent of the technical computer market.

Most of Japan's particular marketing characteristics relate to Japanese culture, language and patterns of social behaviour as applied to business life. If there is any barrier to doing business in Japan, it is the reluctance of foreign company managers to come to grips with these factors. 'The options open to a European manufacturer here are not much different to those found in other countries', says Olivetti's man in Japan, Luciano Cohen. 'People exaggerate the difficulties of doing business in Japan for many reasons. Governments do it for purposes of negotiation, to get better conditions. Many managers send negative reports to their home offices to justify their own inadequacies, or out of an unwillingness to make the necessary effort to keep pace in the fast-moving Japanese business marathon. The easiest thing to do for some is simply to close the books and blame someone else for the failure. I've seen several cases of this. I know of Italian companies who have tried the water, found the temperature too hot and gone home. Others who have taken the plunge, confident they can do business here, find the water very agreeable. Olivetti is among these.'

Olivetti is a 'multinational' manufacturer of typewriters and electronic office equipment, operating on the frontiers of advanced technology. As a multinational, Olivetti belongs to the league of enterprises known for their prowess and international marketing skills such as IBM, NCR, Honeywell, Burroughs and Univac, and the big names of Japan's own emergent data equipment industry, like Fujitsu, Hitachi, NEC and Toshiba.

All-out bid

Within the Olivetti Group there is a total work-force of 73,800 of which some 40,650 work in production and marketing subsidiaries outside Italy. While 11 of Olivetti's 21 factories are in Italy, sales abroad account for fully 76·2 per cent of the group's total turnover, which is rapidly approaching the billion dollar mark. What is more, Olivetti appears to be the only European-based firm in its field to have made a serious all-out bid for the Japanese market. It entered the market without the advantage of support from a government with powerful leverage at the negotiating table. But, despite this handicap, it established a wholly-owned sales subsidiary in Japan at a time when it was commonly believed to be impossible, and, even if possible, not a very sound investment.

Today, Olivetti operates a wholly-owned venture in Japan, and in the twelve years since it established the Olivetti Corporation of Japan it has cornered 25 per cent of the Japanese market for typewriters (37 per cent for portable typewriters) and 38 per cent of the market for technical computers. The company has also gained a solid foothold in Japan's rapidly expanding data processing field. In the first year after Olivetti established its Japan operations it sold more products than the cumulative total of all business previously done in Japan, and sales have been increasing at more than 25 per cent a year; in 1972, they were up 30 per cent over the previous year. As it looks now, by 1980, Olivetti could very easily be doing as much as $250 million, making Japan Olivetti's third largest market in the world–surpassed only by Italy and the United States.

Direct sales

Over the past 12 years, parallel to the indirect sales network that accounts for 15 per cent of total turnover, Olivetti Japan has developed a direct sales and service organization with 72 branch offices (which compares favourably with the 90 Olivetti branch offices in Italy), employing some 2000 highly trained Japanese who account for the other 85 per cent of sales. More than 80 per cent of this spirited team are graduates of some of Japan's finest universities and technical colleges. In addition, these and all other employees are given special courses of instruction at Olivetti's remarkable Kohoku Training Centre, where many take voluntary after-hours courses in electronics, accounting, foreign languages and other subjects designed to develop individual abilities. But, more important, what has moulded these 2000 talented young Japanese into an effective marketing organization is a management system that combines the virtues of Japanese management practices with Olivetti's meritocratic personnel evaluation, and a corporate philosophy that has made it a mark of distinction and a matter of considerable pride to be 'an Olivetti man'.

During the coming decade or so, the Japanese economy can be expected to continue to grow at an average of 8 per cent, at the very least, and may well expand at rates in excess of 10 per cent. Obviously, if the outlook for steady economic growth is good, the prospects for the business machine and data processing equipment market are even better. As Japan moves into an information age, Olivetti finds itself in the mainstream of the future where demand for some types of equipment, such as computer peripherals, is skyrocketing at an annual increment of 35 per cent.

Information industry

According to Luciano Cohen: 'In Japan, some people in key policy-making positions in government and industry have realized that data communications have a central importance for the future of civilization. Like the bullet train, when the Japanese began working on it 15 years ago, no one thought it would be necessary to travel so fast. With the same imagination and foresight, the Japanese are now concentrating energies on communications and the information industry, and I think they are going to get the same kind of results.

'Already, the Japanese data processing market is the largest in the world, in terms of GNP and *per capita*, and there is every reason to believe that its growth will be the fastest in the world for the foreseeable future. Quite clearly, Olivetti's position in this market is of critical importance, not just in terms of the sales and profit opportunities it represents; any data processing equipment maker who is not in this market will find himself out of business one day.'

Perhaps Mr Cohen is over-dramatizing the situation. But the fact remains that Olivetti have acted on the basis of this analysis and found that results prove the thesis correct. Already, with only 1 per cent of the Japanese data equipment market, Olivetti's sales in this field represented 31 per cent of total turnover in 1972; and if sales of technical computers used in factory applications are added, the share jumps to 43 per cent. This achievement in a relatively short period of time is dramatic, in any language.

Direct approach

How was this possible in a market as complex and restricted as Japan? Simply, because Olivetti decided to take the direct sales approach, establishing direct contact with the end user. 'Not only has this made it possible to provide customers with a broader spectrum of services, including software design', notes Mr Cohen, 'it has also provided Olivetti with a feeling for the pulse of the market and, more effective, complete and undistorted feedback so vital to the success of any sales development effort, especially in a market changing as fast as that of Japan'.

With the exception of typewriters and calculators, sold mostly through its dealer network, Olivetti delivers its products directly to the Japanese user. Accounting, computer, and data communications systems, which together accounted for 75 per cent of Olivetti's turnover in 1972, are specially designed by Olivetti sales engineers to meet each customer's needs and are installed by Olivetti's technical service engineers. In the past few years, some 300 software specialists have designed standard packages for ten major Japanese banking systems, nine agricultural co-operatives, several nationwide wholesale organizations, major trading companies, automobile and steel manufacturers, market research organizations and high schools. Software sales, themselves an important new profit centre, now account for 5 per cent of Olivetti Japan's revenue, a share that is on the increase due to mounting sales of data processing equipment and computer systems.

Despite various restrictions and communications problems, Olivetti has found the cost–benefit ratio of investment in the direct sales approach to the Japanese consumer as good as, if not better than, in most markets.

The intangibles

It is true that part of the success of the scheme must be attributed to the fact that Olivetti focused its energies on products of advanced technology. But among the critical ingredients of success in Japan, Cohen rates the intangibles highest. Business philosophy counts much more than strategy, Cohen contends, and he speaks with the authority of experience. Olivetti's management philosophy has provided the human and social foundations on which its Japanese organization has been built, while its corporate philosophy relating to extra-mural activities has fashioned the character of the company as a member of the Japanese community.

At the outset, applying time-honoured Roman wisdom, Olivetti made it a rule to do things the way the Japanese do them. Olivetti Japan is a Japanese company. Of the 2000-odd employees, only three are Italian. Hence, personnel management and the decision-making processes necessarily have to be those which are most suitable to Japanese. The life-long employment system has been fully adopted. Graduates are employed directly from leading universities and colleges, instead of attempting to attract experienced people from other firms. Education and training have been given central importance in building a staff of 'Olivetti personnel'. Remuneration follows Japanese patterns, on the whole, with the system of semi-annual bonuses as an important built-in feature.

Doing things the Japanese way, however, does not inhibit innovation. On the contrary, Olivetti has found that its new 'merit system' of personnel evaluation has been well received by its employees, many of whom find in it much better opportunities for advancement than the rigid seniority system current in most large Japanese companies. Certainly, the number of applicants among university and college graduates, which in Japan is taken as a good barometer of corporate status and prestige, indicates that this is so.

Recruiting

Recruiting is always the most difficult problem for a foreign firm building a Japanese operation. Since fringe benefits such as housing, clubs, special education in traditional Japanese arts and company outings are important considerations in a graduate's choice of a company (the choice of the company for which you will work all your life is tantamount to choice of a career in Japan), foreign firms usually cannot afford to compete with established Japanese companies on this basis for top talent. In their place, other inducements must be found and be made known.

As part of its recruiting programme, Olivetti, like many other companies, produce assorted publications for distribution to students in their last year of university and high school; the company also subscribes to a special careers information service for students. As a result, Olivetti now receive some 2000 applicants for 200 positions that become vacant annually.

Olivetti's appeal to Japanese youth is apparently not solely attributable to what are normally considered career-related factors. The company is convinced that its cultural commitment and social policy are written large in the minds of those who choose Olivetti as a place of lifetime employment.

Olivetti products have, traditionally, been carefully designed for dual effect: to make certain that they are functional as well as beautiful to look at. The simple, clean lines, the choice of colour–these elements have made a strong impression on the Japanese. Likewise, the choice of Japan's dean of architects, Kenzo Tange, to design Olivetti's training centre and warehouses, was in itself an unusual act that has attracted much attention. Few companies give this much importance to a training facility or buildings which house merchandise and service facilities.

Cultural activity

This commitment to culture does not stop with product design, showrooms, buildings and advertising. Olivetti Japan publishes a periodical, called *Spazio*, which includes articles and artistic reproductions from leading Japanese and Italian writers, critics and scientists. The Olivetti Theatre broadcasts five times a week on Japanese commercial radio, featuring the works of Japan's leading authors. A weekly TV programme takes Japanese viewers into the offices and drawing rooms of eminent people throughout the world in a series of half-hour interviews. Since its establishment in 1961, the Olivetti Corporation of Japan has sponsored a continuing flow of calligraphy exhibitions, art film showings, design exhibitions, modern art exhibitions, concerts and music competitions. And, giving still another dimension to its cultural activity, Olivetti Scholarships have been awarded for study in Italy, and an Olivetti Fund was created to support Sophia University in Tokyo.

Public recognition, in the form of awards for advertising by the *Nihon Keizai Shimbun* (Japan's leading financial and business daily) and the Ministry of International Trade and Industry (MITI) have testified to the success of Olivetti's graphics and communications techniques.

Defying the contentions of experts who say it is impossible to 'pull' a product through the Japanese distribution system with effective advertising, and after 12 years of effective TV, radio, newspaper, and periodical advertising, Olivetti has become a household name in Japan. What this means in terms of market prowess is best reflected in portable typewriter sales. Olivetti's share of the total Japanese market is a very considerable 37 per cent, and is expected to reach 45 per cent by 1975.

On the other hand, Olivetti's social policy has no such direct sales effect. For the past several years, for example, Olivetti has concentrated much of its extra-mural activities and resources on an extensive programme of assistance for handicapped children, which includes special annual summer schools, and a new form of typewriter for the handicapped which has enabled many to communicate in the written word for the first time in their lives.

Communications is, of course, what Olivetti is all about, and in a very real sense the Olivetti management has sought to respond to the demand of modern Japan for business with a human face, through a creative philosophy that seeks the harmonious unity of industry, culture and society. As one of Olivetti's top Japanese executives put it: 'To reach the Japanese people today, the way is not to put primary emphasis on the quality of your products, or the high technical achievements of your laboratories. People expect this from business, and have found that all hardware is produced pretty much to the same high quality standards. The most important thing today is to differentiate the company, rather than the product. These features of our corporate philosophy are not mere public relations afterthoughts, but intrinsic to our character and to our corporate objectives'.

PEZ

(CONFECTIONERY)

Eduard Haas IV would have smiled incredulously (in 1971) if someone had told him that Japan would be his leading foreign market for Pez confectionery in 1973. Nor would the president of Ed. Haas Nahrmittelfabrik, whose Pez-Haas subsidiary in Linz is Austria's leading confectionery manufacturer, have believed that, in 1972, his orange and lemon lozenges would account for virtually all of the 21 per cent increase in Austria's exports to Japan in 1972.

Today, Eduard Haas, the fourth in line of a pioneering family of Austrian food industrialists, wears a smile of an entirely different sort. In the past two years, Pez lozenges have become the largest selling single brand of this kind of confectionery product in Japan. This outstrips the rather remarkable performance recorded by Haas's illustrious forefathers who built a company from a small family baking-powder factory into one of Austria's emergent multinational enterprises.

Trade barriers

Prior to liberalization of confectionery imports, in October 1971, Japan was a very small pin on the map of Pez International's marketing strategist, Horst F. Schafelner. Quotas, limited to

$10,000 annually, were sold in a matter of a few weeks by a small trading company that had been serving as the Pez distributor in Japan. But when the trade barriers came down, Eduard Haas IV and Horst Schafelner were in Tokyo to see what could be done to expand their position in the market.

They were, of course, fully conversant with the common wisdom on the complexities and difficulties of the Japanese market, and aware that among foreign marketing specialists food distribution in Japan has a reputation for being the most anachronistic, cumbersome, and labyrinthine of business structures–rather like a medieval system of fortification that had somehow remained impervious to most modern marketing strategies. But Haas and Schafelner, both of whom have been around the world markets enough to know never to underestimate the problems which any market presents, had little time for generalities of this sort.

When it became clear that imports of confectionery products were to be liberalized, Haas and Schafelner set about separating myth from reality to find the proper ingredients for a positive marketing strategy. They studied distribution systems to understand fully how Japanese confectioners managed to do so well with such 'out-dated' distribution facilities. They subjected every manufacturer and major wholesaler in the business to intensive analysis. Sales promotion and advertising techniques and services were surveyed; customer tastes and buying habits carefully reviewed.

Choice of partner

In April 1972, Haas paid his first call on Tahei Morinaga, the dean of Japan's confectionery industrialists. A leading manufacturer of confectionery products, with eight major factories in Japan and a nationwide marketing organization involving 72 branch offices, Morinaga seemed the ideal choice as licensee for Pez confectionery production. Morinaga was already producing several European and American confectionery lines for the Japanese market, and had the kind of international experience that makes for effective co-operation with foreign partners.

But Haas had eliminated both licensing and a joint venture from his range of options. Instead, his proposal was that the Morinaga company depart from its established pattern of operation and take on its first imported confectionery speciality.

By September 1971, Morinaga decided that Haas was right: importing seemed to make good business sense. Pez was a product not available in Japan, and its original packaging ideas and imaginative sales promotions approach would appeal to Japanese youth. What is more, an imported product of this kind would have decidedly more appeal than a locally manufactured product of the same kind, and could be sold at the higher end of the price spectrum.

Significantly, Morinaga's decision came just one month before the liberalization of confectionery imports and, in December 1971, Morinaga placed the first order of 35,000 cartons of Pez lozenges–intended as a market teaser.

Initial promotion

Although no distributor contract was yet concluded between the two companies, both Morinaga and Haas threw the full force of their resources into the initial marketing effort. A huge reception at Tokyo's Prince Hotel was the occasion for introducing Pez to more than 200 leading confectionery wholesalers in Japan. Pez films were shown. At the end of the proceedings, there was no doubt in anyone's mind that Pez lozenges are produced by the country that gave us the Strauss family, Karajan, and the Tyrolean hat.

Pez International's advertising subsidiary, Parkring Werbegesellschaft, and Dentsu of Japan, who has the Morinaga account, designed special advertising and point of sale materials for the Japanese market. Pez shipped in liberal quantities of promotional materials–Tyrolean hats, Austrian flags, Cantonal crests, ballpoint pens, placards and window stickers from Vienna, and Morinaga allocated a healthy share of their TV advertising time to launch Pez on the Tokyo, Nagoya and Osaka markets. Special promotional events were organized at 300 department stores and supermarkets, together with children's competitions which introduced the galaxy of international patented Pez characters to the younger generation.

By September 1972, it was clear to both Morinaga and Pez that they had a winning formula, and on 27 October Morinaga's Senior Managing Director, Mr T. Matsuzaki, signed the distributorship agreement. Following the formal appointment of

Morinaga in spring 1973, both firms stepped up their promotional effort, with more intensive TV advertising, special film productions for children, more Pez girls passing out Pez samples at department stores and supermarkets. In short, Morinaga-Pez promotions successfully applied the same marketing techniques and gimmicks that served so successfully to introduce Pez in foreign markets since the 1920s. Of course, there were refinements and adaptations for the Japanese market. But essentially Pez found that what works elsewhere works even better in Japan.

Collaboration

Horst Schafelner sums up: 'We never try to push water uphill. We have a good product, and one that we believe will sell well in any market. The problem is to develop the best possible distribution network at the lowest possible cost. In Morinaga we have the most powerful partner of any in our worldwide organization. They know the market, and have the personal relationships and resources necessary to develop it'.

Collaboration and complementary attributes of the two parties were clearly a vital ingredient in the spectacular success of Pez confectionery in Japan. These two well-established family confectionery firms from opposite ends of the earth seemed to hit it off well from the outset. Both know their business. Each knew they had much to learn from the other. And each added vital power to the marketing mix: their recognition of the prestige of an imported product; the focus on the younger consumer, and the concentration of their marketing energies on the three big urban conglomerations which embrace fully 50 per cent of the Japanese market; and the right mix of advertising and promotional techniques and resources.

This is synergy at its best–a case where one plus one makes millions.

PHILIPS

(HOUSEHOLD PRODUCTS)

The announcement in June 1973, by the Nihon Philips Corporation, the multinational giant, that it had decided to make a serious bid for a share in the booming Japanese consumer electrical market, was clearly not such good news for certain elements of the Japanese business world. For the past 20 years the Japanese electrical manufacturers have had things pretty much their own way in their home market. In the 1960s, when refrigerators and washing machines ranked with cars as the three main consumer durables in a Japanese household budget, Japanese manufacturers offered products designed to fit both modest budgets and small households. Then, when colour television receivers and audio equipment took their place among the priority items on the Japanese consumer's shopping list, foreign competitors were, for the most part, excluded by dint of higher prices and a decided lag in product design, if not in applied technology. Import restrictions only added a margin of safety to what was already a solid market position of the Japanese industry.

Suddenly, all this has changed. Not only have import liberalizations and two upward revaluations of the yen radically affected the competitive power of Japanese electrical and electronic products at home and abroad, but Japanese manufacturing costs have risen sharply over the past three years. The result: instead of self-sufficiency in electrical and electronic products, Japan is now seeking international collaboration, which means the internationalization of supply to the Japanese domestic market.

Quality demand

At the same time, Japanese demand for quality consumer durables has been increasing at a rate that even the Japanese industry has been unable to match, leaving large gaps in product lines and sales channels without a supply of products because of lagging output. With the rapid growth of *per capita* income, demand is shifting to more semi-luxury and luxury items. Although households are not becoming that much more spacious, larger-sized appliances and fixtures have become fashionable. Add to this a notable upsurge of preference for imported internationally-branded products of almost every conceivable variety, and what European and American manufacturers now are finding is a market of a size, accessibility and profitability that is downright irresistible.

Philips, of course, is not new to the Japanese market. For years it has had a close association with the Matsushita Electric group, and is still a major shareholder in, as well as source of technology for, several Matsushita companies. In 1953, Philips established Nihon Denshi Kaihatsu KK for import and sales promotion of various kinds of industrial and professional products in the Japanese market, with Matsushita holding 50 per cent interest in the company. Philips has still another joint venture with Matsushita and Japan Victor, called Nippon Phonogram, which markets recordings in Japan. Over these, as a kind of administrative holding company, is Philips Industrial Development and Consultant Co., which also conducts market research and organizes new activities. But so far as home electrical and electronic appliances are concerned, Japan was, until 1973, the only country in the free world where Philips products were not sold.

A year's study

By 1970, however, the handwriting was there for all who would read. Still, Philips did not rush in to get a piece of the action. Japan was too important and Philips' management knew Japan well enough to appreciate that involvement in the market had to be an all or nothing engagement of resources. After more than a year of careful study, Philips Products Sales Corporation of Japan (the successor of Nihon Denshi Kaihatsu) was transformed, in 1972, to the Nihon Philips Corporation, with Philips as the main shareholder, and reorganized to develop the market for home appliances, as well as for an increasing number of industrial and professional products. Even after the formation of Nihon Philips, more than a year was spent in recruiting, training and market study to determine product strategy, pricing policies and the most effective approach to distribution. In all, Philips spent two-and-a-half years in market analysis and building their consumer sales organization before they sold a single item.

Since Philips realized that a Japanese sales organization must, in the main, be manned and managed by Japanese for maximum efficiency, it set out to recruit top quality product managers with experience in the electronics field. Under the direction of Chieo Kitagawa, who joined Philips in 1970 as

National Sales Manager (of what has now become the Consumer Products Division of Nihon Philips), and Marketing Manager, Einar Kloster, a tight headquarters staff of specially trained executives was developed. With his wide contacts in the industry, Kitagawa, who had been in the electronics industry for 15 years before joining Philips, proved his ability to select and get good men.

Each product group was staffed with a technical man and a commercial man at the head. The various product groups, which from the outset have taken a long-term approach to the market, conduct continuing market research, competition surveys and product design work. They are, of course, ultimately concerned with sales promotions and support for Nihon Philips' nationwide distributor network.

Japanese management

To be a Japanese organization, clearly it is not enough that a company simply be staffed by Japanese personnel. Most important, the personnel must feel that they are not working for a foreign organization and this means that the management system and corporate philosophy must be familiar to them. Fortunately, many of the main features of Japanese management have their counterpart in Philips' policy. Life-long employment, for example, is the rule at Philips factories everywhere: once a Philips man, always a Philips man.

Still, like almost all newly established foreign firms, Philips has found it very difficult to find good people; recruiting through advertising works occasionally. But as a general rule, good people do not leave the companies that they have joined 'for life'. And young high school or university graduates tend to select companies that are well known, large and growing rapidly. The company, with more than 200 factories in 50 countries and more than 250 affiliates or subsidiaries throughout the world, is well known abroad, although, curiously enough, it is hardly known by Japanese consumers, and almost not at all by Japanese students. Philips is just beginning in Japan, and suffers from the handicap of not having a track record for university and high school graduates to use as a standard by which to measure their life-long career prospects within the company. But Philips is moving towards a systematic policy of recruiting, begun in 1973, with its first intake of graduates from the universities.

Training

While not a decisive factor, the difficulties posed and time involved in staffing, training and developing a large nationwide sales organization were an important consideration for Philips in evaluating the question 'How can we get a solid share of the booming Japanese market?' Or, more precisely: 'How should we organize our Japan sales operations to achieve this objective?' A direct approach to the Japanese retailer, bypassing complex multi-tiered wholesale structures, was not feasible for several reasons. One was that most retailers would require a consignment of inventories or other credit facilities that would entail heavy financing costs and substantial risks, and Philips did not know local dealers throughout the country well enough to select the best credit risks. Some intermediary solution, which would provide Philips with maximum control over marketing activities and at the same time enlist the services of competent Japanese distributors, was necessary.

Maze of intermediaries

Most foreign manufacturers of consumer electric and electronic products selling in Japan have been struggling uphill through a maze of intermediaries, with far from satisfactory results. The usual formula is for the foreign exporter to sell to a Japanese trading company, who, in turn, sells to a primary wholesaler. Contrary to general impressions, general Japanese trading companies are not really the most effective marketing organizations. Instead, they may organize and finance marketing companies to sell a product, or line of products. But they normally rely on established wholesalers, who, in turn, may sell to secondary wholesalers or retail outlets. Most primary wholesalers tend to supply only major retail organizations, such as department and chain stores, leaving secondary wholesalers in each region or large locality to service small appliance shops.

Philips found this route unsuitable for attaining its long-range objectives in the Japanese market. Not only would any uniform and consistent marketing policy be rendered impossible, but these traditional channels are both costly and cumbersome. What is more, Philips would be faced with the competitive power of major Japanese manufacturers who have developed their own more direct marketing channels. Radical solutions were clearly called for. In the process of finding them Philips will have blazed a trail others are certain to find useful.

Economies were achieved by streamlining distribution in two ways. Nihon Philips, in addition to its role as marketing policy maker and marketing activities co-ordinator, now imports directly from various Philips factories in Europe and Singapore, eliminating the intermediary trading company. Then, in a most important move to distribute these products throughout Japan, Philips has appointed five exclusive regional distributors and eight regional wholesalers.

The regional distributors are new companies, formed specifically for the purpose of distributing Philips products directly to local department stores and retail shops in Tohoku, Niigata, Kanto, Chubu and Kansai.

Nihon Philips has no capital participation in these companies, but it provides them with consulting and co-ordinating services, as well as full sales support activities. The eight local wholesalers distribute Philips consumer products in those areas not covered by the five regional wholesalers–Chugoku, Shikoku and Kyushu.

Product strategy

Perhaps the most indicative and significant feature of the Philips sales organization is that Japanese businessmen are sufficiently convinced of the profitability in selling Philips products that they are investing substantial amounts of money to obtain an exclusive franchise for restricted areas. In short, Philips' product strategy has met the first important test: distributors are betting that the market potential for the products which Philips intends to offer is a lucrative one, and that the variety of products is large enough to devote their resources exclusively to Philips. Without this kind of confidence from its distributors, any possibility of success would be quite remote.

Philips is not rushing in with its full line of products, however. The strategy is to select a few products at the top of their line, and expand step-by-step once they have a toehold in the market.

Their launch products include shavers, coffee-makers, mixers, blenders, juicers, toasters, knife-sharpeners, irons, electric clocks, radiators and a range of beauty-care products–mostly in the small domestic appliance range.

Higher quality products have been selected, wherever possible with features not offered by Japanese manufacturers. Design is also an important element in this selection process–the company making certain that the aesthetic quality of each product placed on the market appeals to Japanese taste.

Trade launch

With a good distribution network and the right product strategy, Philips believe that half the battle is won. In the final analysis, however, Philips also recognize that it is the judgements made as business develops that will be decisive. A pull-push sales promotion effort has been launched to introduce Philips products to the trade and to consumers, which includes back-up advertising to generate the kind of demand that will pull products through the distribution network. The problem is to design advertising that especially appeals to rapidly changing Japanese tastes and consumption patterns.

The initial dealer meetings in Tokyo, in June 1973, clearly showed that Philips had already generated considerable steam behind its push. Of the 600 representatives of department stores and retailers invited from around the country, an impressive 92 per cent attended the full-day affair. This kind of turnout indicates that either the dealers smell gold or Nihon Philips has done a very successful selling job.

While they are leading with top quality products at present, purposefully avoiding head-on competition with local products, Philips will eventually move down into the medium-priced field.

At least for the foreseeable future, the company plans to stress the European character of its products–taking full advantage of the current preference for imported goods.

Top management in Holland is fully aware that Japan is not the place for half measures. Either you do it, or you don't. And Philips will succeed to the degree that they throw their full energies behind the bid for the Japanese consumer yen. By 1976, in fact, they expect annual sales in Japan of around $30 million.

ROUSSEL-UCLAF

(PHARMACEUTICALS)

For any pharmaceutical company executive, the Japanese market is bound to have an irresistible attraction, especially for the chief executive of an established international company not yet in the market. It was inevitable, then, that Jean-Claude Roussel, President and Managing Director of Roussel-Uclaf, should decide after his first visit to Tokyo in 1958–a brief two-day stop-over *en route* from Sydney to Paris–that Japan represented a tremendous untapped opportunity for his company's expansion. Here was a booming new frontier with demand for ethical pharmaceutical products far beyond the supply capacity of Japanese industry.

In retrospect, statistics provide dramatic evidence to support his assessment. The industry has continued to grow explosively during the past 15 years. So swift has been its annual production increase that, by 1970, it had become the world's second largest producer of ethical drugs, surpassed only by the United States. And in terms of the number of pharmacists per 100,000 population, by 1970 Japan was the unqualified world leader with more than twice as many as France, the United Kingdom or Sweden, and about 20 per cent more than the United States where the corner drug store is a representative national institution.

Amazing development

But this is only part of the picture. Even more significantly, during the ten years 1960–70, gross national medical expenditure rose almost sixfold and the percentage claimed for drugs increased sharply from around 25 per cent in 1961 to over 40 per cent in 1970. Accounting for this amazing development of pharmaceutical consumption is a combination of two parallel factors: the phenomenal growth in consumers' buying power resulting from rapid overall national economic growth, and continued expansion of Japan's insurance-based medical services. As a result, with consumption far outstripping production, imports skyrocketed from around yen 10 billion in 1962, to over 90 billion a decade later, a ninefold increase in ten years.

It is true that the liberalization of imports made this development of trade in pharmaceuticals possible. But it was the sheer limitations of the Japanese pharmaceutical industry that made it inevitable. With production highly fragmented between 2200 firms, about 60 per cent of the industry's output is accounted for by companies with a work-force of ten or less. A mere 1 per cent of the total, that is only 20-odd companies, are major enterprises staffed by 500 or more personnel, and even these are dependent upon wholesalers for the distribution of their products. Because of production fragmentation, therefore, the industry tends to be dominated by its commercial distribution channels. For example the largest pharmaceutical wholesaler has more than 2350 employees and an annual turnover equal to the gross revenue of many major manufacturers.

Added stimulus

As a result of limitations imposed by size and the intermediate gap between producer and consumer, production tends to be unresponsive to changes in market demand. Outlays for R & D are limited to an average 4 per cent of turnover for the industry as a whole. And resources available for expansion of production are equally constricted.

Under these circumstances, it is understandable why Jean-Claude Roussel took the initiative to establish Nippon-Roussel hardly a year after his initial visit. His findings were sustained by the then French Ambassador in Tokyo, whose complaint that French businessmen were missing a great opportunity in Japan's rapidly expanding market provided Roussel with that added stimulus needed to take the plunge.

From all appearances his beginning could hardly have been better. As a matter of principle he had rejected licensing as a possible route into the market. Although licensing had the advantage of being the easy, no-risk way in, not only was it likely to assure only a temporary participation in the market, ending just as soon as a Japanese licensee saw no further benefits in its continuing; it would also not be nearly as profitable as an active role in one of the world's largest and fastest growing markets, where profit rates of leading pharmaceutical firms are frequently over 50 per cent and have been as high as 184 per cent. What was called for, quite clearly, was a sizeable investment and, given the compelling logic of having a good Japanese partner as well as the Japanese regulations governing foreign investments then in force, that meant a joint venture.

This decision came quite naturally to Roussel. But the company had other joint ventures throughout the world that were operating most satisfactorily. And, fortuitously, the critical problem for any foreign investor in Japan–the choice of the right Japanese partner–presented no great difficulties.

Powerful partners

In Chugai Pharmaceutical Company, a leading company with plans to expand its sales of products to hospitals and physicians, Roussel had found an interested and powerful Japanese partner. And, after some debate as to who was to have the majority equity in the new venture, Chugai accepted a 20 per cent minority position, with Air Liquide taking another 20 per cent through its Japanese affiliate–Teikoku Senso KK, leaving Roussel-Uclaf with a comfortable 60 per cent holding.

On paper, at least, Roussel had plenty of reason to be pleased with this arrangement. He had succeeded in hammering out an agreement which assured his company what seemed to be unequivocal control over the new subsidiary. Air Liquide, with 60 years' experience in the Japanese chemical market, brought to the venture a storehouse of knowledge and excellent contacts in the Japanese business community. And Chugai provided a ready-made distribution system for products of the new manufacturing facility that was to be developed, as well as managerial experience in pharmaceutical production.

An excellent piece of business strategy, it seemed. And yet, four years later, Jean-Claude Roussel was on his way back to Japan to do away with a company that had really never got off the ground. Sales had risen to yen 100 million in the first year of operations, and stayed there for the next three. Chugai, whose responsibility for managing production as well as distribution of the products of Nippon-Roussel meant that they had ultimate control over the success or failure of the venture, failed to produce results. The original agreement, Chugai's President Kimio Ueno complained, was simply not workable.

New agreement

So, the agreement was scrapped and another negotiated. But the new arrangement was no more satisfactory than the old. Nor, for that matter, were the results of the six rounds of negotiations that took place during the intervening three years. Apparently, the match was a non-starter from the outset. At least that is how it looked to the very dejected Roussel-Uclaf chief executive when he deplaned at Tokyo's Haneda airport on a dreary October day in 1963.

There seemed to be no alternative but to cut losses by getting out of the market he still considered to represent a great opportunity for his company. The busy chief executive of an international firm the size of Roussel-Uclaf would not be expected to be aware of the one element in the picture that was to change his mind about future outlook and strategy of the Japanese subsidiary. It had never occurred to him, of course, that he would find the answer to his problems in a divinity-student-turned-language-professor whom the company had engaged as a translator to put the steady flow of renegotiated agreements into good Japanese business prose.

Japan, argued André Bouilleux, is, after all, one of the new economic centres of the world. And one of the largest. What is more, it is an excellent platform from which to launch Roussel's operations in other parts of Asia, including China. A company the size of Roussel could not ignore Japan and stay in the international league for long. None of this was news to Roussel, but, though it did not solve his problems, he found in Bouilleux's enthusiasm the first sign of encouragement in what hitherto had been a consistent pattern of gloom.

The situation was critical, Bouilleux admitted. But it was not desperate. And there was nothing basically wrong with Roussel's strategy. The problem was basically one of communications. There was misunderstanding on both sides about the nature and objectives of the venture and there was no clear, common understanding about the appropriate means for achieving those objectives.

It is often the case that a Japanese partner in a joint venture may view the partnership, not as a first step in combining capabilities and experience, but rather as a short-term means of allowing him access to some specific technology that he needs.

Most of the manufacturing joint ventures formed in the 1950s were intended to be little more than a means of capitalizing technical know-how, by either party. But broader ventures that involve the foreign partner in engineering activities or technical development, marketing, financial and personnel activities as well as manufacturing, require a genuine co-operative effort working towards common goals. And more often than not, new joint ventures in Japan are not properly staffed to work out marketing programmes, formulate pricing policies, finance growth or perform the myriad other management tasks needed to achieve profits and growth.

The right man

What was needed to work out these programmes and policies were not just technical people who knew how things were done in France or some other country, but someone who knew the Japanese situation well enough to adapt and interpret Roussel's thinking and experience in terms that were meaningful and acceptable to the Japanese partners. This required a knowledge not only of the Japanese industry and market, but, more important, of how things were done in Japan. It meant, above all, a thorough knowledge of Chugai's operations and its various relationships–and especially its web of informal relations–in the pharmaceutical field and in the Japanese business community in general. Finally, and formally, it needed someone who understood the Japanese way of doing things, Japanese thought processes, and Japanese social patterns. In a word, what was needed was someone who understood Japan and who could command the confidence and respect of the Japanese partners.

Only then could a new division of labour be achieved that would at once combine Roussel-Uclaf's experience in ethical drug sales promotion and marketing strategy with Chugai's knowledge of the market itself. Since Japanese pharmaceutical manufacturers commonly play only a limited part in marketing operations, with sales left exclusively to trading companies and wholesalers who are not capable of providing the kind of sales organization and promotional services modern drug marketing demands, it would be necessary for Nippon-Roussel to play a more direct role in marketing operations–adapting Roussel-Uclaf strategies and techniques to the Japanese market situation.

In short, the real question at issue was not how much equity Roussel-Uclaf owned in the company, but rather what kind of influence it exercised in the policy area and how effectively it could work with its Japanese partners to achieve common accord and full co-operation towards realistic and well-understood objectives, utilizing each partner's resources and experience to the fullest.

Roussel got the message. Convinced that the problem was primarily one of communications failure to develop closer relationships with their Japanese partners, he returned to Paris with the unprecedented proposal to his Board of Directors that André Bouilleux, the company's translator and a wholly unknown quantity in the Paris boardroom, should be made the President of Nippon-Roussel. Bouilleux spoke Japanese, knew Japan, and had a plan for a new division of labour between the partners that he believed would work. Predictably, the Board, for the first time ever, refused to endorse a specific proposal of its President. Never had such a position of trust been placed in anyone who had not risen in the ranks of the company, and who did not have the proper technical background. And they just could not see how a translator with no business experience, much less a track record of successful international management, could save a situation much more experienced men found beyond their capabilities.

Roussel's response was immediate and unequivocal. Breaking with precedent a second time that day, he overruled his Board and took full personal responsibility for the Japan operations.

Own distribution

Bouilleux was appointed to the top managerial post of Nippon-Roussel, and the process of reorganization began. While Chugai remained responsible for manufacturing, Nippon-Roussel assumed wider responsibilities for sales and promotion. From a work-force of 20 in 1963, the staff was expanded to 260, mostly detail men and other promotional personnel who were carefully trained to make Roussel products known to hospitals and doctors in every city, town and village of Japan. For this purpose the company was decentralized, operating from seven new offices throughout the country. Rather than rely on Chugai wholesalers as in the past, Nippon-Roussel set up its own distribution network using more than 100 local and regional wholesalers to blanket the country systematically with an intensive sales network. A new factory was built to keep up with rising sales.

In the meantime, a second company has been formed, Nippon-Uclaf, a wholly-owned sales subsidiary, selling bulk chemicals to the vast majority of Japanese pharmaceutical houses that are dependent upon outside sources of supply for basic materials, which they mix or simply package for resale.

While Roussel-Uclaf still trails the large American, German and Swiss pharmaceutical firms in the Japanese market, both Nippon-Roussel and Nippon-Uclaf are expanding at a rate in excess of 15 per cent a year and showing a profit. Both companies have established themselves firmly in the market, and have now passed the take-off stage.

Future prospects for expansion are good. The basic demand for medical care in Japan should continue to increase steadily for years to come, as demand is strengthened by increasing disposable income, and the proportion of the population in the age group over 55 years* becomes larger. Nippon-Roussel expects to respond to rising demand and the changing pattern of disease in Japan. Preventive medicine will be among the fields of development in coming years. And there is a growing market for medical equipment which Bouilleux considers to offer interesting opportunities for the company.

Costly process

The introduction of new pharmaceutical products is a particularly difficult and costly process in Japan. Standards imposed by the Japanese health authorities tend to be much higher than in France and most other European countries. And since an increasing amount of medical care is being provided under various types of health insurance programmes, the degree of socialization and control of drug usage is proportionately

*The normal age of retirement and the end of company medical care.

higher. In response to this new challenge, Nippon-Roussel has appointed a special medical adviser as assistant to the President, raising the number of foreigners to two.

Nippon-Roussel's past success, in Bouilleux's view, is due largely to the company's ability to attract top-level personnel and mould them into an effective operating team. In a country where one of the best indexes of a company's future is the career opportunities it offers, as seen by well-informed university graduates, the appeal which Nippon-Roussel has generated for graduates from the best universities in Japan augurs well for its future. After a very difficult beginning, Nippon-Roussel has succeeded in combining the French partner's technology and philosophy of sales promotion management with the Japanese partner's knowledge of local market conditions and production management, into an effective business organization propelled by a dedicated Japanese staff of sales and administrative personnel.

TRIUMPH

(WOMEN'S CLOTHING)

Despite liberalization of trade and investments, Japan's complex distribution channels and the distinctive characteristics of the Japanese female form have combined to discourage most European and American clothing manufacturers from direct entry into the Japanese market. As a result, some western garment makers have chosen the licensing route, making their trademark and designs available to Japanese manufacturers against a royalty on gross sales turnover.

Direct investment

Triumph, Germany's leading foundation garment, lingerie and swimwear manufacturer, was the first European firm in its field to see the opportunities of direct investment in production and marketing facilities in Japan. Today, the company has locally-based manufacturing units and produces a wide variety of European-designed clothing especially tailored for Japanese women. And, contrary to the belief that existing distribution channels in Japan are a major impediment to new entrants in the market, Triumph began selling directly to department stores from the outset, and has grown to second rank in the Japanese industry–all in less than 10 years and without reliance on intermediary wholesale distributors.

To be sure, Triumph's task was not an easy one. As one of the first foreign garment makers to enter a field that had for so long been synonymous with Japanese industrial enterprise, and one which was particularly sensitive politically, Triumph took every precaution to do things correctly. And, fortunately, they had the advantage of good Japanese partners to advise and assist them in making the right moves at the right time.

Triumph approached Carolina, a well-established, traditional textile company, with a proposal to form a joint venture for garment manufacture. Carolina was manufacturing hosiery and other ladies dress materials, but saw in an increasingly affluent Japan a growing demand for high quality internationally acclaimed merchandise. Guenther Spiesshofer, whose ancestors founded Triumph and built it into one of Germany's most successful businesses, found Carolina's future promising and their common experience the essential ingredients for a successful partnership. Nippon Rayon was brought in as a third partner and, on 10 October 1964, the International Foundation and Garment (IFG) Co. Ltd was formed with a majority Japanese holding. At that time, Toshio Takemura of Carolina was President and Guenther Spiesshofer was Vice-President.

An auspicious day

The day could hardly have been more auspicious. It had been carefully chosen by a selected council of *Shinto* priests as the most appropriate day for the opening of the Tokyo Olympics. The stars and other elements, the Japanese partners reasoned, were certain to be favourable for launching the new venture. And the timing proved to be perfect. The Japanese economy, then emerging from its most serious recession since the end of the Korean War, was moving into a period of sustained high rate of growth–a period in which wages and salaries were to climb at a rate of 15–20 per cent a year.

Need for quality

Triumph's objective, from the beginning, was to appeal to the ever-increasing market wanting high quality garments with international names. When Triumph entered the market in 1964 they chose the department stores as a single, direct route to this upper segment of the market. Following Japanese custom, they employed trained Japanese girls as 'foundation consultants' to staff their counters, providing a personalized introduction of their products to Japanese ladies eager to have the latest in international fashions. All Triumph counters in department stores are staffed with Triumph's own sales personnel, as are the counters of leading internationally-known Japanese cosmetics manufacturers. As is also the custom in Japan, Triumph agreed with the department stores to accept the return of all unsold merchandise, whether this was as a result of changing styles or sudden shifts in market conditions.

Speciality shops

Once Triumph had gained a solid footing in the market through leading department stores, and a competent sales-force had been trained, speciality shops were added to the growing list of outlets. Aggressive sales promotions directed at the retailer were supported by nationwide advertising through press, women's fashion magazines and television. And, in 1970, Triumph flew in a plane-load of international models for the Osaka Expo to introduce their new line of special creations by designer Heinz Oestergaard.

Significantly, while Triumph has tailored its products to fit the Japanese figure, it has carefully maintained a European identity of design and quality. At first, a local Japanese flavour was added (in the days before liberalization) by combining the Triumph logo with a transliteration in Japanese *kana* characters and displaying the garments on Japanese models. But, in 1973, Triumph switched to a European image, dropping the Japanese characters and using European models, with an English language slogan 'Be A Progressive Beauty'.

Triumph, quite obviously, has decided that its greatest asset is its international leadership in the field. Japanese women want to be fashionable internationally. They have a definite preference for products that are *à la mode* in Paris, Düsseldorf and London.

European image

It is worth noting that the switch to a total European image was made in response to a recent phenomenon in Japan that has special significance for foreign manufacturers of quality merchandise. It is not just that Japanese women are attracted to international fashions, but it is generally fashionable in Japan to be international. Quality imported products are the vogue in Japan of the 1970s, just as the latest Japanese products were the status symbols of the 1960s. Where imported products previously had to be 'pushed' to gain access to the limited space in prime retailer outlets, today the 'pull' of Japanese demand for quality foreign merchandise prompts retailers to give primacy of place to the wares of leading European and American manufacturers.

While other manufacturers of foundations, lingerie and swimsuits in Japan are also now selling directly to retail outlets, most of them, unlike Triumph, still rely on wholesalers for some part of their distribution, and this reliance tends to increase with the concentration of sales in the lower ranges of the price spectrum.

Among the advantages of Triumph's international organization is a fully computerized production/planning and logistics facility. Changes in Japanese demand patterns and production cost advantages have prompted increasing imports of higher quality swimwear fashions from Europe and shifted more production to Taiwan and Hong Kong.

With the Japanese market growing at more than 20 per cent a year, and labour supply becoming rapidly inaccessible to the garment industry which is no longer able to bid successfully for a diminishing supply of labour, Triumph anticipates a continuing upward trend of imports from both its European and other Asian points of supply, maximizing the advantages of its global rationalization of sourcing and production for its Japanese operations.

Management of IFG is controlled by Triumph. Yet there is only one German executive in the company's top management, and the total number of expatriates, out of a total of more than 1000 IFG employees, is only three, one of whom is a secretary. While Triumph had difficulty in competing with some of the large advanced technology companies in mounting fringe benefits offered to employees (these include housing, and often free instruction in golf, tea ceremony, flower arrangement, as well as wedding arrangements) it assures its employees of life-long employment and other characteristic features of Japanese personnel policies.

'When in Japan . . .'

'Our policy is very simple', states Triumph International's Tokyo Branch Manager, Karl Rummel. 'When in Japan do as the Japanese do–even if it costs a little more. The cost–benefit ratio is what counts.'

'We wouldn't think of doing business here on any other basis', adds Rummel. 'The key to success in Japan is being a permanent part of the Japanese business world. There is no short cut.'

The increasing sophistication of the Japanese market may not have been the most compelling reason for Triumph's choice of the joint venture formula for its 1964 debut, but it is certainly the cement that keeps the joint venture together. Although there has been a change in the Japanese partners, with Toray replacing Nippon Rayon when the latter was merged into the new Unitika combine, the common objectives of the partners, upon which the joint venture was founded, still sustains the joint endeavour.

What was conceived of legal necessity now thrives on mutual advantage.

SUPPLEMENT: SINCLAIR

(ELECTRONIC CALCULATORS)

David Gribbin

As with any market, luck can play its part alongside strategic marketing efforts and long-term endeavours. In the case of Sinclair, the British electronics company, the element of luck came about in a most startling way, yet herein lies a lesson to all potential exporters to Japan. As if this were not amazing enough in itself, the actual product being marketed in Japan is a pocket calculator: a rare combination of ironies–but also involving a good deal of resolve.

When it was announced that the aggressive young Sinclair company from St Ives, Huntingdonshire, had sold $1,500,000-

worth of electronic calculators to the Japanese, the *Financial Times* described it as a classic case of taking coals to Newcastle. The same phrase was used by the trade press and also by the local newspaper in Cambridge, home of David Wilson, the man who negotiated the deal.

When one considers the proliferation of calculating machines on the Japanese market and the fact that the Sinclair Executive is selling in Japan at approximately six times the price of an indigenous pocket calculator (which has been given the kind of saturation TV advertising reserved for beer and fish fingers in Britain), perhaps Sinclair's success is more a case of selling refrigerators to the Eskimos.

The groundwork

Wilson, 34, head of David Wilson & Partners, a specialist in selling technical and semi-technical products to the Japanese, began laying the groundwork for Sinclair in November 1972, and almost immediately ran into difficulties. 'I did not realize how hard it would be to explain to the Japanese that the Executive, despite its smallness, is not just a calculator but an electronic slide rule capable of performing extremely sophisticated calculations. The Japanese are very quick on the uptake, but they are very conservative, both individually and as a group. In fact, no Japanese, in my experience, is happy when placed in a situation where he has to take an original stance. Maybe that's why all the companies with whom I discussed the possibility of a Sinclair agency–and they ranged from a well-known trading company to a well-known electronics giant–all reacted in precisely the same way.

'In other words, they all insisted the Executive was just a super-small electronic calculator. Then they looked at the prices of calculators in the department stores in Tokyo and reported that the Executive couldn't possibly be a viable proposition in Japan because it would be too expensive at the yen equivalent of approximately $168.'

Conviction

At this point, having heard the same story from six different sources, Wilson would have been justified, perhaps, in packing his bags and heading for home. But he was convinced that his product was right for the Japanese market.

As a result of the initial communication problem, Wilson was in the unhappy position of being unable to report back to his client with anything resembling even a glimmer of hope.

Ironically, while David Wilson was in Japan trying to interest the Japanese in the Sinclair Executive, the man he was looking for was actually in London. The Van Jacket Company of Tokyo, a go-ahead company specializing in trendy clothes for Japanese men, were taking a look at the clothing scene in Europe. As part of this operation, a Van man was looking over Austin Reed in Regent Street and noticed the Sinclair Executive offered for sale as a kind of executive toy.

The Van man was impressed by the calculator and obviously lost no time in communicating this fact to head office, since a letter arrived at Sinclairs shortly after saying that Van Jacket would be interested in acting as their Japanese agents.

'Initially, Sinclair didn't respond all that positively', Wilson recalls. 'For one thing, Van Jacket seemed to be straying quite a bit away from their main line of business. For another, they appeared to be too close to their product and I don't think they liked the fact that Van Jacket might see it as an executive toy.'

Follow through

Nevertheless, Sinclair agreed with Wilson that the approach was worth following up, and back he went to Japan. Having been through similar situations earlier, he was not particularly surprised when Van, too, preferred to consider the Executive as nothing more than a very small pocket calculator.

'I'm fairly sure that I was only able to get across to them finally because their man had seen the product in a sophisticated setting in London', said Wilson.

Despite this initial advantage, the Van discussions were protracted. 'I don't care what anyone says', Wilson remarked. 'It is very difficult for a *gaijin* – "outside person", the word the Japanese use indiscriminately when referring to all non-Japanese – to arrive in Japan and start telling the Japanese how to do a job.

'As a *gaijin* negotiator the art lies in dropping hints until the

Japanese finally catch on and suggest the thing you wanted them to do all along.

'Once the Van people began suggesting that the Executive was, in fact, so much more than an electronic calculator, it wasn't long before I could expose them to the thinking behind our latest advertising in Europe and the United States.'

Having finally realized how very much superior the Executive was to their indigenous electronic calculator in terms of performance, Van Jacket responded with typical Japanese enthusiasm, even abandon.

Decision to buy

And so, they placed their first order for Executives worth $1,500,000. From then on, having committed themselves to buying, the Japanese began to spin off selling ideas by the dozen. As well as the obvious outlets in department stores and their own boutiques, other possibilities were Diners Club, give-aways for car purchasers and golf clubs. The product may even be sold into the motor trade as a de-luxe give-away and there are plans for a special version expressly designed to appeal to top-échelon Japanese management.

'If you like, this was the honeymoon stage', says Wilson. 'Inevitably, it was followed by a down phase. As everyone who has been exposed to the Japanese knows, they are the most group-orientated people in the world. I knew that Van Jacket, having jumped in to the tune of $1,500,000 in what for them was a totally new product field, would be having doubts.

'Although you would never think it from their impassive faces, the Japanese are actually a very emotional people. While they are feeling well motivated they work like nobody else in the world. But if doubts and uncertainties set in they can go off an idea just as quickly as they latched on to it.

'Another complication is that they are convinced they are a unique people with a unique culture. For that reason, I knew it would be pointless to try and bolster the Van people up by telling them how well the Executive is doing in Europe and the United States.'

Wilson solved the problem by making frequent trips back to Japan to regenerate enthusiasm for the project by a kind of osmosis.

Understanding the system

Wilson's close scrutiny and study of Japan convinced him that the modern Japanese businessman, unlike his western counterpart, is more attracted by the competitive aspects of business than by mere profit.

The Sinclair company itself is headed by a genuine innovator in the person of Clive Sinclair. A self-educated electronics genius, Sinclair is every schoolboy's idea of the typical boffin, who started in the electronics business making do-it-yourself hi-fi kits. These experiments were not exactly a flop, but the company has only really begun to make its presence felt internationally with the introduction of its calculator.

An exceptionally large and sophisticated monolithic integrated circuit enables the Executive to perform a number of sophisticated functions. But the real secret of its success is Clive Sinclair's elegantly simple (and readily patentable) idea of having the illuminated display switch itself on and off at high speed. This subliminal flickering is too fast for the human eye to detect, but it dramatically reduces the power consumption. So much so that, whereas conventional calculators require either mains power or bulky batteries to keep their displays permanently lit up, the Executive can work off tiny power cells as used in hearing aids or electronic cameras.

Sinclair's founder, according to David Wilson, possesses a rare combination of inventive and entrepreneurial talents. He is also sensible enough to know when to call in specialized help. Which is why Wilson was hired in the first place–and given a free hand in his negotiations with the Japanese.

Choice of representative

If a company feels it really must have a man permanently based in the world's most expensive city, what should he be like?

'Above all, he must be a sensitive character able to detect very subtle changes in stance and react quickly to them', says Wilson. 'A steamroller type might do well in other parts of the Far East but he is going to be a disaster in Japan.

'So far as the Japanese are concerned your man *is* your company. Send the same man out to Japan so he has time to develop personal relationships with your client companies.

Personal relationships are very important, but they take time to grow.

'Before sending a man to Tokyo, be sure he is interested enough in the country and its people to learn about Japanese history and culture. The modern Japanese are motivated much the same as they were a thousand years ago.

'And if you can't afford to let your man have enough time to digest the Japanese way of life, and maintain himself at an impressively high level while doing so, it would be better to forget about the Japanese market.'

What about the potential for other companies in Japan?

'The number of opportunities being thrown away is heartbreaking.'

12 Japanese Business Etiquette and Behaviour

GEORGE FIELDS

INTRODUCTION

In a society as formalistic and as tightly structured as Japan's, one would naturally expect to find numerous rules and codes of practice governing business behaviour. Yet it would be a grave mistake to talk about business etiquette or even business ethics as if they were completely divorced from the general social and personal codes that govern society as a whole. Business behaviour, like personal behaviour, is solidly based on the Japanese socio-cultural environment. It is not surprising, therefore that, while the structure of Japan's general social etiquette and mores is well documented, very little exists that relates specifically to behaviour patterns in the business world.

Let it be said immediately that good manners in inter-personal business dealings in Japan are no different from good manners expressed in normal social situations. Thus, understanding 'etiquette' in the personal sense also helps to understand business etiquette. However, it is the basic underlying principles which one should try to grasp and not simply their manifestation in manners. It is also worth pointing out that it is quite unnecessary for the visitor to Japan to try to master all the intricacies of Japanese etiquette; if he tries he will probably not do this at all well and might end up making himself look foolish. In any case, and more important, he will not be expected to try and behave like a Japanese.

Know your counterpart's 'company style' (*shafu*)

There are three key words which sum up the Japanese concern for 'style'–*kunigara* (national characteristic), *kafu* (family style) and *shafu* (company style). It is automatic for a western salesman to set out to know something about his clients' *personal* life-style in order to establish a worthwhile rapport. The Japanese word for style, *fu,* however, applies generally to a collective body, the smallest unit being the family. In Japan, a good salesman has a grasp of his customer's *shafu (*company style)–considered the crystallization of the organization's traditional spirit and *esprit de corps.* Of course, a newly established company has no *shafu* in this sense but follows the lead of the president's life style–the head of the company household.

It is obviously very difficult, if not impossible, however, for the Japanese to know your particular western *shafu*–assuming you have one. So they resolve the dilemma by simply substituting *kunigara*–the national stereotype. If your behaviour seems to conform naturally to this stereotype, you are fairly safe. Safer, in fact, than trying too hard to act the Japanese way, although this may not necessarily be such a bad thing, since it could create a certain amount of light amusement and be to everybody's pleasure, not embarrassment. The point is that so long as you conform to the stereotype image, you need not worry too much about offending your Japanese counterpart simply because you have not observed strict Japanese protocol. In my opinion, many foreign businessmen are too sensitive about this issue–in the long run it only serves to cramp their natural style and so puts them at a disadvantage in the context of human relations. The Japanese have fairly fixed stereotype images of major nationalities–the Americans, the British, the Germans, the French, the Russians, etc.–and it might almost be worth your while to find out what these are!

Take your name card (*meishi*) seriously

It is not difficult for one Japanese to *place* his relationship with another Japanese in clear perspective. But it is another matter when it comes to a foreigner, and vice versa. The well-known Japanese custom of exchanging name cards is an essential first step. Having said this, remember that titles differ, not only between Japan and the West, but between western countries themselves; for instance, the chief operating executive is termed president in the United States, but managing director in the United Kingdom. In Japan, like the United States, the president is the chief operating officer but, unlike the United States, where he is sometimes all-powerful, the role of chairman in Japan is virtually an honorary retirement position, allocated to a senior company statesman.

Basically, the Japanese have far more titles and rankings than we do and they find the often ambiguous western titles frustrating. A recent article in the *Nihon Keizai Shimbun* (Japan's leading financial daily) discussed this question very seriously and mentioned the chagrin of a Japanese businessman who entertained a 'vice-president in charge of the Far East', only to discover subsequently that the man had arbitrarily upgraded himself to this title for his visit to Japan but was 'no more than a *kacho'* (division manager reporting to a division head). To the Japanese businessman concerned, this was one of the most serious breaches of business etiquette. Thus the article went on to warn that the vice-president title was most likely to be equivalent, at best, to that of *bucho*– 'division head'. Now, there is nothing wrong in the title of *bucho,* and it is a very important one; however, one must remember that in the Japanese decision-making process, which is generally a collective one for *major* issues, he *does* report to several levels of directors and finally, of course, to the president. The division head, of course, is an important part of the decision-making process but is seldom *the* decision-maker. While it may seem a trivial matter, the Japanese translation of your title and position should be checked and double-checked to indicate your true position *vis-à-vis* the *Japanese* management structure, *not* yours.

Establishing rapport–the Japanese way

Entertainment is a universal tool for establishing a rapport between businessmen; but, unlike the West, business luncheons in Japan are a rarity–they disturb the work flow and, in any event, the Japanese hate drinking during the day if for no other reason than the fact that alcohol often affects their complexion. What is more, evening entertainment almost never takes place in the home.

What is left is evening business entertainment, for which Japan is renowned. In 1972, for example, 1·5 per cent of Japan's impressive GNP was spent on (declared) entertainment. Entertaining is not limited to clients but is also extended to one's employees and subordinates as a social lubricant. Here, the Japanese have a saying, *hito no kokoro wa yoru wakaru* – 'You get through to a man's soul at night'. *Asobi* (literally, 'play') is supposed to be an integral part of the Japanese management system; in a structured society, this provides the necessary outlet for personal feelings. In turn, the superior obtains vital information for the efficient management of his department but must *never* be offended by what he hears on these occasions.

As a general rule, inter-company business entertainment basically adheres to this principle although it naturally differs in nuance. As in the West, the purpose of wining and dining in Japan is to establish rapport and friendship but it is also to gain *information*. The information thus gathered may be perceptive rather than tangible, but this does not make it any the less important. Of course many a contract is signed, many a joint venture deal is concluded in this context, but the final stage was almost certainly preceded by a number of 'information gathering (and exchange)' type of night-time meetings–*hara no saguriai* (literally, 'searching each other's stomachs', i.e., minds–but more on this later).

Rules of status governing business entertaining

To be able to entertain at the company's expense is a privilege earned by seniority which, in a Japanese organization, is derived mainly from many years of service. This privilege may be abused at times but it is never taken lightly. Should it ever happen that a junior company executive is entrusted with the task, he will not only lower the status of the company but, worse still, offend the dignity of the guest. As a rule, etiquette demands that you do *not* personally invite someone senior in status to yourself; the ideal situation is that you invite someone who is one rank or so below you. If a division head is to be invited, it is preferable that a director, *torishimariyaku*, plays host, since this invariably flatters the guest's ego.

In Japan husband and wife entertaining in the business context is still rare, although, if you are a visiting dignitary, your

Typical seating arrangements at a Japanese restaurant

(a) 'Zen': the most formal with individual tables

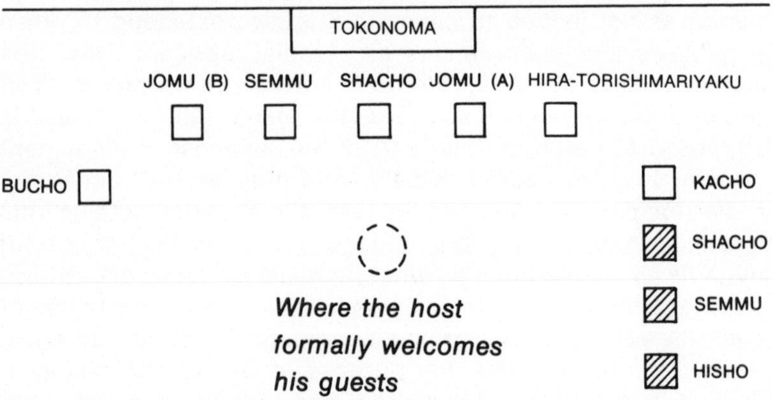

(b) Less formal with centre table

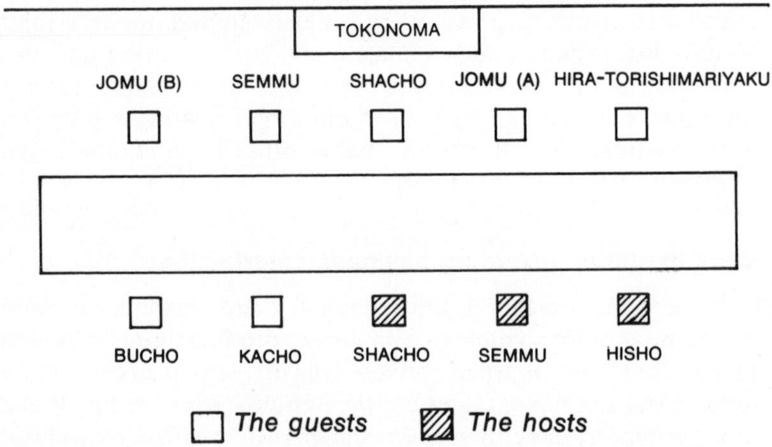

Glossary of terms

Tokonoma	The recess in a Japanese room in which scrolls are hung and flower arrangements placed
Shacho	President
Semmu	Senior managing director
Jomu	Managing director
Hira-torishimariyaku	Director
Hisho	Literally 'secretary', but more akin to executive assistant to the president

wife will most definitely be invited. The chances are, however, that the Japanese hosts will turn up without their wives and, apart from the *geisha* or hostesses, your wife will be the only female present. If you are entertaining your Japanese business associates, the best way is to entertain in the style that, paradoxically, requires the least protocol–namely the American-style cocktail party. Many Japanese businessmen actually dislike these affairs, since they consider that having to stand up to eat and drink is a barbaric custom. Nevertheless, this western tradition is perfectly acceptable since this is *your* way. On the other hand, if you are a Japan-based branch manager or a local representative and you have visiting dignitaries who want to experience a traditional Japanese feast, and you also decide to invite your Japanese business associates along for the occasion, then it would be useful for you to know the protocol of seating arrangements. If you do it *properly*, your Japanese guests will be highly impressed and will respect the depth of your knowledge concerning their country.

The entertainment ladder

The Japanese word *hashigozake* means 'drinking up the ladder', but it can also imply drinking down the ladder–depending on where you fit in to the little hierarchy amongst those drinking with you. Another word relating to this situation is *ichijikai* (the first get-together), then *nijikai* (the second get-together); and remember that no night out can be said to be off the ground and a good rapport established unless everybody adjourns to at least one other bar–the *nijikai* stage. Incidentally, the concept of going 'up the ladder' is not really very appropriate since, as the night progresses, you move on to places feeling increasingly relaxed–roughly corresponding to the general degree of inebriation!

Remember, however, that the first get-together, the *ichijikai*, is a most important occasion and should be approached with the formality befitting the guest's position (ranking). Ignore this, and you are highly unlikely to progress to the *nijikai* stage, and so on.

One word of caution: if, after having been lavishly entertained at the first get-together, you decide to reciprocate at the *nijikai* level, don't use this opportunity to drag your host off to your favourite bar simply because you want to renew acquaintance with your favourite bar hostess. Your local bar contact for these occasions should be impersonal and business-like; a good Japanese hostess understands this and will make sure that your guest is the centre of attention.

Form versus substance

The words *tatemae* (the front face) and *honne* (one's real intention) are the basis of a very important issue in Japanese business etiquette. An entire book in Japanese has been devoted to this subject. Although to the westerner this may seem a cynical form of duplicity, basically there is no difference between the two. The essential point is that 'front face' affords a rule of behaviour which gives continuity from the past and a unified measure to judge the behaviour of others. It is also considered necessary to maintain social harmony and in that sense it acts as an individual's safeguard.

The problem is that these rules of behaviour have actually become increasingly complicated rather than simplified because the social structure itself has become more involved. The individual is not nearly as clearly positioned in society as he once was; thus, the rules of behaviour have become more intricate. Ironically, in this sense, the democratization of Japan has made the Japanese even more difficult to understand. (Admittedly a heretical view, as most people seem to think that Japan's visible westernization–instant foods and golf–means that the Japanese are actually becoming western.)

Respect for the other's social style and values

A simplistic conclusion would be to say that the division of *tatemae* and *honne* is an admission of duplicity–the West's raw interpretation of social behaviour. The *tatemae* view is that 'to reveal that making money is bad form' may also strike westerners as a form of business hypocrisy. After all, one may reasonably ask, is there any other reason for being in business than to make profits? The Japanese 'true' answer to this question might be that there is more than one reason for running a business, although he may laugh and agree with you since that may be how *you* feel. *Tatemae*, therefore, is respect for the other's social style, with the clear recognition that there is very often no *one* right or wrong way. If respect for another's sensitivity is *the* consideration, camouflaging one's true intention is not necessarily duplicity.

In their overseas dealings, the Japanese thought that they were conforming to local standards by *not* bothering about *tatemae*, which they presumed did not exist. Thus they unashamedly revealed their determination to achieve trading success and now feel hurt that they have been branded as 'economic animals'! It seems unfair, therefore, that the foreigner has to cope with Japanese *tatemae* in Japan, when the Japanese do not have this problem overseas. It is no consolation, but we have to accept the fact that we are talking about the home ground of the Japanese businessman – and this is how things are done in Japan.

Behaviour versus true intention

The manipulation of *tatemae* and *honne* – surface appearance versus true intent – evolved before the days when direct verbal communications were possible, which is a subject on its own. It all revolves around the renowned Japanese *haragei* (stomach art) concept. In essence, this concept concerns the pit of the stomach – the place where one feels and, yes, makes basic decisions and communicates; it is similar to but rather more complicated and subtle than the western 'gut feeling'. In the business situation, I suspect that the most important *haragei* may be the decision as to when to reveal one's *honne* (true intentions). It is at this critical point that the game is decided. There is a parallel in Japanese sport, where originally there was no second chance; even now the *sumo* bout is over very quickly by a throw or push out. Under the circumstances, the two parties do a great deal of strategic 'feeling out' – in order not to reveal their tactics to the opponent too quickly: it is undoubtedly a practice which seems to have been carried into the area of business negotiations.

'Ambiguity'

There are Oriental sayings such as 'There are idle moments during busy times' or 'Stillness within movements'. What may seem to be ambiguity to the westerner may not be perceived as such by a Japanese who is irritated (although he may not show it) by the western businessman's noughts-and-crosses approach to strategy and his penchant for analyzing everything in logical terms. In the West, being busy means being fully occupied within a time-frame; so the busier you are, the less free time you have. The 'idleness' referred to in the East has nothing to do with such a time-frame and refers to the need to relax the mind–no matter how busy you are. In other words, the mind should be idle from time to time so that you can deal with the situation properly. The point is simply that against this backdrop of basic cultural differences, which are in turn reflected in attitudes, irritations and frictions are almost bound to occur in East-West business situations. The best business etiquette is not to show your irritation, since difficulties probably derive from cultural differences, and are not a deliberate ruse created by your business counterpart in order to frustrate you and your business objectives.

13 The International Businessman and Japan

HERBERT GLAZER

INTRODUCTION

Living and doing business in Japan presents the foreign businessman with an enormous personal and domestic challenge. This challenge is centred on his capacity to evolve relationships in his business and private life based on a completely new set of ground rules and within the framework he has never before experienced in the West. This 'relationship factor' does not imply anything artificial or superficial, nor does it suggest that one is playing a part. Certain Japanese customs, mannerisms and behaviour patterns, however, will undoubtedly be the source of confusion, consternation and even amusement. But time and desire to understand will place them in perspective.

In this chapter, Herbert Glazer considers some of the more fundamental implications of the foreign businessman living in Japan; his observations, however, are essentially just as valid for the visitor on a two or three week business trip. What is of the essence is the capacity to communicate oneself and one's business objectives within Japan's own terms of reference. This philosophy provides the only building materials that could possibly form the bridge which every businessman knows he has to build.

INTERPERSONAL RELATIONSHIPS

Living in Japan, one cannot help but be struck by the contrast between the western façade of Japanese industrial society and the fact that business in this society is conducted in a traditional Confucian manner where civility, politeness and the search for constructive relationships is of the essence. It is this Confucian tradition and not race, as is so commonly assumed, that links the countries of East Asia.

The foreign firm in Japan, therefore, should be represented by executives with authority who are allowed to remain there for a considerable period to develop the vitally important human relationships that are fundamental to Japanese business life. Continuity is extremely important; personnel changes in the foreign firm involving key men can destroy the contacts and understanding that have been carefully forged over a period of time; the new representative is thus forced to create from scratch a new set of relationships all his own. Even after these personal relationships have been established, extended discussions and negotiations become part of daily life. The relationship is simply a vital precondition for regular business dealings: by itself this relationship is not the *sine qua non* of a business deal. Furthermore, the friendship that arises between a foreign and a Japanese businessman will not generate business, in and of itself, or swing business in the direction of the foreign businessman. The friendship opens the door to the possibility of a successful business arrangement, but thereafter the hard reality of the benefits to be gained and the risks to be run will take over. Often enough, the toughness of the man on the Japanese side may seem to belie his friendship and fondness for the foreign businessman with whom he had previously established a warm personal relationship. But one must remember all the time the fact that the Japanese businessman is representing his firm and his primary loyalty is to his enterprise. Nothing will change that. It is for his company that he bargains hard and attempts to achieve what will create maximum benefit or return to the enterprise. This in no way diminishes his admiration, respect and affection for his foreign business friend, of whom he expects similar demonstrations of loyalty and business acumen in representing the foreign firm.

Silent language

The major problem facing many foreign businessmen arriving in Japan ready to engage in business discussions is that they are not prepared to operate within this 'two-tier' business structure. Typically, the foreign businessman is ready to move quickly, mainly for reasons of limited time and financial resources, to the second stage of actual business negotiations. He is suspicious of an approach that requires him first to become acquainted and then friendly with his Japanese counterpart. He may feel that the Japanese side is attempting to take unfair advantage of him, or he may simply feel that friendship and business are separate and that he does not wish to mix the two. Yet the idea that there is more to international business negotiations than business is not some spectacular discovery of the twentieth century and it is certainly not the prerogative of Japan.

Hall coined the expression, 'the silent language' to describe the numerous variables of foreign behaviour and custom that the western executive must learn to deal with.* The behaviour patterns of the peoples of Latin America, the Middle East and the Far East seem exotic to the newly arrived western businessman, whereas (to the European and the American) life-styles and business methods that one encounters in London, Paris, Rome, Düsseldorf and New York are now fairly standardized and relatively uniform. And despite the fact that Tokyo looks like a modern industrial capital, its business life-style has a form of 'silent language' that has no close parallel to the experience of most western businessmen.

Hall speaks of a five-dimensional cultural framework within which the international businessman must learn to operate. The dimensions are: time, space, things, friendship and agreements. Typical examples might be: A western businessman expects a reply to a letter within a reasonable period of *time*. Similarly he expects a phone call to be returned without being expected to wait too many hours or days. In Japan, when delays occur in replies, or when replies never take place, then there is a hidden or silent message in the delay or non-reply, which only the perceptive are aware of. The message is simply that there is an obstacle facing the Japanese side that delays or prevents a prompt reply. The perceptive western businessman must now apply diagnostic techniques to ascertain what the obstacle is and then try to overcome it. The obstacle may be a simple one

*Edward T. Hall, 'The Silent Language in Overseas Business', *Harvard Business Review* (May–June 1960) pp. 87–96.

such as the fact that the information requested is not available, or it may be a complex problem, such as when the Japanese side require extensive deliberation and consultation before being in a position to reply.

The language of *space* in Japan is communicated in many ways, but most vivid is the manner in which the Japanese executive will arrange his subordinates in a semi-circle on either side of him when confronting the foreign businessman. It seems feudal and hierarchical but it is, of course, extremely useful in providing the executive with ready advice and it certainly does not reflect unfavourably on him to have specialists at his side. The western businessman often attempts to act as an expert in numerous areas and assumes that his position and title require him to do so. The contrast is striking. Another example is the fact that the limited space of the Japanese home means that an enormous amount of business entertainment has to be done outside the home. The western dinner party has no close counterpart in Japan,

The language of *things* in Japan immediately suggests a contrast between overt materialism and the traditional values that are epitomised in the tea ceremony and in the *tatami* mat room with its absence of furnishings except for an alcove containing a hanging scroll and a vase of carefully arranged flowers. The underlying *zen* values in the tea ceremony room are still dominant throughout Japan, and many Japanese businessmen take much more pride in their *zen*-related artistic accomplishments than in their material wealth. In fact several of Japan's top businessmen are known for their frugal and austere life-style.

The language of *friendship* is one that has already been referred to earlier. Suffice it to say here that friendships take more time to form, are deeper and last longer than in the West, and may involve real obligations of a sort not normally known in the West.

The language of *agreements* in Japan is to be seen less in the written document and more in the reciprocal obligations inferred from an agreement of which the written document may be only a minor part. It is important here to distinguish two points. First, agreements are honoured but, second, flexibility and ambiguity are often sought to allow the Japanese side the ability to adjust to unforeseen future circumstances. This should not be interpreted by the western businessman as an attempt to violate legal contracts, but rather the desire of the Japanese side to open up room for manoeuvre. The western businessman should be clear in his own mind as to how much ambiguity would be beneficial to both sides; he should also be clear as to how much detail is actually necessary. This suggests that the agreement requires significant elements of diplomacy that are not normally involved in the drawing up of business contracts.

Business and night life

The cramped living quarters of the average Japanese family largely preclude entertaining at home. In apartment blocks the average area per person is only 12·5 square feet. The night life of Japan clearly reflects this fact. Men leave the office together and go to restaurants, bars and cabarets, while their wives remain at home watching television, having dinner and caring for the children. Night life is a man's life and although young office girls can be seen in coffee shops and the like, it is rare to see mature women out in the evening. Bars and cabarets have hostesses to entertain their male customers. Sunday afternoon and early evening is an exception, in that one may see younger married couples at restaurants with their children. During the week, men are out either with their colleagues or business clients–business and the company being the main topic of conversation. One Japanese writer referred to these restaurants and bars as 'night offices'. Japanese companies have been spending over $3·5 billion (yen 1000 billion) each year on entertainment.

Thus the western businessman will have to adjust himself to the rhythm of evening business life in Japan; but perhaps even more importantly so will his wife, as she will often be excluded from evening activities. There is also another and important side to the 'night office'. I refer to the group drinking of the Japanese businessman. The business office is an intense place where lunch is consumed quickly (often a bowl of noodles delivered to the office) and everyone is extremely busy or at least must appear to be busy to avoid the opprobrium of his fellows. The evening meal at a restaurant, lubricated with many bottles of beer and *sake*, provides the necessary release from the tensions of the day. When a client is entertained, it becomes much easier to break down the natural reserve of both sides and to develop the sort of interpersonal relationship that is a necessary prerequisite to a lasting business relationship.

I remember talking about this subject to an advertising executive who had lived in Tokyo for three years. He described the typical evening in a hostess bar, or the more exceptional *geisha* party, as 'ritualistic' and not 'end-oriented', the latter tending to be the general conclusion of many newly-arrived western businessmen when confronted by the hostess system for the first time.

Thus, whereas the Japanese wife accepts her husband's separation from the home in the evening, albeit begrudgingly, the western wife usually finds it difficult to be quite as accommodating. Consequently, quite drastic adjustments on both sides have to be anticipated. A western businessman who spends the majority of his evenings with his family and is still successful in business in Japan is something of an exception.

Domestic life

In many ways the life of a businessman's wife is not unlike that of the expatriate diplomat's wife, in that there is an international circle of friends who entertain each other and share each other's company. Some form of domestic help is usually necessary, not only to assist with the shopping, food preparation, care of the home and children and so on, but also to act as a form of guide and interpreter. It should be remembered, however, that the labour shortage in Japan and Japan's high rate of inflation has made domestic help increasingly scarce.

Neighbourhood shops selling fresh produce of all kinds are plentiful in Japan; supermarkets carry extensive lines of imported foods (including such things as air-shipped French Brie cheese), and the numerous large department stores offer a highly comprehensive range of goods and foodstuffs. Similarly, pharmaceutical products are readily available in small local pharmacies and there are some which specialize in imports.

Schools for younger children are available and pre-university education in a number of European languages is possible. But the number of such schools is small and the cost is high. Housing costs are extremely high and the company should be expected to bear the cost of housing, or a significant portion of it. Transportation via the company car is a privilege most wives of Japanese executives share with their husbands and is also desirable for the western wife, where feasible.

In the evening the Japanese wife dines at home with the children, supervises their TV watching time and study time, and then retires, without waiting for her husband to return home. At times her husband will remain in Tokyo overnight. Consequently, except for the circle of western friends and 'international' Japanese friends whom the western wife can entertain at dinner parties and the like, she is not likely to be able to share many of her husband's evenings. It is unfortunately true, however, that when the western wife seeks to entertain her husband's business associates and their wives, she will fail in her purpose–all too often because she has forced her Japanese guests to accept her invitation as a couple and thus made them miserable. As so often happens, even after an invitation to dinner or cocktails has been accepted, the Japanese businessman will show up without his wife (without prior notice) and then make some embarrassed excuse about his wife's indisposition that evening.

As a result of these readjustment problems, there is a natural tendency to become over-dependent and over-reliant upon the company of the other expatriates whose life styles are the same, and this, in turn, results in a narrowing of the range of opportunities for a meaningful relationship with the people of Japan. Since really close foreign–Japanese friendships are rare and take a lot of time and trouble to establish, even under the best circumstances, the wife may find herself rather isolated and lonely. So it is worth while for the wife to become as involved as possible in activities outside the home, activities of a participatory nature. The teaching of one's native language, formally or informally, to Japanese school children or university students, for example, is probably one of the most effective ways of surmounting the cultural barriers which separate western wives from 'the real Japan'. The teacher or *sensei* in Japan is highly respected and treated as an honoured guest in the homes of his pupils. The wife of a western businessman who does take up teaching often finds her most treasured experiences and memories of Japan relate to her Japanese students. They open to her a dimension of Japanese life that would otherwise be difficult to attain.

A VIEW ON JAPANESE AND WESTERN MANAGERIAL PHILOSOPHIES

The western view, as presented in a long and excellent case study of a western–Japanese joint venture in Japan,* basically assumes that the western manager must go more than half-way in his partnership with Japanese business interests. The study ends with a list of general recommendations for the foreign executive in Japan:

Recognize that Japan is a monolithic society.
Recognize that the Japanese economy is highly developed and is directed by energetic and capable leaders.
Recognize that, while business in Japan is highly competitive, it is not western-style free enterprise.
Recognize that doing business in Japan is considered by the Japanese to be a privilege for a foreign company.
Recognize that compromise is a way of life in Japan.
Recognize that the financial and profit standards of the average Japanese company are considerably lower than in western companies and 'obligations' to employees and customers often outweigh profit 'obligations' to shareholders.
Devote time to the study of Japanese language and culture.
Recognize that foreigners are viewed with reserve.
Recognize that there is an enormous amount of information about important business, economic, and political issues in Japanese publications.
Recognize the indirect nature of the Japanese language.
Be extremely patient, but firm and foreceful at appropriate times when you have 'all the facts'.

Young Japanese manager's view

A graduate student from Sophia University, Tokyo, who was employed as a junior executive with a western Japanese joint venture, was asked to list what he considered to be the positive and negative aspects of working for western management. On the positive side he indicated:

*The American Chamber of Commerce in Japan, *High Adventure in Joint Ventures*, 2nd ed. (Tokyo, 1972).

Higher salary.
Merit system for promotion and salary increases.
Shorter daily working hours.
No Saturday work (5-day week).
Overseas travel.
English language conversation practice.
Non-office free time.

The negative aspects were:

No chance of promotion to a top management position.
Chance of being fired.
Lower status of foreign firm employment.
Language and other cultural barriers.
Lower fringe benefits.

Obviously, the western manager in Japan has the opportunity in a case such as this to enhance those aspects of employment that are viewed positively and actively to seek to minimize the negative elements. In doing so, the western executive would, in effect, be working towards a synthesis of western and Japanese-style personnel policies in a direct and effective manner.

Young western manager's view

The following observations are based on an interview with a young western businessman who held the position of assistant manager of a major joint venture advertising firm in Japan. The interview took place about one week prior to the man's departure from Japan in 1973, after four years' service in Japan. Japan was the executive's first overseas assignment. Since his company's policy was to avoid prejudicing the man in any direction prior to his arrival in Japan, there was no particular effort made to prepare him for life in Japan. He adjusted well, as did his wife and small daughter. He also adjusted easily within the organization and developed good working relationships with the Japanese and expatriate staff and executives. At the same time, he managed to work hard and late in the office as required, without following the Japanese night-life pattern of eating and drinking with his office staff. His night life was more of the western sort, entertaining clients and the like. He managed to avoid the excesses of the entertainment world of Japan, while developing an understanding of the role it plays in the lives of others.

As he looked back on the experience, he felt that he had gained a great deal that would serve him well in the future. Surprisingly, this concerned less the specifics of the Japanese situation and more the broadening and maturation of the man's outlook and point of view. The cross-cultural experience changed him significantly. It changed him by teaching him how to deal effectively with people whose total cultural experience was different from his own. He recognized that this is one of the few generalizations that appears to be valid in the area of cross-cultural training. Taking the point to an extreme, the westerner who is successful in adapting to ways of doing business in Saudi Arabia will find that same adaptability serving him in good stead in Japan. One man put it this way–the sheep's eye and *sashimi* (raw fish), when first encountered as local delicacies in Saudi Arabia and Japan respectively, produce the same reaction in both cases. Once either of these experiences has been adapted to, the other is less difficult to deal with.

SUMMING UP

Not all western visitors to Japan leave the country with a sense of fulfilment. Some have the sense of an unrequited love affair with the country. Edward Seidensticker described this love affair in great detail.* He notes that there are special dimensions that the love affair assumes with different western nationalities. The French use the word *tatamisé*, indicating that the expatriate has taken extremely well to the straw mat flooring of the traditional Japanese room. The British used to speak of 'piggotry', making reference to Gen. F. S. G. Piggott, an English Japanophile. Seidensticker notes that the American love affairs with Japan are painful and tortured, and with a little tongue in cheek suggests the word 'hearnia' after Lafcadio Hearn. But the expatriate, despite his love for the country, often finds that the life of an outsider in Japan, for one who really loves Japan, is often too difficult to bear and he leaves with his love unrequited. Seidensticker tells the delightful story of the westerner who

*Edward Seidensticker, *Japan – an expatriate's love affair*, Holiday (Oct. 1961) p. 32.

resolved to bridge the gap between himself and the Japanese–having failed to do so via a monastic and then an academic life–by shoplifting, in order to have himself thrown into the totally Japanese life of a Japanese jail. But here, too, he was disappointed, as he discovered that there was a special jail in Tokyo for foreigners. He was later deported.

Kurt Singer, former German Professor of Economics at Tokyo University, who became a pre-Second World War refugee in Japan, focused on the underlying continuity of the Japanese people.* He noted that he would turn to the *Tale of Genji*, an 11th century novel describing courtly life during the Heian period, whenever he needed help in understanding the habits, customs and manners of the people around him in the 1930s.

The western businessman in Japan today is faced with the challenge of operating in a culture that has had well over a thousand years of continuous development and still bears a remarkable similarity, in the area of interpersonal relationships, to the traditional Japan of former times. The challenge facing all visitors to Japan is to come to grips with this culture on modern terms while appreciating the importance of the traditional. It is not a challenge which is easily resolved, but there is no alternative.

*Kurt Singer, *Mirror, Sword and Jewel* (London: Croom Helm, 1973).

Supplement

A Businessman's Guide to Japan

INTRODUCTION

To the visiting or resident businessman, the Japanese cityscape, particularly that of Tokyo itself, presents a formidable challenge. There is the steamy heat of summer, for example, the sudden storm and typhoon in the autumn, and everywhere teaming crowds as if there were no space left anywhere in Japan. There is also the challenge of loneliness and isolation in the midst of this alien culture.

There may have been no host to help you in your initiation into Japan. If there is no ready-made connection or potential business associate waiting for you, try to avoid arriving completely unannounced, since there are few things that throw the Japanese more than being taken by surprise. You cannot just appear out of the blue and knock on what looks to be a suitable Japanese door, expecting that everyone behind it will be willing to slot you promptly into an appropriate business arrangement. The rules of status, the forms of decision-making, the complex contours of business groupings and the whole ambience of the established conventions of Japanese society militate against this.

At the same time, do not let the battery of do's and dont's that older hands will hurl at you make you nervous and ill at ease. One of the most often asked questions concerns the distinctive etiquette of the Japanese, both business and social; what dire consequences would follow, people ask, if a foot–or several feet–were put wrong? Of course, anyone can commit a number of social gaffes, just as the Japanese often do when they leave their own country. But this does not spell the end of all hope for you and your venture. If, above all, you act naturally and openly, if you observe the normal courtesies of your own society, if you indicate your interest in whatever your host or potential business partner has to show you (and remember how inordinately proud he might be of his country's uniqueness), and if you can reveal that you have bothered to learn about Japan, you will have opened the most important door of all. For you will have demonstrated your *sincerity*–and this is just what your Japanese host or business contact will have been seeking to discover in you.

To restore your equilibrium, there is the calm of your hotel (if you have selected wisely). Do not forget that you may be judged partly according to your choice of hotel. Some of Tokyo's hotels have managed to hit the mean of a workable balance between East and West in decor, furnishing and so on. As a result, westerners can feel relaxed and Japanese also find the 'mood' is right for them.

The Japanese are proud of their heritage and sometimes slip back involuntarily into line with it: the bar hostess, loud-voiced, with a raucous laugh and garish western dress, caught in the sad limbo between cultures–yet revealing the pull of her own tradition with every posture and movement of her long, slender fingers.

The zeal, the panache and the sheer professionalism of those who serve you in a land in which, still today, service is considered an honour, sometimes have an almost hypnotic effect. The swank of the cook, the sure swagger of the sweeps of his knife as he slices a fish and prepares the batter in a *tempura* house, are a treat to marvel at. The meal tempts not just the palate; it also tempts the eye–for it has often been said, so rightly, that the true Japanese cook panders to your eye, your heart, or wherever your sense of beauty lies.

Life in Japan can be very demanding, it can leave you completely wrung out; it can end up as a love–hate relationship. The extraordinary thing is that you cannot remain unmoved and uninvolved once you have encountered this distinctive culture and unique rhythm of life. Few visitors wish never to return. Japan, you might say, is yet another aspect of the phenomenon of man. It also happens to have a very large market-place consisting of some 108 million people.

P.N.
G.B.

CONTENTS OF SUPPLEMENT

Note: All commodity prices quoted in this guide were correct at the time of going to press. However, as there has been a steep upward movement in prices since the end of 1973, price fluctuations will be even greater than would normally be expected. In any event, it is hoped that the prices given will act as a useful indicator for the purpose of estimating travel budgets, etc.

TOKYO
N
SUMIDA RIVER
Kokugikan Hall
Meijiza Theatre
RYOGOKU
ASAKUSABASHI
AKIHABARA
KANDA
Mitsukoshi Dept Store
Shin Ohashidori
Tokyu Dept Store
Takashimaya Dept Store
Kiyosumidori
TOKYO
Chuodori
Showadori
Matsuya Dept Store
Kabukiza Theatre
Ginzadori
Mitsukoshi Dept Store
Matsuzakaya Dept Store
YURAKU CHO
Harumidori
Hotel Nikko
Hibiyadori
Palace Hotel
Nicolai Dome
OCHANOMIZU
Nohgakudo Hall
Hakusandori
SUIDO BASHI
Imperial Hotel
SHINBASHI
IMPERIAL PALACE
Double Bridge
Budokan Hall
IIDABASHI
Yasukuni Shrine
Uchiboridori
Kasumigaseki Bldg.
Tokyo Hilton Hotel
Hotel New Japan
Diet Bldg.
National Theatre
Hotel New Otani
Hotel Okura
Tokyo Prince Hotel
Tokyo Tower
Sotoboridori
ICHIGAYA
YOTSUYA
No.3 Expressway
SHINANOMACHI
National Stadium
Aoyamadori
Okubodori
Yasukunidori
Shinjukudori
Shinjuku Gyoen Garden
SENDAGAYA
Isetan Dept Store
Meijidori
SHIN OKUBO
SHINJUKU
YOYOGI
HARAJUKU
SHIBUYA
Meiji Shrine
National Gym.

Airport*

Tokyo International Airport–Haneda (12 miles to central Tokyo).

Minimum check-in time for Haneda is 60 minutes (international) 20 minutes (domestic). Tel: 747 3131.

There are several methods of getting from Haneda to central Tokyo. (If you have any contacts at all in Japan, remember that airport meeting and sending off are integral parts of a business relationship, so inform your contacts of flight time and number.) If you have no such contacts, then you may go by:

taxi costing about yen 2000, including yen 200 expressway toll; about 30 minutes to most central Tokyo hotels in normal traffic conditions;

'airport limousine' so-called, although the limousine turns out to be a bus which tours the main hotels, and is very slow if your hotel should be at the end of the route (ticket yen 400);

monorail (the world's longest commercial monorail) to Hamamatsucho, eight miles from Haneda. Journey takes 15 minutes, frequent service, yen 190. But there are snags: if you are carrying the normal air traveller's luggage, there is little storage space inside the carriages, there are long walks at the end of the line, and porters are few and far between. Also, the terminal at Hamamatsucho is four miles from the central hotel area, business sector etc.

However, the *monorail is recommended* as the most reliable route to get you from Tokyo to Haneda on time when the expressway and main roads to the airport are likely to be subject to heavy traffic delays (mainly Saturday afternoon and Sunday morning in the summer or at national holiday periods, and some evening rush-hour periods throughout the year). Remember that all roads from Tokyo to Haneda carry on to Yokohama and other commuter cities, and go beyond to the coast resorts and Fuji National Park area.

Banks

Banks are open 9.00 to 3.30; 9.00 to 12.00 on Saturday (when no foreign business is transacted). A selected list of foreign banks located in Tokyo is carried in Appendix 2.

Chemists

American Pharmacy, Hibiya Park Building (formerly Nikkatsu International Building), Yurakucho. Tel: 271 4034.

Fuji-Rexhall Pharmacy, Sankei Newspaper Building, Otemachi. Tel: 231 0745.

Mill Pharmacy, 23 Azabu, Imai-cho, Minato-ku. Tel: 583 5044.

Churches/synagogues

Cathedral of the Immaculate Conception (Catholic), 9 Sekiguchi-daimachi, Bunkyo-ku.

*The new international airport at Narita, 40 miles to central Tokyo, is due to open in the near future.

Sacred Heart Chapel and St Ignatius Church (Catholic), 2–37, 4-chome, Roppongi (on the campus of Sophia University Franciscan Chapel Centre).

Tokyo Union Church (Interdenominational), Yoyogi Sando, (Harajuku).

St Albans Church (Anglican), opposite the Masonic Building, Tokyo Tower, Shiba.

Tokyo Baptist Church (Baptist), 33 Hachiyama-cho, Shibuya-ku.

Nikolai-do Cathedral (Orthodox), near Ochanomizu Station.

Jewish Community Centre (Jewish), Hiroo-cho, Shibuya. Tel: 400 2559.

Climate and clothing

To somebody from Western Europe, Tokyo and Kyoto winters seem short and are not really cold, but summers are stifling and humid.

January–March: in the daytime and in the sun, less cold than expected, but often biting dry winds from the Asiatic mainland, with the likelihood of snow. Cold at nights.

April, May and October: the weather is usually mild, similar to the average Western European early summer day.

Mid–June: the rainy season sets in, for three weeks or a month. The rain varies from drizzle to downpour, though there may be dry rainy seasons (as in 1973). Humid and energy-draining.

July, August and September: hot and humid, with the daily high temperature averaging well over 80°F.

November and December: usually dry, with fairly warm days and cool to cold nights.

Typhoons are most likely to strike in September, though Japan is vulnerable from early July onwards in most years.

The most clement seasons for a visit are April and May (coinciding with cherry blossom): also remember that late April and early May are national holiday periods. October and November are also good visiting months.

Tokyo weather (temperature in degrees fahrenheit)

	Jan	Feb	Mar	Apr	May	June	July	Aug	Sep	Oct	Nov	Dec
daytime high	47	48	54	63	71	76	83	86	79	69	60	52
night low	29	31	36	45	54	63	70	72	66	55	43	33
humidity (%)	61	60	64	70	74	79	80	79	80	76	72	64
days with rain	5	6	10	10	10	12	10	9	12	11	7	5

Hotels, banks, major business offices, restaurants, department stores and larger shops, taxis, cars and super-express trains are air-conditioned/centrally heated, so that the problem of clothing appropriate to the climate is no longer as great as, for instance, ten to fifteen years ago.

In summer lightweight suits, and cotton rather than man-made fibre dresses or shirts. Japanese businessmen dress quietly and formally;

almost invariably they turn out in dark charcoal greys or navy blue. Shirts are nearly always white, and ties are very conventional.

In winter, dress as you would for an English or European winter, bearing in mind that Japanese central heating is often over generous.

An umbrella is a must in the rainy season and is useful at most times of the year since the weather is extremely changeable. (One of the favourite weather forecasts in the English language press in Japan reads: cloudy, bright; winds north, later south.)

Currency

Coin denominations: yen 1, 5, 10, 50, 100.
Note denominations: yen 500, 1000, 5000, 10,000.
No entry or exit restrictions on currency.

Dentists

All leading hotels have English-speaking dentists and doctors on call. Also, in Tokyo there is:

Japan-American Dental Clinic, Takano Building, 2, 2-chome Kanda, Kajicho, Chuo-ku. Tel: 251 7555

Hardy Barracks Dental Clinic, 8-11 Akasaka, Minato-ku (near Roppongi Crossing). Tel: 408 2020.

Drinking in Japan

Scotch whisky, malt, brandy, etc. are very expensive, although not as ridiculously so as in the pre-1971 days. These, especially malt, still make highly acceptable gifts to friends and colleagues. Expect to pay yen 400 to yen 600 per measure for gin and Scotch whisky in hotels, bars, restaurants, etc. If you do not wish to pay such prices, insist on Japanese brands. The most renowned Japanese whisky is *Suntory* which is quite agreeable. Japanese gin is rather less expensive; *High and Dry*, made under licence in Japan, is available at just under yen 600 per bottle.

Even the cheapest of European wines, are also ridiculously expensive. Japanese wines (as well as Australian and Californian wines) are much more reasonable in price and, on the whole, are much improved in taste since about the middle 1960s.

Sake, the traditional rice wine (15–22 proof) often served cold in summer but always hot in winter, is very difficult to describe; it has something like the tang of sherry while on the palate, and a slight whisky kick as it goes down the throat. *Sake* mixes excellently with Japanese food, though not so well with other drinks. Japanese hosts often order *sake* and beer to go with a meal, and usually mix whisky with it, both before and after.

There is a wide variety of local Japanese beer which is largely a lager-type beer. Such is the popularity of beer (and now wines) in Japan that the *sake* brewers are said to be rather concerned about the future of their market share.

Duty-free allowances (*for non-residents*)

alcohol	3 bottles
tobacco	500
or cigarettes	400
or cigars	100
perfume	2 oz.
watches	2

and, in addition, articles to the value of yen 50,000 (*excluding* personal effects).

Eating out

Water is normally perfectly safe throughout Japan and sometimes has quite a lively taste. Even in the cheapest of restaurants or coffee shops the standard of cleanliness is unexpectedly and pleasingly high.

Tokyo, Kyoto and Osaka offer restaurants in which you can eat the world's food–at far higher prices, of course, than you would pay outside Japan. Occasionally, you will be served what might be called a Japanese variation on a western theme: roast beef, for example, often turns out to be a slim version of a sirloin steak, while Yorkshire pudding is, to say the least, different.

For business appointments, lunch and dinner in hotels and top-class restaurants, it is conventional to wear a suit or jacket and tie, even at the height of the hottest summer.

When eating in Japanese restaurants, try to use chopsticks (*hashi*). Even a not very promising effort in your eyes will bring rapt attention and vocal approval from the restaurant maids, and will gratify your host. When offered *sake*, beer, etc. at a Japanese dinner party or in a club, lift your cup or glass an inch or two from the table.

There is a wide variety of Japanese dishes, the most popular usually being available in the hotels' specialist restaurants. Among the most popular and the easiest to eat are:

Sukiyaki–thin slices of beef, cooked at your table in a soya sauce and *sake*, along with green vegetables, fungi, bamboo shoots, bean curd and so on. When cooked, the meal is served in individual bowls containing a whisked egg.

Shabu-shabu–thin beef slices, again like *sukiyaki*, with vegetable, bean curd, etc. dunked by you in a funnelled cauldron with water on the boil, and transferred to your mouth via a variety of piquant sauces (sometimes with ginger or sesame base).

Tempura–a range of fish, including shellfish, and some vegetables, sliced into small, thin portions and deep fried in batter.

For the more cultivated and acclimatised palate there is:

Sushi–rice rings with wafer-thin seaweed surrounds and fillings including raw fish. Ideal for a summer lunch, with a little beer or *sake*.

Sashimi–raw fish slivers, dipped in a pungent horse-radish dressing (which, until you acquire the taste, helps you to get it down).

But, if you cannot bring yourself to try, or have become wearied of, Japanese dishes, there is always steak (like fish and chips in a Chinese restaurant in England), which has become the national staple eating-out dish. Japanese steak, from animals reputedly fed and massaged with beer, is very fine-quality meat and very expensive (yen 5000 for a medium-sized sirloin in a first-class restaurant).

A meal that is quite inexpensive, by Tokyo standards, yet very filling and varied, can be had in the Viking restaurants (for instance, the top floor of the Imperial Hotel, the ground floor of the Tokyo Hilton). Viking is a typical Japanese happening–a twist to, and an extension of, smorgasbord. Average prices are around yen 1750–yen 2000 for lunch, and yen 2500–yen 2750 for dinner; there is the choice of a variety of soups and hors-d'oeuvres, hot and cold meat and fish, salads, sometimes hot Chinese main course dishes, sweets and cheeses. You can return to the serving table, of course, as often as you wish.

Electrical

100 volts AC 50 cycles in eastern Japan; 100 volts AC 60 cycles in western Japan.

Embassies

See Appendix 3.

Entry requirements

All visitors require smallpox vaccination. Cholera innoculation is necessary in the case of those journeying from or travelling through infected areas.

There is no restriction on the amount of foreign currency, travellers' cheques, etc. that may be taken into Japan.

Customs requirements are as follows: for accompanied baggage, an oral declaration; for unaccompanied baggage, a written declaration form. (See also section under 'Visas', below.)

Etiquette in a Japanese house or restaurant

If you are entertained in a traditional Japanese restaurant, or go into a Japanese house, shoes come off at the entrance and are replaced by thin-soled slip-ons, which should be worn as long as the floor is plain wood; as soon as you reach the *tatami* (thick straw mat) floor areas, these slip-ons come off, and you walk around in stockinged feet only.

In this situation, slip-on shoes are obviously much more convenient than laced shoes.

Fukuoka

The largest city of the southern island of Kyushu, and its commercial centre.

Airport: Fukuoka International. Tel: (092) 65 4031.

Hotels:

Hakata Tokyu Hotel, 1-16-1 Tenjin Chuo-ku (Tel: 78 7111).

Nishitetsu Grand Hotel, 6–60 Daimyo 2-chome, Chuo-ku, Fukuoka-shi, Fukuoka-ken (Tel: 77 7171).

Hotel New Hakata, 1-1, Chuo-Gai, Hakata-Eki, Hakata-ku (Tel: 43 1111).

Hospitals (in Tokyo)

All leading hotels have English-speaking doctors and dentists on call.

Tokyo Medical and Surgical Clinic, Masonic Building (next to Tokyo Tower) Shiba, Minato-ku. Tel: 431 3692.

Seventh Day Adventist Clinic, Yoyogi and Aoyami-dori. Tel: 401 1171.

St Luke's International Hospital, 10-1 Akashi-cho, Chuo-ku. Tel: 541 5151.

St Mary's Hospital, 2-chome, Naka-Ochiai, Shinjuku-ku. Tel: 951 1177/9.

Japan Red Cross Central Hospital, Hiroo, Shibuya-ku. Tel: 400 1311.

Keio University Hospital, 35 Shinanomachi, Shinjuku-ku. Tel: 353 1211.

Jikei University Hospital, 3 Nishi-Shimbashi, Minato-ku. Tel: 433 1111.

Hotels

Advance booking: it is essential to book your hotel in advance, for, even with a rapidly increasing total number of hotel beds, the most popular hotels in, say, Tokyo, Kyoto and Osaka are recording averages of 95 per cent occupancy *the year round*. At seasons when the western businessman is not inclined to visit, his place is taken by the package dealer or the business visitor from South-East Asia. Try to avoid the Japanese holiday periods–early January, early April, 'golden week' (the holiday period at the end of April and the start of May) and the whole of August.

Some of the major hotels have European or American representatives or are part of or related to a worldwide chain. Of the Tokyo hotels Okura, Imperial and Palace are generally ranked as luxury; among hotels rated as first class are Keio Plaza, New Otani, Tokyo Prince, Takanawa Prince, Hilton and New Japan. In Kyoto the two leading hotels are the Miyako and Kyoto Hotel.

Hotel bars close at 11.00 or midnight, but there is usually an all-night room service (with a significant mark-up) for drinks, light refreshments, etc., unless you have one of the new self-contained refrigerated self-service 'bars' in your own room.

To make sure of getting back to your hotel, always carry the hotel's card (or a postcard, or the hotel's matches) to show to a taxi driver to reinforce your spoken words: for some taxi drivers are not able to make sense of even impeccably pronounced names like Otani or Okura. It's partly because they *expect* not to understand; there can also be a kind of phobia about foreigners which produces a nervousness not unlike that in foreign business visitors afraid of offending against Japanese business and social rules and etiquette.

Below is a list of the major Tokyo hotels, their special features and services, and the tariff for 1974 (correct at the end of 1973). This follows the generally-accepted classification of luxury (in the case of Okura, Imperial and Palace) and first class (the remainder of those listed). Remember to add 10% service charge to all prices quoted; there is also a 10% tax levied on all food and beverages.

Key
1 address
2 telephone number
3 cable address
4 telex address
5 access (to Haneda Airport, Tokyo Station and central business area)
6 number of rooms, banquet and reception/conference facilities, shopping arcade, postal, etc. facilities, airline and travel offices.
7 car parking
8 room and meal tariff

Hotel Okura

1 3, Aoicho, Akasaka, Minato-ku, Tokyo 107
2 582 0111
3 Hotelokura Tokyo
4 J 22790
5 10–15 minutes Tokyo station; 20–25 minutes Haneda Airport (in normal traffic conditions), yen 1500 (including yen 200 expressway) by taxi; especially convenient for US Embassy and American Trade Centre, Kasumigaseki Building business area and Ministries (including MITI and Foreign Ministry)
6 980 guest rooms (550 main building, 430 new extension: lobbies and reception, accounts, etc. computer linked)
shopping arcade (including branch of Takashimaya store)
barber, beauty parlour
steam bath, all-year indoor pool, gymnasium and health club
secretary, photo-copying services, free typewriter loan, worldwide telex news services, post office, packing and shipping facilities
JAL, Panam, North-West Airlines
JTB, Hankyu and American Express travel services
membership of Okura International Club (in return for showing your loyalty by staying serveral times) brings priority in room booking, even at peak times, simplified checking in/out procedures.
7 restaurants (including one Chinese, one Japanese)
5 bars and lounges
banquet rooms: Heian (1500 buffet-style, 800 seated) with full international conference facilities, simultaneous translation
Akebono (1200 buffet-style, 600 seated), latest acoustics and lighting devices (situated in extension, opened November 1973) 35 other meeting/banquet rooms
7 parking for 1000 cars

8 tariff (from October 1973):

single	yen 4200 upwards
studio twin	yen 5900–8600
double	yen 8600–9900
superior twin	yen 8400–9900
semi-suite	yen 14,500
suite	yen 22,000 upwards

(suite can be used for conferences, etc: sitting-room has chairs for six, tables and desks can be moved in, and there is a refrigerator and mini-kitchen for refreshments and drinks)
all rooms have private bath/shower, radio, colour TV, telephone, air-conditioning/heating
meals: breakfast yen 800 (continental yen 500), lunch yen 2200, dinner yen 3000

Imperial Hotel

1 1–1 Uchisaiwaicho, 1-chome, Chiyoda-ku, Tokyo
2 504 1111
3 Impho Tokyo
4 Tokyo 2222346
5 five minutes by taxi Tokyo Station or Marunouchi business area. Ginza shopping and entertainment area and some business head offices (including air lines)–walking distance. 20–25 minutes Haneda Airport (in normal traffic conditions); yen 1500 by taxi (including yen 200 expressway toll)
6 1300 guest rooms
40 shops in one of the largest hotel arcades
barber, beauty parlour
doctor's clinic and dentist in attendance
no swimming pool
secretarial, translation, etc. facilities available at Nagashima Associates, in one of hotel's shops and offices
limousine service, with English-speaking chauffeurs
post office, packing and shipping services
JAL, Lufthansa, North-West Airlines, National
American Express, Fuji Tours International, JTB, Fujita Travel Service, Travel Centre of Japan
9 restaurants (including two Japanese and one Chinese)
5 bars and lounges
convention and banqueting facilities:
Peacock (2000 banquet style, 3500 cocktail, 2400 theatre)
Fuji (800 banquet, 1500 cocktail, 1200 theatre)
Sakura (180 banquet, 300 cocktail, 350 theatre)
(see below for specimen charges)
Fuji International Convention Hall–'the best facilities in the Orient'–has recording control room, 6 booths for simultaneous translation, BGM and TV relay equipment, ITV, etc. Fuji and Peacock Halls can be used for banquet/convention simultaneously. 40 other reception, conference, etc. rooms

7 parking for 700 cars
8 tariff (effective March 1974):

	East Building	Main Building	Tower
single	yen 5000	yen 7500	yen 8500
double	yen 7000	yen 12,500	yen 12,500
twin	yen 7000–7500	yen 9500 to yen 15,000	yen 12,500 to yen 15,000
suite	yen 13,000	yen 18,000 to yen 28,000	yen 20,000 to yen 48,000

presidential suites (monthly rates) yen 300,000, 450,000, 540,000 and up to 1,200,000

meal tariff (1 March 1974 to 28 February 1975):

breakfast	yen 900	(coffee house yen 600, continental yen 800):
lunch	yen 2500	(coffee house yen 1800)
dinner	yen 3000	(coffee house yen 2300)

specimen charges for meals, refreshments etc. for conventions, banquets etc. (for a minimum of 20 persons)

cocktail	yen 2000	per person upwards (food only)
buffet	yen 3500	
lunch	yen 3000	
dinner	yen 3500	

Palace Hotel

1 1–1 Marunouchi, 1-chome, Tokyo 100
2 211 5211
3 Palacehotel Tokyo
4 222 2580
5 2–3 minutes Tokyo Station; 20–25 minutes Haneda Airport (in normal traffic conditions), yen 1500, including expressway toll. Especially handy for banking and finance-house head offices
6 407 guest rooms
good arcade, with 20 shops
barber, beauty parlour, turkish bath
doctor on duty 24 hours
interpreting, secretarial, translation, etc. facilities through ISS (see p. 309)
typewriter rental
hotel hire-car service with English-speaking chauffeurs
JAL, Varig, China Air Lines, Mexican Air Lines, Arabia Air Lines
JTB
6 restaurants, including:
Crown (roof floor) 3 bars, 2 lounges
Rose Room (3500 cocktail style, 1000 dinner style)
Cherry Room, with international conference facilities, seating for 400
17 other banquet/conference rooms
high reputation as a meeting place for lunch
7 adequate car parking

8 tariff (from 1 January 1974):

single yen 6000
regular twin yen 9400 (with alcove dressing-room in bathroom entrance)
deluxe twin yen 15,000
suite yen 30,000 (facilities for small conference, mini-kitchen, etc.)

rooms are spacious, and a special feature of the Palace is wide, 'semi-double' beds

Tokyo Hilton

1 10–3 Nagatacho 2-chome, Chiyoda-ku, Tokyo
2 581 4511
3 Hiltels Tokyo
4 222 3605
5 Tokyo Station 8–9 minutes; Haneda Airport 25–30 minutes (in normal traffic conditions). Well situated for US Embassy, Japanese Foreign Ministry and MITI
6 478 guest rooms
arcade
swimming pool in summer season; steam bath; good traditional garden; interpretation, translation, etc. through ISS desk (see p. 309) on reception floor
free typewriter loan facilities (hotel)
JAL
JTB, American Express
2 restaurants (one Japanese), including lunch-time 'Viking' service; cocktail and tea lounge; bar
Pearl Ballroom, with permanent stage (Hilton and Keio Plaza alone have this facility); 850 conference or banquet style, 1200 cocktail, 1500 meeting style; no permanent audio-visual facilities etc., but hotel will hire in
Silver Room, 130 cocktail, 100 banquet style
7 other banquet/conference rooms
7 adequate car parking
8 tariff (January to December 1974):

single yen 7600, 8000, 8600 (traditional Japanese screen partitions are part of decor; rooms larger than average)
standard twin yen 8000 single, yen 9200 double
studio twin yen 8600 single, yen 9800 double
corner suite yen 26,000 (spacious living-room has sofas, chairs, desk, table; mini-kitchen and bar, twin bedroom)

Tokyo Prince Hotel

1 3–3–1 Shiba Koen, 3-gochi Minato-ku, Tokyo 105
2 434 4221
3 Hotelprince Tokyo
4 242 2488
5 five minutes downtown Tokyo; 25–30 minutes Haneda Airport (in normal traffic conditions)

6 510 rooms
arcade with large number of shops, some specialising in a wide variety of imported luxury and high-quality goods
barber, beauty parlour
swimming pool (open-air, summer season only)
interpreter, translation, secretarial, etc. facilities through ISS, arranged by hotel (see p. 309) free typewriter service in some rooms and suites
7 restaurants (including two Japanese, one Chinese, one 'Viking')
2 bars, coffee shop
Providence Hall, for conference/banquet, seating up to 2000 conference style; excellent international conference facilities and equipment. Sunflower and Magnolia Halls (combined capacity up to 3000 conference style)
Camellia Hall and 30 other private conference/banquet rooms
7 parking for 1000 cars
8 tariff
wide 'semi-double' beds are a feature of all rooms
deluxe single yen 6000–6500
standard twin yen 7000–7500
deluxe twin yen 8000–9500
business suite yen 25,000 (double occupancy): large sitting-room, large bedroom and two bathrooms.

Keio Plaza Hotel

1 2–1, Nishi Shinjuku 2-chome, Shinjuku-ku, Tokyo 160
2 344 0111
3 Keioplatel, Tokyo
4 J 26874
5 Tokyo Station area 20 minutes (costing about yen 1200 by taxi, including expressway toll) Haneda Airport, 25–30 minutes
Very close to the centre of the Shinjuku area (department stores, other shopping, night life). Shinjuku is a growing business area, and Keio Plaza Hotel is part of a whole new complex, with additional restaurants and facilities in other new buildings in the complex.
6 47 floors, yet well planned for swift movement within the building (25 elevators)
1057 guest rooms
arcade, including Keio department store branch
barber and beauty parlour
dental clinic, house doctor
open-air swimming pool (summer only), sauna, massage
ISS service (for interpretation, secretary, translation, copying, guide, etc. facilities)
hotel typewriter loan
airline and travel offices
hotel hire-car service
10 restaurants (including one Chinese, three Japanese)
coffee shop, with good major snack meals, open 24 hours a day all week

9 bars and lounges
Convention Hall, (Concord), 3000 cocktail style, 2000 theatre style, 1800 conference style, and 1500 dinner style (see below for further particulars)
12 executive banquet rooms and 11 party rooms (42nd–43rd floors)
7 parking for 800 cars
8 tariff for 1974:

economy yen 5500–6500 single, yen 6500–7000 double
standard yen 7500–8000 single, yen 8000–9000 double
deluxe yen 9500–11,000 single, yen 11,000–12,000 double

every room has outfacing windows (the building is a thin skyscraper), and all rooms are air-conditioned, with colour TV, private bath and shower, etc.
deluxe suite (in three sections–office, sitting room, bedroom–with two bathrooms) yen 25,000.

Specimen convention and banqueting room charges:
Concord (maximum cover 3000 persons) can be sectioned off into three rooms: whole day (9.0 a.m. to 9.0 p.m.) yen 1,500,000, meeting, first two hours yen 300,000, additional time, yen 150,000 per hour, waiting use yen 150,000 per hour
Hana (banqueting/conference room, maximum cover 800 persons) whole day (9.0 a.m. to 9.0 p.m.) yen 800,000, meeting, first two hours yen 150,000, additional time yen 80,000 per hour, waiting use yen 80,000 per hour
smaller banquet/conference room, maximum cover 50 persons whole day (9.0 a.m. to 9.0 p.m.) yen 150,000, meeting, first two hours yen 30,000, additional time yen 15,000 per hour, waiting use yen 15,000 per hour
banquet/conference meal charges:

breakfast yen 750 }
lunch yen 3000 } and upwards
dinner yen 4000 }

cocktail party charges: yen 3500 per person, based on local drinks, bar open for one hour, three glasses per person average, and selection of hot and cold hors d'oeuvres
yen 4500 per person, imported drinks, same average intake, same food snacks
prices for cocktail party include room charge, flower arrangements, etc.; add 10 per cent service charge, 10 per cent tax

Hotel New Otani

1 Kioicho, Chiyoda-ku, Tokyo
2 265 1111
3 Hotelnewotani, Tokyo
4 Htlotani 124719

5 10 minutes Tokyo Station and business centre; 25 minutes Haneda Airport; 5 minutes Akasaka and Government office areas; also convenient for Shinjuku area (shopping, night life)
6 2100 guest rooms

Fuyo Hall	2800 theatre style	1500 dinner	3000 cocktail style
Kiri	450 theatre	260 dinner	360 cocktail
Katsura	210 theatre	120 dinner	180 cocktail

and 18 other banquet, etc. rooms
Fuyo is equipped with international conference facilities, 6-channel simultaneous interpretation, complete AVF, etc.
7 restaurants (including one Japanese, one Chinese)
17th floor revolving lounge (cocktails, buffet, etc.) with magnificent views
and two other bar/lounges
arcade with 26 shops, including branches of Takashimaya and Matsuya department stores
dental clinic, beauty salon, barber, baby-minding room, steam bath
ISS desk for interpretation, translation, photocopying, typewriter rental, etc.
indoor swimming pool, health club
7 parking for 800 cars in banquet car park
8 2100 guest rooms, including new Tower Block, opening 1 September 1974 (1000 Tower Block, 1100 main building)
Tower Block is designed to include a family floor, ladies' floor, executive floor, etc. (executive floor facilities include quiet, jack telephones, special lighting, wide desk-tables, magic-eye security)
residential floor for longer-term residents
tariff (no inside rooms, always a view, all rooms with private bath/shower, colour TV, radio) January to December 1974:

single yen 5200 single and sofa yen 7600 double yen 7500 up
twin yen 8200 up semi-suite yen 18,000 up luxury suite yen 50,000
table d'hôte meal tariff:
breakfast yen 900 lunch yen 1800–2500 dinner yen 2500–3500

Tower Block (opening September 1974):
40 floors (40th floor, Sky Restaurant)
7th to 39th floor, guest rooms
6th floor, lobby, main dining-room, bar, lounge
5th floor, banqueting rooms
4th floor, Trader Vic's restaurant
2nd and 3rd floors, sports, swimming pool, etc.
1st floor, shops, snack bar

Hotel New Japan

1 13–8, Nagatacho, 2-chome, Chiyoda-ku, Tokyo 100
2 581 5511
3 Hotelnewjapan
4 NEW JAN J2 2499 (domestic: 222 2422)

5 Tokyo Station 8–10 minutes, Haneda Airport 25 minutes; very convenient (walking) for Akasaka–bars, clubs, shopping, and for US Embassy, main government offices
6 Main banqueting hall, cocktail style 1000, conference style 450–500, no in-house simultaneous interpretation, etc. facilities, but can be ordered in without difficulty
7 restaurants (including one Chinese, two Japanese and one Polynesian)
coffee shop, lounge, bars
arcade with 20 shops
packing service
free hotel typewriter loan
JAL
JTB
7 small car park
8 506 rooms (including 100 apartments)
tariff (1974):

single yen 4400–4500 (quite narrow and small accommodation)
twin yen 6300–6800 (single *or* double occupancy)
standard twin (semi-double beds) yen 7000 (single or double)
de luxe twin yen 10,000 upwards
suite for two (twin bedroom, separate sitting-room) yen 20,000
apartment for long-term guests (not less than 6 months) in seven different classes and sizes:
from yen 185,000 per month standard twin with kitchen (one room, including heat, cooking, etc. but not cleaning), to yen 400,000 per month (three-room suite)

all rooms have air-conditioning, bath, radio, TV, etc.
specimen business lunch in Grill Villa (yen 600):
choice of sea food or pork and green vegetables
tossed green salad and French dressing
ice cream
roll and butter or rice
coffee

Takanawa Prince Hotel

1 3–13–1 Takanawa, Minato-ku, Tokyo
2 445 5311
3 Prinsotel Tokyo
4 242 3232
5 Situation near Shinagawa (5 minutes walk to Shinagawa station, with direct suburban trains 12 minutes to Tokyo station), about midway between central Tokyo (20 minutes) and Haneda airport (15–20 minutes); not as convenient as more central hotels for business and government offices
6 Excellent conference/banquet facilities
6 restaurants (four specializing in Japanese food) plus a tea salon serving all the world's teas and coffee shop
7 Adequate parking

8 tariff (1974):

single yen 4000–5500
twin yen 7300–9500
double yen 7300–8300
group rate: single yen 4800, twin yen 6000–6500
no group meal rates
breakfast yen 500–900, lunch yen 2000, dinner yen 2500–3000

Information (*research and contacts*)
Preparatory reading at home before you leave is a must. The Marketing Series published by JETRO makes very useful supplementary reading. A growing list of books giving a broad background picture of Japanese society and history is now available–any of which will help to put Japanese business practices in their proper context. (See Bibliography, p. 338.)

For more specific sources of information for the businessman see Appendix 4 p. 337.

Whether or not you already possess contacts in Japan, and however small your operation may seem, it is always advisable to inform your Embassy (Commercial Section) in Tokyo well in advance of your visit. Requests for suitable contacts or advice (in the case of Britain channelled through the special Japan Export Unit office in the DTI) are often quite productive. (See page 332 for addresses and Tokyo telephone numbers of the main western Embassies.) In Japan the role of go-between that an Embassy official can play is a point not to be missed; he has his network of contacts and can achieve results through a mutual third-party connection in the intricate web of interlocking relationships within the Japanese business world.

Interpreters/translators
For interpreting, secretarial, translation facilities, etc., there are several specialist bureaux. International Secretarial Services (ISS) has desks on the reception floor of several of the major hotels (New Otani, Hilton, Keio Plaza, etc.) and Nagashima Associates has an office at the side of the Imperial Hotel. (*Note*: the price of such services in Japan is very high indeed.) If you are in touch with your Embassy, it might be as well to inquire whether the Commercial section can put you in touch with a specialist agency catering for such requests in your particular sector of industry or business.

Kyoto
The capital of Japan until 1868 and still the cultural capital. It was founded in A.D. 794 on the classical Chinese model and has over 600 shrines, 1400 temples (some impressive Zen temples) and innumerable Japanese gardens. It is full of historic buildings and has a calm, old-world atmosphere in marked contrast to Tokyo. A convenient base for visits to Osaka, Kobe and Nara.
Airport: Osaka International. Tel: (068) 56 7033 (international) or (068) 56 7022 (domestic)

Hotels:
Hotel Fujita, Kamo Riverside, Nijo Kyoto (Tel: 222 1511).
Kyoto Hotel, Kawaramachi Oike, Nakagyo-ku (Tel: 211 5111).
Miyako Hotel, Sanjo-Keage (Tel: 771 7111).
Kyoto Grand Hotel, Horikawa-Shionokoji, Shimogyo-ku (Tel: 341 2311).
International Hotel, 284 Nijo Aburanokoji, Nakagyo-ku (Tel: 222 1111).
Nara Hotel, 1096 Takabatake-cho, Nara-shi (Tel: (0742) 23 4101).
All leading hotels have English-speaking doctors and dentists on call, and will advise on churches, theatres and hospitals etc.

Language

On the whole the Japanese, like the English, are poor speakers of languages other than their own. However, it is more than likely that many of the people you meet will be able to read and write English much better than they can speak it; so when in difficulties, do attempt to write down the word or phrase which you cannot communicate verbally.

English has always been the second language in Japanese schools so that everyone has at least been exposed to it; and there are a great many 'English hours' on most of the television and radio channels.

The main hotels provide efficient spoken English at all service levels, including the reception desks, restaurants, bars and telephone switchboard. But very few Japanese speak or understand French, German or other European languages.

There are three English-language dailies–*The Japan Times*, *The Mainichi Daily News* and *The Yomiuri News*–and one evening paper, *The Asahi Evening News*. Most hotels deliver a free copy of one of the morning papers under your bedroom door. But there are no foreign-language papers other than English, and western dailies arrive at least three or four days after the date of publication.

Almost all English and other foreign language programmes on Japanese radio and television are educational and aimed at the Japanese audience. But the American Forces Network (which can be received all over Japan) broadcasts regular news programmes and also provides first-class coverage at times of emergency–as when, for example, a typhoon is in the area.

Most public places are furnished with adequate English language directions and signposts. Most stations used regularly by foreigners provide English as well as Japanese directions. On the roads and railways, place names are often written in Roman letters as well as Japanese characters.

At business discussions, your Japanese counterparts will usually bring in a member of their staff whose English is adequate for interpretation. You would probably do best to use him too, even though you feel that your own interests may not be represented fully and to your best advantage. (When you have yourself faced the problems of finding reliable and swift translation facilities, secretaries capable of working in English and other foreign languages, and so on, you will readily realize the problems facing the Japanese businessman in getting off prompt replies in English. And remember how hard it would be for you to conduct anything like a regular correspondence in Japanese!)

There is no doubt that the language barrier constitutes a major hurdle, and that very little can be done about it. It would cost you two years at least of hard study to be able to read or discuss your own particular business matters (and precious little else) in Japanese. But if you take the trouble to learn just half a dozen greetings or polite phrases, the acknowledgement you get will make the trouble you went to worth while. Do make sure you get the pronunciation and lilt correct–listen and practise for a day or two. And if you have no ear for language, let well alone!

Name cards (*visiting cards*)

Cards should have English on one side and a Japanese translation on the reverse. Arrangements should be made well ahead for visiting cards to be printed and prepared for your arrival in Japan. It now takes about five days even for a rush job in Japan, and in those first five days it is essential for you to have a stock of cards to swop with all the new contacts that you make. This is so that not only can they have a written record of your name and firm, but also they can understand the slot you occupy in your organization. This will help your opposite number to deal with you at the equivalent and appropriate level. You will soon learn how important 'level' is in Japan: it is essential for a Japanese to be able to 'place' anyone he is dealing with.

It thus becomes more than a matter of academic accuracy that your title be properly translated into the appropriate Japanese term. Japan Air Lines offer a card service, with delivery to your hotel ready for your arrival. To be on the safe side allow for a hundred cards a week, and order accordingly. Remember that your visiting card is your first personal link with a Japanese: it will remain an important reference for him long after you have gone.

Some time each day try to put your collection in order, with notes about each card-owner either on the card itself or in a special booklet; you will be very pleased you took the trouble after you return home. Name cards are also invaluable as repositories of telephone numbers that no hotel operator can find for you, and they will often come in useful as guides for hotel porters and taxi drivers if you are visiting the office shown in the address. While in Japan try and purchase name card holders–a small album in which you can slot all those you receive.

The name card–your own, the hotel's, that of the person or the business you are to visit–often helps to solve the language problem. If you have to visit an address quite unknown to you, for instance, show the card at the hotel reception desk (or, if you have no card, PRINT the address) and ask the hotel porter to be informed. He will then pass on the information to the taxi driver–and you may be lucky enough to find one who knows his Tokyo fairly well. But do not expect anything like 100 per cent success, for Tokyo addresses frequently fox even seasoned Tokyo drivers.

National holidays

1 January	New Years Day (with most businesses closed until 4 or 5 January)
15 January	Adults Day
11 February	National Foundation Day
21 March	Vernal Equinox Day
29 April	Emperor's Birthday
3 May	Constitution Day
5 May	Children's Day
mid-August	*Bon*
15 September	Respect for the Aged Day
23 September	Autumnal Equinox Day
10 October	Physical Culture Day
3 November	Culture Day
23 November	Labour Thanksgiving Day

With three national days in the week, the period from 29 April–5 May (called 'Golden Week') usually becomes a continuous holiday. (Note: if a national holiday falls on a Sunday, the holiday is automatically transferred to the Monday.)

In addition, the Japanese do quite a lot of travelling and sightseeing during the cherry-blossom and autumn-leaf seasons. These vary according to the area and the weather, but are usually at the start of April and November.

Night life

Bars in the Ginza and other central areas usually open at 6.00 or thereabouts and close at 11.00. In Shinjuku, Shibuya and other centres, bars often remain open until 2.00 a.m. Clubs usually close at 11.00 or 11.30. Perhaps the single most important thing to say about this subject is that Japanese night life is largely geared to business expense-account budgets, which are phenomenally high by western standards.

Office hours

Most offices are open from 9.00 or 9.30 to 5.00 or 5.30. The tradition is a $5\frac{1}{2}$ or $5\frac{3}{4}$ day week, though more and more businesses are moving over to a 5 day week norm (especially on the production side). But do not forget the *kaigi*–the conference–and its integral part in Japanese business life. Conferences in Japan seem interminable, and one follows another in rapid succession. If the man you want on the phone is a middle-ranking executive, he will start the conference soon after he gets to the office, so try hard to get him between 9.15 and 9.40. After that the reply will be, 'His seat is vacant for a while'. It is not that you are being put off, just that this pressing need to relate with colleagues in conference is a root fact of Japanese business life. Unless a Japanese businessman is right at the top, he is not served by a personal secretary who will take messages and make sure there is a reply. But just keep trying!

Osaka
The second largest city in Japan, predominantly industrial and commercial.
Airport: Osaka International. Tel: (068) 56 7033 (international) or (068) 56 7022 (domestic)
Hotels:
The Plaza Hotel, 2-2 Minami, Oyodo, Oyodo-ku (Tel: 453 1111).
Osaka Grand Hotel, 22, 2-chome, Nakanoshima, Kita-ku (Tel: 202 1212).
Osaka Royal Hotel, 1, 2-chome, Tamae-cho, Kita-ku (Tel: 448 1121).
Toyo Hotel, 1-21 Toyosaki-Nishidori, Oyodo-ku (Tel: 372 8181).

Presents
At certain times of the year (New Year and midsummer, for instance) it seems as if everyone in Japan is giving and receiving presents. Present giving plays an important part in business etiquette, and you will almost certainly be on the receiving end from those with whom you already have an association or those whom you have arranged to meet. So it is as well to go prepared.

You will probably never be able to match your Japanese host's presents in value, so you should try to show that, before you left home, you *bothered*, you thought about a suitable present. If your home town or area produces something typical or well known, this would be very suitable. (In the same way, the Japanese often proudly give their local *meibutsu* – special product.)

Now that Japanese taste has extended to all manner of European antiques or *objets*, there is a wide variety of suitable and acceptable presents, such as pottery, glass or prints.

Full use can be made as presents of the duty-free allowance on entry into Japan of three bottles of spirits. Quality blended whisky, malt whisky and brandy are still eminently acceptable to most Japanese, although sophisticates would be flattered to receive a gift of fine wines. The accent is firmly on luxury.

Shopping
The leading hotels in Tokyo, Kyoto, Osaka, etc. have shopping arcades, with an average of twenty stores, often including a branch of a department store (Takashimaya in Hotel Okura and New Otani, Keio in Keio Plaza, for instance). In the larger arcades, there is usually at least one store which covers the majority of items on the list below.

In addition, in Tokyo, Sukiyabashi Shopping Centre, International Arcade and Nishi Ginza Electric Centre (all between Imperial Hotel and Yurakucho Street) offer tax-free items and are geared for foreign shoppers. There is a growing number of arcades in new office blocks (Kasumigaseki Building, Nikkatsu, etc).

In Kyoto, much of your souvenir hunting can be concentrated in the area around Kawaramachi between Sanjo and Shijo.

Back in Tokyo, there are department stores in the main shopping centres of Ginza, Shinjuku and Shibuya. Department stores have floor plans in English and assistants and information counters to cope with language problems. They offer an extensive range of goods and have money-changing facilities.

Some arcade shops may offer a discount, particularly if you make a return visit; department and other large stores work on fixed prices, *sometimes higher than the smaller, specialist stores.*

Many items (pearls, etc. over approximately yen 20,000, and electronic items) are sold tax-free to foreign tourists or businessmen on short visits, on production of a passport. A certificate of tax-free purchase is issued and attached to your passport: it must be surrendered to customs on exit from Japan, when you will also be asked to produce the tax-free item in question (so do not pack it in checked luggage). Arcades, department stores, etc. sell electronic models adaptable to European and US voltages. Although prices are considerably cheaper in the Akihabara area in Tokyo, for instance, where you find row after row of electronic and electrical stores, models are often obsolescent and you may find that you have bought a domestic (and therefore unadaptable) model.

Main Department Stores

Tokyo	*Ginza* area: Matsuya, Matsuzakaya, Sogo, Wako
	Nihombashi area: Mitsukoshi, Tokyu, Takashimaya
	Shinjuku area: Isetan, Keio, Odakyu
	Shibuya area: Tokyu
	Tokyo Station: Daimaru
Kyoto	Daimaru, Fuji-Daimaru, Marubutsu, Takashimaya
Osaka	Daimaru, Hankyu, Hanshin, Kintetsu, Mitsukoshi, Matsuzakaya, Sogo, Takashimaya
Nagoya	Matsuzakaya, Meitetsu

Almost all department stores are open on Sunday. (Wako, a very high quality store, is one of the few exceptions.) Opening hours of department stores, arcades, etc. are usually 10.00 a.m. to 6.00 p.m. Closing day is staggered between department stores in a particular area. (See also below, 'Souvenirs'.)

Souvenirs

Among the best and most popular buys are:

pearls and other jewellery and accessories; bracelets, ear-rings, chokers, strings, brooches, etc; and for men, cuff-links and tie-pins
silk by the yard (there is nearly always a sale somewhere, with good reductions)
purses, handbags, scarves, shirts and pyjamas
kimono, happi coats
fans
umbrellas
wood-block prints, antique and modern; also attractive as Christmas and greeting cards and calendars

pottery (including a wide selection of modern folk)
bamboo ware
lacquer ware, including trays
ivory, coral
dolls (in plastic cases–the apocryphal last-minute airport present)
tea ceremony bowls and kits
flower arrangement kits
origami kits (paper and explanatory books)
photograph albums
cameras, still and cine
projectors
binoculars
microscopes
transistor radios
televisions, portable etc., black and white, colour
tape recorders
record players
stereo equipment
watches and clocks

(See also previous section, 'Shopping'.)

Taxis

Taxis can in most cases be recognised by the garish colouring of the car body and the roof lamps which advertise the company name. The 'free' sign is in red, in front of the passenger seat. There is usually a line of taxis at the rank at the main hotels, the airport, terminal stations, etc. Taxis can also be flagged down on the streets, but empty taxis cannot always be relied on to stop.

If you are starting from your hotel travelling alone, and do not know the route to your destination, ask the local hotel enquiry desk to write it in Japanese and have the door porter explain it to the driver.

There are some taxi drivers who are newcomers to Tokyo; they may be more recent arrivals than you, and do not even know basic landmarks such as the Imperial or Okura Hotels, Tokyo Station, the Central Post Office, etc.

If you have the choice, travel with an owner driver (*kojin* in Japanese). His sign is two characters, black on a green/yellow background on the taxi roof, and the colours of his car body are more subdued than the company fleets. He does not wish to die either!

All taxis have automatically-opening rear nearside doors. Remember not to try to close the door behind you when you get in or out. There are no extras for additional passengers (normally up to four passengers are accepted) and there is no tipping. There is a 20 per cent surcharge (at least) after midnight.

Late at night, particularly in the Ginza and Akasaka bar and club areas, you may be asked exorbitant fares and find that drivers are reluctant to accept any but long journeys. Try to establish, before you start such late night journeys, that you will be charged only the meter figure and legitimate extras. If you cannot be sure, get out and try again. As a last resort, flag the driver down with two or three fingers raised, indicating that you are willing to pay twice or three times the normal fare.

In Tokyo, traffic is usually exceptionally heavy and taxis are difficult to find:

1 from 11.00 p.m. onwards, particularly in the entertainment areas
2 in rainy weather
3 on dates which include five (i.e. 5th, 15th, 25th) which by tradition are the dates when accounts are closed
4 on wage day (25th–27th of the month)
5 at the summer and winter bonus seasons (mid-June to mid-July and December).

Carry an hotel card in Japanese for an easy return home. And, as may well happen in the suburbs, if the driver loses his way, telephone (or ask him to telephone–*denwa* is the word) your destination from a call-box, to receive directions.

Fares:

Basic yen 220 in Tokyo for the first 2 km., and yen 30 for each additional 435 metres (or 150 seconds). (An increase in fares is expected in 1974.)

Telephone calls

Japan has an all-figure dialling system. Public coin boxes (near the door in many shops, stores and restaurants) can be used for local calls–yen 10 for three minutes. Place the yen 10 coin in the slot before dialling. Coin boxes cut out with little or no warning and cannot be re-fed. For long distance domestic calls it is better to use a private telephone, as coin boxes feed insatiably on yen 10 or yen 100 pieces.

There is a variety of international telephone services, including person to person (to a named individual) and station (to a specific phone number); the station call is cheaper, and adequate for most purposes. There are also collect (reverse charge) and credit services to most parts of the world. Check prices from your home country before your departure, as it often turns out (as with the UK for instance) that it is cheaper to place a call collect.

The hotel's telephone operator will book international calls from your room (with a 10 per cent handling charge added).

From central Tokyo (not coin boxes) dial 109 for international calls.

Specimen charges: Tokyo to Hawaii and North America, person to person, yen 4320 for first three minutes: station to station, yen 3240 for first three minutes; Tokyo to Europe, yen 4300 to 4500 for first three minutes.

Time

GMT plus nine hours.

Tipping

Almost totally unknown as service is invariably included and the concept is alien to Japanese society. Between 10 and 15 per cent will be added to all hotel, restaurant and nightclub bills in addition to tax.

Tours
Package tours, by bus or by private car, are organised from all the main centres. Examples from Tokyo are a two-day trip to Kyoto and Nara, inclusive, for yen 33,390 (by bus) or yen 57,470 per person (two people sharing a car); or a two-day tour of Kamakura and Hakone for yen 15,400 (by bus) or yen 36,500 per person (two sharing a car).
Hotels will advise on package tours.

Trade organizations (Japanese)

Japan External Trade Organisation: JETRO
Japan Trade Centre, 2 Aoi-cho,
Akasaka, Minato-ku.

Tokyo Chamber of Commerce and Industry
22, Marunouchi, 3-chome Chiyoda-ku.
Telephone 221 4411.

Trains
Japan National Railways (JNR) has a national network covering the four main islands. Various private railways cover smaller areas, both long distance (such as Kyoto to Nagoya) and commuter services. Reservation in advance is advisable on JNR, particularly during the Japanese holiday seasons–the end of December to about 10 January, late April and early May, most of August but particularly 10th–20th, and early November. Tickets are available one week before date of departure and Japan Travel Bureau (JTB) offices have a limited quota of tickets available up to three weeks in advance. Reservations can be made through JTB and other travel agency offices in your hotel. The JTB head office is located in Marunouchi, 4 minutes' walk from Tokyo Station–Marunouchi north exit.

Meals and refreshments are available on most express and all super-express services. The *Shinkansen* (New Trunk Line, or Bullet Train) services all have refreshment-car facilities, buffet style, and snacks are sold throughout the journey by trolley sales-girls. The Japanese always eat early–lunch at 12.00 noon, dinner at about 6.00 p.m.–and, it seems, eat even earlier than usual on trains. Sandwiches, drinks, cigarettes, fruit, etc. are also available from platform vendors at stations (but don't leave the *Shinkansen* en route: stops are rarely more than a minute).

Most notices ('exit', 'tickets', etc.) are duplicated in Japanese and English, and platform indications ('for Nagoya, Tokyo', etc.) make travel comparatively simple. There is also a most useful practice, used almost on the whole network, of indicating the next station in each direction (in both Japanese and Roman script). This also applies to the underground (subway) system.

There are Green Car (first class) services on most trains. There is also a range of supplements, varying with the speed of the train, for ordinary, limited and super-expresses (see table of specimen fares below).

Shinkansen trains run at present from Tokyo to Okayama. The Tokyo-Osaka section was opened just before the Tokyo Olympics in 1964, and the line will go right through to Hakata (Fukuoka) in north Kyushu by December 1974. Coaches are sealed airtight, and are air-conditioned throughout the year; all doors are automatic. The speed is such that, as the train really picks up speed about six miles out of Tokyo, you find yourself reaching involuntarily for your seat belt, ready for take-off! Telephone services to and from the train are available for the main centres en route–Tokyo, Yokohama, Nagoya, Kyoto, Osaka and Okayama. There are taped announcements of stops in English.

The fastest service (called *Hikari)* stops only at Nagoya, Kyoto, Osaka and Okayama and does the 733 km. run in 4 hrs. 10 mins. Other *Hikari* services stop also at Kobe and Himeji (4 hrs. 20 mins. to Okayama). *Kodama,* a slower service, makes 16 stops between Tokyo and Okayama, including (as well as *Hikari* stops) Yokohama, Shizuoka, Hamamatsu, Gifu. Some services terminate at Osaka.

The first Tokyo–Osaka service is at 6.00, Tokyo–Okayama 6.15. There is a half-hourly service to Osaka from 6.00 to 20.30. The last through-service to Okayama departs Tokyo 19.00, arrives Okayama 23.30.

Hiroshima (changing from *Shinkansen* at Okayama) is just over two hours beyond Okayama by ordinary express–a total of 6½ hours from Tokyo. Hakata (Fukuoka) is 10½ hours from Tokyo. (These timings will be drastically reduced by the introduction of the through *Shinkansen* service.) All *Shinkansen* services start from Tokyo (Central) Station.

Going north, from Ueno Station, Sendai is 4 hours, Aomori (for ferry to Hokkaido) is 8 hours, Sapporo is about 18 hours (including 4 hours ferry). Nikko is about 2 hours by JNR from Ueno Station.

Specimen fares quoted below are for ordinary (i.e. second class) seats. There is an additional Green Car (first class) charge, which varies with the distance travelled.

Shinkansen	*fare*	*Kodama supplement*	*Hikari supplement*	*Hikari total*	*Green Car supplements*
Tokyo–Nagoya	1560	1100	1500	3060	1400
Tokyo–Kyoto	2150	1500	1900	4050	2000
Tokyo–Osaka	2230	1500	1900	4130	2000
Tokyo–Okayama	2560	1900	2300	4860	2600

(*Note*: These fares and supplements were current at the time of going to press. Fare increases, between 10 and 20 per cent, are expected to be introduced during 1974.)

Visas

Transit visas are valid for up to 15 days. Tourist visas are valid for 60 days. Visas are not required by:

(*a*) nationals of Argentina, Belgium, Canada, Denmark, Finland, France, Greece, Italy, Luxembourg, Netherlands, Norway, Pakistan, Spain, Sweden, Tunisia and Turkey, for periods up to three months;

(*b*) nationals of Austria, Switzerland, United Kingdom, Ireland and West Germany, for periods up to 180 days.

All other nationalities must apply for a visa.

All visitors who stay in Japan for more than 60 days *must* register with the Municipal Office of the district of residence (e.g. Ward-*ku*-office in Tokyo).

An alien registration card will be issued which is surrendered on exit.

Appendix 1

JAPANESE TRADING COMPANIES

Below, shown alphabetically, is the complete members' list of the **Japan General Merchandise Importers' Association** (a member of the Japan Federation of Importers' organizations), which was established in May 1971 with the immediate aim of promoting import trade.
For further details see *Japan Trade Index* or write to:
Japan General Merchandise Importers' Association
World Trade Centre Building
4–1, Hamamatsu-cho 2-chome, Minato-ku, Tokyo 105, Japan

Ace Co.
58, Bakurocho 5-chome, Higashi-ku, Osaka
Alaska Umbrella Co., Ltd
8, Takaida-hondori 6-chome, Higashi–Osaka, Osaka
Apollo Trading Co., Ltd
Nihon Bldg, 79 Kyomachi, Ikuta-ku, Kobe
Arai & Co., Inc.
14, Kandacho 1-chome, Chigusa-ku, Nagoya
Seitaro Arai & Co., Ltd
8, Onoecho 1-chome, Naka-ku, Yokohama
The Asadashin Co., Ltd
1, Shinden–Asahimachi, Daito, Osaka
Asahi Corporation
4–5, Hirakawacho 2-chome, Chiyoda-ku, Tokyo
Asahi Mats Co., Ltd
4–3, Ninomiyacho 4-chome, Fukiai-ku, Kobe
Asian Mercantile & Co., Ltd
Kyodo Ginza Bldg, 3–19, Hamadacho 3-chome, Nada-ku, Kobe
Associated Lumber & Trading Co., Ltd
Furukawa Bldg, 8, Nihonbashi–Muromachi 2-chome, Chuo-ku, Tokyo
Associated Merchandise Co., Inc.
Ginyu Bldg, 13–12, Ginza 1-chome, Chuo-ku, Tokyo
Aurora Famous Sales
88, Motomachidori 3-chome, Ikuta-ku, Kobe

Bergman & Co.
Chartered Bank Bldg, 9–2, Kaigandori, Ikuta-ku, Kobe

Carbatex International Ltd
1–1, Izumidori 5-chome, Nada-ku, Kobe

T. Chatani & Co., Ltd
Sanwa Bldg, 55, Kawaracho 2-chome, Higashi-ku, Osaka
Cosmos Products Co.
6–10, Mita 1-chome, Minato-ku, Tokyo

Daimaru Kogyo Kaisha Ltd
Konoike Bldg, 27, Kita-Kyuhojicho 4-chome, Higashi-ku, Osaka
Daimyo Bussan Co., Ltd
40, Sakaemachi 2-chome, Ikuta-ku, Kobe
Dainan Kooshi Ltd
1–1, Otemachi 2-chome, Chiyoda-ku, Tokyo
Daisho Co., Ltd
9, Uchiawajicho 2-chome, Higashi-ku, Osaka
Daishowa Sangyo Co., Ltd
Tsuchiya Bldg, 8, Takaracho 1-chome, Chuo-ku, Tokyo
Duco Company Ltd
Idachu Bldg, 8, Takaracho 1-chome, Chuo-ku, Tokyo

Echo Trading Co., Ltd
Onozuka Bldg, 25, Kanda-Sudacho 2-chome, Chiyoda-ku, Tokyo
Empire Trading Co. (Tokyo)
Shin-Tokyo Bldg, 2, Marunouchi 3-chome, Chiyoda-ku, Tokyo
Ezaki Bamboo Inc.
2–5, Shimoyamatedori 3-chome, Ikuta-ku, Kobe

Fuji Industries Co., Ltd
Meikai Bldg, 32, Akashimachi, Ikuta-ku, Kobe
Fumi Trading Co. Ltd
7, Kyobashi 1-chome, Higashi-ku, Osaka
Futagawa Kaisha Ltd
37, Kita-Kyuhojicho 4-chome, Higashi-ku, Osaka

Gepe Trading Co., Ltd
13, Awazakamidori 2-chome, Nishi-ku, Osaka
Gitokin Company
Shin-Matsuoka Bldg, 27, Awazakamidori 1-chome, Nishi-ku, Osaka
Gunji Trading Corporation
27, Shimoyamatedori 4-chome, Ikuta-ku, Kobe

Hachiya Brothers
13, Shirakabecho 4-chome, Higashi-ku, Nagoya
Hakko Shoji Co., Ltd
25, Kanamoricho, Chigusa-ku, Nagoya
Hakkoh Co., Ltd
10, Hannancho 3-chome, Abeno-ku, Osaka
Hiraoka & Co., Ltd
Matsuoka Bldg, 70, Kyomachi, Ikuta-ku, Kobe
Z. Horikoshi & Co., Ltd
22–17, Nishi-Gotanda 7-chome, Shinagawa-ku, Tokyo

Ida-Ryogokudo Co., Ltd.
9–2, Asakusabashi 1-chome, Taito-ku, Tokyo
Ideal Co., Ltd
11–15, Misuji 1-chome, Taito-ku, Tokyo
Y. Ikemura & Co., Ltd
1, Kobaicho, Kita-ku, Osaka
K. Inoue Co., Ltd
22, Sannomiyacho 3-chome, Ikuta-ku, Kobe
S. Ishimitsu & Co., Ltd
8, Kotonocho 2-chome, Fukiai-ku, Kobe
C. Itoh & Co., Ltd
68, Kita-Kyutarocho 4-chome, Higashi-ku, Osaka
Iwata Boeki Kabushiki Kaisha
7–1, Isobedori 4-chome, Fukiai-ku, Kobe

Japan Quality Products Co., Ltd
Iino Bldg, 1–1, Uchisaiwaicho 2-chome, Chiyoda-ku, Tokyo
Japan Trading Co., Ltd
16, Nagaheicho 6-chome, Higashi-ku, Nagoya

Kamatani Watt & Co., Ltd
Takasago-Shoko Bldg, 100, Edomachi, Ikuta-ku, Kobe
Kanda Enterprise & Co.
46, Yashiromachi 2-chome, Kita-ku, Nagoya
Kaneroka
2096–1, Dachicho Toki, Gifu
Kashima Trading Co., Ltd
Hasegawa Bldg, 40, Hiranomachi 5-chome, Higashi-ku, Osaka
Kasuga & Co., Ltd
3, Isogamidori 5-chome, Fukiai-ku, Kobe
Katoh & Co., Ltd
Ryoshin Bldg, 221–1, Sasajimamachi 1-chome, Nakamura-ku, Nagoya
Kishi Merchandising Corporation
Nisshin Bldg, 12, Oimatsucho 3-chome, Kita-ku, Osaka
Kobayashi Industrial Co., Ltd
11–35, Minami 5-chome, Tsubame, Niigata
Kobe Taiyo Trading Co., Ltd
Asahi Bldg, 59, Naniwamachi, Ikuta-ku, Kobe
Kokusai Boeki Kaisha Ltd
41–6, Kameido 6-chome, Koto-ku, Tokyo
Kokusai Mingeisha Co., Ltd
1, Kotonocho 5-chome, Fukiai-ku, Kobe
Kongo Lite Works Ltd
1–20, Nishiooi 3-chome, Shinagawa-ku, Tokyo
Koshin Co., Ltd
10–1, Kawarayamachi 3-chome, Minami-ku, Osaka
Kowa Co., Ltd
6–29, Nishiki 3-chome, Naka-ku, Nagoya

O. Kurokawa Umbrella Co., Ltd
Shinya Bldg, 33, Shiamachidori 3-chome, Minami-ku, Osaka
Kyo Trading Co., Ltd
Sanjodori-Jingumichi-Higashi-iru, Higashiyama-ku, Kyoto

Marubeni Corporation
3, Honmachi 3-chome, Higashi-ku, Osaka
Marui Cycle Trading Co., Ltd
45, Motomachidori 4-chome, Ikuta-ku, Kobe
Maruichi Trading Co., Ltd
14–2, Hatazukadori 7-chome, Fukiai-ku, Kobe
Marumatsu & Co., Ltd
71, Kyomachibori 4-chome, Nishi-ku, Osaka
Masudaya Toys Co., Ltd
6–4, Kuramae 2-chome, Taito-ku, Tokyo
Matsui Shoji Co., Ltd
95, Higashiyoshinomachi 1-chome, Higashi-ku, Nagoya
Meiji Seika Kaisha
8, Kyobashi 2-chome, Chuo-ku, Tokyo
Mikasa Trading Co., Ltd
Nihon Bldg, 6–2, Otemachi 2-chome, Chiyoda-ku, Tokyo
Million Trading Co., Ltd
Taniguchi Bldg, 24–8, Asakusabashi 2-chome, Taito-ku, Tokyo
N. Minami & Co., Ltd
95, Hachimandori 5-chome, Fukiai-ku, Kobe
Minami Sangyo Ltd
9–26, Higashishinagawa 4-chome, Shinagawa-ku, Tokyo
Mitsubishi Corporation
6–3, Marunouchi 2-chome, Chiyoda-ku, Tokyo
Mitsuboshi Boeki Ltd
Asahi Bldg, 59, Naniwacho, Ikuta-ku, Kobe
Mitsuboshi Cutlery Co., Ltd
5178, Shimouchi, Seki, Gifu
Mitsugiri Kogyo Co., Ltd
4–13, Kiyosumi 2-chome, Koto-ku, Tokyo
Mitsui Bussan Kaisha Ltd
2–9, Nishishinbashi 1-chome, Minato-ku, Tokyo
Mitsuyu & Co., Ltd
18, Minamihonmachi 1-chome, Higashi-ku, Osaka
Kay Miyazi
Mercantile Bldg, 5–15, Nishiki 1-chome, Naka-ku, Nagoya
Mogi Trading Co., Ltd
Shinsankyo Bldg, 6–7, Kita-Ueno 2-chome, Taito-ku, Tokyo

N & K Co., Inc,
13, Oisodori 3-chome, Minami-ku, Nagoya
D. Nagata Co., Ltd
Sanwa Bldg, 50, Sakaemachidori 2-chome, Ikuta-ku, Kobe

Nakagawa & Co., Inc.
29–7, Yanagibashi 1-chome, Taito-ku, Tokyo
Nanri Trading Co., Ltd
Iimura Bldg, 9–5, Kotobuki 3-chome, Taito-ku, Tokyo
Tsusho Nanri Co., Ltd
6–1, Gokodori 1-chome, Fukiai-ku, Kobe
Nanyo Boeki Co., Ltd
10–21, Marunouchi 3-chome, Naka-ku, Nagoya
Narukawa & Co., Ltd
7–16, Nishiki 2-chome, Naka-ku, Nagoya
New Japan Products Co., Ltd
22–2, Yanagibashi 2-chome, Taito-ku, Tokyo
Nichibo Shoji K.K.
Mizushima Bldg, 2–11, Uchikanda 3-chome, Chiyoda-ku, Tokyo
Nichiyo Trading Co., Ltd
6, Toyosakinishidori 3-chome, Oyodo-ku, Osaka
Nippon Fishing Tackle Co., Ltd
21, Miyamotodori 7-chome, Fukiai-ku, Kobe
Nippon Rubber Co., Ltd
Bridge–Stone Bldg, 1, Kyobashi 1-chome, Chuo-ku, Tokyo
Nippon Trading Co.
Bridge–Stone Bldg, 1, Kyobashi 1-chome, Chuo-ku, Tokyo
Nippon Yo-ko Boeki K.K. (N.Y.K. Trading Co., Ltd)
11, Shindekimachi 1-chome, Higashi-ku, Nagoya
Y. Nishida & Co., Ltd
5, Honcho 1-chome, Naka-ku, Yokohama
Nishimoto Trading Co. Ltd
14, Kaigandori 3-chome, Ikuta-ku, Kobe
Nishizawa Limited
8, Bingocho 3-chome, Higashi-ku, Osaka
Nissho–Iwai Co., Ltd
30, Imabashi 3-chome, Higashi-ku, Osaka
Nosawa & Co., Ltd
Shin–Kokusai Bldg, 4–1, Marunouchi 3-chome, Chiyoda-ku, Tokyo

Okuda Co., Ltd
3, Karaboricho, Tennoji-ku, Osaka
K. Onishi & Co., Ltd
8, Higashikozu-machi 3-chome, Tennoji-ku, Osaka
Ono & Co., Ltd
Asahiseimai Bldg, 9, Imabashi 1-chome, Higashi-ku, Osaka
Oriental Trade Agencies Ltd
Chushin Bldg, 3–5, Uchikanda 3-chome, Chiyoda-ku, Tokyo
Osaka Boeki Kaisha Ltd
Koraibashi–Nomura Bldg, 9, Koraibashi 2-chome, Higashi-ku, Osaka
Ose Boeki Co., Ltd
Daiichi–Kinko Bldg, 1–10, Komagata 1-chome, Taito-ku, Tokyo
Owariya Trading Co., Ltd
60–7, Ozonecho, Higashi-ku, Nagoya

Pentel Company Limited
12, Nihonbashi–Koamicho 2-chome, Chuo-ku, Tokyo
Pink Button Co., Ltd
152, Sannomiyacho 1-chome, Ikuta-ku, Kobe

Royal Praying Co., Ltd
13–14, Kuramae 3-chome, Taito-ku, Tokyo
Royal Trading Co., Ltd
125, Higashiyoshinocho 2-chome, Higashi-ku, Nagoya

Sakai & Co., Ltd
15–7, Kuramae 3-chome, Taito-ku, Tokyo
Sakura Color Products Corporation
10–17, Nakamichi 1-chome, Higashinari-ku, Osaka
Sakurai Co., Ltd
2–7, Komagata 2-chome, Taito-ku, Tokyo
Sanei Sangyo Co., Ltd
Daisen–Shibata Bldg, 20–9, Taito 4-chome, Taito-ku, Tokyo
Sanwa Cutlery Co., Ltd
9–3, Iwamotocho 3-chome, Chiyoda-ku, Tokyo
Sanyei Merchandise Co., Ltd
36–14, Hashiba 1-chome, Taito-ku, Tokyo
Sassa Brothers
18, Maenocho, Higashi-ku, Nagoya
Sato Shoji K. K.
13–10, Hacchobori 1-chome, Chuo-ku, Tokyo
Seki Cutlery Mfg Co., Ltd
Shimomura Bldg, 6, Kyobashi 3-chome, Chuo-ku, Tokyo
Shimoi & Co., Ltd
19, Sagiyama, Naka-ku, Yokohama
Shin Nihon Tsusho Co., Ltd
Nihonbashi Asahiseimei Bldg, 2, Nihonbashidori 2-chome, Chuo-ku, Tokyo
Shinei Kaisha
77–1, Kyomachi, Ikuta-ku, Kobe
Shinko Mengyo Co., Ltd
9, Kawanishidori 5-chome, Nagata-ku, Kobe
Showa Tsusho Co., Ltd
Showa Bldg, 14, Shinsakaemachi 5-chome, Naka-ku, Nagoya
Sudo & Company, Inc.
69, Ozonecho, Higashi-ku, Nagoya
Sugiyama Industrial Co., Ltd
9–14, Minamicho 5-chome, Tsubame, Niigata
Suzuki Trading Co., Ltd
6, Hyankunincho, Higashi-ku, Nagoya

Taikyo Sangyo Co., Ltd
Kezuka Bldg, 27–3, Taito 2-chome, Taito-ku, Tokyo

Taiyo Trading Co., Ltd
Kaigan Bldg, 3, Kaigandori, Ikuta-ku, Kobe
Taiyo Trading Corp.
Kuramae–Kaikan, 1–1, Kuramae 3-chome, Taito-ku, Tokyo
Taiwa Co., Ltd
Towa Bldg, 10, Awajicho 4-chome, Higashi-ku, Osaka
Takasago Shoko Ltd
100, Edomachi, Ikuta-ku, Kobe
Takashimaya Co., Ltd
5, Nihonbashidori 2-chome, Chuo-ku, Tokyo
Takebayashi Trading Co., Ltd
Boeki Bldg, 123–1, Higashimachi, Ikuta-ku, Kobe
Takemura Trading Co., Ltd
Mitsuibussan Bldg, 14, Nihonoodori, Naka-ku, Yokohama
Taki & Co., Ltd
123, Higashimachi, Ikuta-ku, Kobe
Tamasho Kaisha Inc.
16–8, Shioikecho 1-chome, Nakamura-ku, Nagoya
Tamba Trading Co., Ltd
32, Kitanakadori 3-chome, Naka-ku, Yokohama
Tanimura & Co., Ltd
70, Kobaicho, Kita-ku, Osaka
Tashima & Co., Ltd
7, Isobedori 4-chome, Fukiai-ku, Kobe
Tohwa Electric Co., Ltd
3–6, Kitashinagawa 3-chome, Shinagawa-ku, Tokyo
Tojo Electric Co.
13–13, Yagumocho 2-chome, Meguro-ku, Tokyo
Toki Electric Industrial Co., Ltd
2–6, Higashishinagawa 4-chome, Shinagawa-ku, Tokyo
Tokyo Mutual Trading Co., Ltd
11–8, Kanda-Sudacho 2-chome, Chiyoda-ku, Tokyo
Toshoku Ltd
3, Nihonbashi–Muromachi 3-chome, Chuo-ku, Tokyo
Toyo Bussan Co., Ltd
43, Ishiicho 3-chome, Hyogo-ku, Kobe
Toyokawa Denki Co., Ltd
7–15, Higashiooi 4-chome, Shinagawa-ku, Tokyo
Toyoshima & Co., Ltd
14–27, Nishiki 2-chome, Naka-ku, Nagoya
Tozai Electric & Industrial Co., Ltd
P.O. Box 286, Merchandise Mart, Tokyo 141
Tsunoda Trading Co., Ltd
16–3, Kotobuki 3-chome, Taito-ku, Tokyo

United China & Glass Co.
12, Maenocho, Higashi-ku, Nagoya
United Trading Co., Ltd
21–10, Honjo 1-chome, Sumida-ku, Tokyo

Universal Trading Corporation
Tosho Centre, 1–9, Yanagibashi 2-chome, Taito-ku, Tokyo

Wakabayashi Co., Ltd
2–4, Nihonbashi-Bakurocho 2-chome, Chuo-ku, Tokyo
Watanabe Sporting Goods Co., Ltd
30–7, Asakusabashi 3-chome, Taito-ku, Tokyo

Yamanaka Industries Co., Ltd
128, Daikokucho 1-chome, Naniwa-ku, Osaka
Yasuda Import Co., Ltd
22, Sugimuracho 7-chome, Kita-ku, Nagoya
Yoshikawa Seisakusho Co., Ltd
4–10, Hacchobori 2-chome, Chuo-ku, Tokyo
Yutaka Trading Co., Ltd
5, Daikocho 2-chome, Higashi-ku, Nagoya

EUROPEAN TRADING COMPANIES

E. Amram & Sons	French
Caldbeck Macgregor & Co. Ltd (wines and spirits only)	British
Cornes & Co. Ltd	British
C. Correns & Co. Ltd	German
Dodwell & Co. Ltd	British
East Asiatic Co. Ltd	Danish
Gadelius KK	Swedish
Jardine Matheson & Co. Ltd	British
Kjellberg KK	Swedish
Lieberman Waelchi & Co. S. A.	Swiss
Olivier S. A. Compagnie	French
Price Mason & Co. Ltd	British
Siber Hegner & Co. Ltd	Swiss
Soficomex	French
Swire & Maclaine Ltd (associated with Butterfield & Swire Ltd and Swire Mackinnon)	British

Appendix 2

FOREIGN BANKS IN TOKYO

(*Note: this list is not all-inclusive*)

Algemene Bank Nederland N.V.
Fuji Bldg, 2–3, Marunouchi 3-chome, Chiyoda-ku, Tokyo
Allied Bank International
Asahi Tokai Bldg, 6–1, Otemachi 2-chome, Chiyoda-ku, Tokyo
American Express International Banking Corporation
Toranomon Mitsui Bldg, 8–1, Kasumigaseki 3-chome, Chiyoda-ku, Tokyo
Australia & New Zealand Banking Group Ltd
Room 1109, New Yurakucho Bldg, 11 Yurakucho 1-chome, Chiyoda-ku, Tokyo

Banca Commerciale Italiana
Nippon Bldg, Annex 7–1, Otemachi 2-chome, Chiyoda-ku, Tokyo
Banco de Comercio, S.A.
Shin-Kokusai Bldg, No. 8424–1, Marunouchi 3-chome, Chiyoda-ku, Tokyo
Banco di Roma
Joint Representative office Banco di Roma/Commerzbank AG/Credit Lyonnais, Rooms 521–2, Fuji Bldg, 2–3, Marunouchi 3-chome, Chiyoda-ku, Tokyo
Bank of America NT & SA
Sumisho Mitoshiro Bldg, 6th-Floor 1 Mitoshiro-cho, Kanda, Chiyoda-ku, Tokyo
Bank of India
Mitsubishi Denki Bldg, 2–3, Marunouchi 2-chome, Chiyoda-ku, Tokyo
Bank Indonesia
Hibiya Park Bldg, 310 & 311, Yurakucho 1-chome, Chiyoda-ku, Tokyo
The Bank of Korea
Room 611, Hibiya Park Bldg, 1, Yurakucho 1-chome, Chiyoda-ku, Tokyo
Bank of Montreal
Suite 419, New Tokyo Bldg, 3–1, Marunouchi 3-chome, Chiyoda-ku, Tokyo
The Bank of Nova Scotia
Palace Bldg, 1–1, Marunouchi 1-chome, Chiyoda-ku, Tokyo
Banque Française et Italienne pour l'Amerique de Sud S.A.—SUDAMERIS
Nippon Bldg, Annex 7–1, Otemachi 2-chome, Chiyoda-ku, Tokyo

Banque de l'Indochine
French Bank Bldg, 1–2, Akasaka 1-chome, Minato-ku, Tokyo
Banque de l'Union Européenne
Nihon Gas Kyokai Bldg, 38, Kotohiracho, Shiba, Minato-ku, Tokyo
Banque Nationale de Paris
918 Kokusai Bldg, 1–1, Marunouchi 3-chome, Chiyoda-ku, Tokyo
Barclays Bank International Ltd
Room 916, Kokusai Bldg, 1–1, Marunouchi 3-chome, Chiyoda-ku, Tokyo
The Barclays Group of Banks
Far East Representative Office (as above)
Bayerische Vereinsbank
Tokyo Prince Hotel Suite 516/517, 3–1, Shiba Park 3-chome, Minato-ku, Tokyo

The Chartered Bank
Fuji Bldg, 2–3, Marunouchi 3-chome, Chiyoda-ku, Tokyo
The Chase Manhattan Bank, N.A.
Tokio Kaijo Bldg, 2–1, Marunouchi 1-chome, Chiyoda-ku, Tokyo
Commerzbank AG *see* Banco di Roma
Credit Lyonnais *see* Banco di Roma

Den Danske Landmandsbank
Room 509, Fuji Bldg, 2–3, Marunouchi 3-chome, Chiyoda-ku, Tokyo
Deutsche Ueberseelsche Bank–Deutsche Bank Gruppe
Mitsubishi Shoji Bldg, Annex, 3–1, Marunouchi 1-chome, Chiyoda-ku, Tokyo
Dresdner Bank AG
Room 818, New Yurakucho Bldg, 11, Yurakucho 1-chome, Chiyoda-ku, Tokyo

First National City Bank
2–1, Otemachi 2-chome, Chiyoda-ku, Tokyo

The Hongkong and Shanghai Banking Corporation
1–2, Marunouchi 2-chome, Chiyoda-ku, Tokyo

The International Commercial Bank of China
4–2, Marunouchi 1-chome, Chiyoda-ku, Tokyo

Kleinwort Benson Ltd
Room 713, Kokusai Bldg, 1–1, Marunouchi 3-chome, Chiyoda-ku, Tokyo

Lloyds & Bolsa International Bank Ltd
Room 242, New Yurakucho Bldg, 11, Yurakucho 1-chome, Chiyoda-ku, Tokyo
Note: This office also represents Bank of London and South America Ltd, Bank of London and Montreal Ltd, and Lloyds Bank Europe Ltd.

Manufacturers Hanover Trust Company
21st Floor, Asahi Tokai Bldg, 6–1, Otemachi 2-chome, Chiyoda-ku, Tokyo
Marine Midland Bank–New York
Room 261, New Yurakucho Bldg, 11, Yurakucho 1-chome, Chiyoda-ku, Tokyo
Mellon Bank N.A.
Room 243, New Yurakucho Bldg, 11, Yurakucho 1-chome, Chiyoda-ku, Tokyo
Morgan Guaranty Trust Company of New York
New Yurakucho Bldg, 11, Yurakucho 1-chome, Chiyoda-ku, Tokyo

National and Grindlays Bank Ltd
Room 242, Shin Kokusai Bldg, 4–1, Marunouchi 3-chome, Chiyoda-ku, Tokyo
The National Bank of Australasia Ltd
Room 332, Chiyoda Bldg, 1–2, Marunouchi 2-chome, Chiyoda-ku, Tokyo
The National Bank of New Zealand Ltd
Room 630, New Tokyo Bldg, 3–1, Marunouchi 3-chome, Chiyoda-ku, Tokyo
National Westminster Bank Ltd
Kokusai Bldg, Suite 920 1–1, Marunouchi 3-chome, Chiyoda-ku, Tokyo

Philippine National Bank
Room 710, Kokusai Bldg, 1–1, Marunouchi 3-chome, Chiyoda-ku, Tokyo

The Royal Bank of Canada
Room 602, Fuji Bldg, 2–3, Marunouchi 3-chome, Chiyoda-ku, Tokyo

Skandinaviska Enskilda Banken
509, Fuji Bldg, 2–3, Marunouchi 3-chome, Chiyoda-ku, Tokyo
Note: This office also represents Banque Scandinare en Suisse and Scandinavian Bank Ltd.
Société Générale
Room 502, Fuji Bldg, 2–3, Marunouchi 3-chome, Chiyoda-ku, Tokyo
The Standard Bank Ltd
Suite No. 122, Fuji Bldg, 2–3, Marunouchi 3-chome, Chiyoda-ku, Tokyo
Swiss Bank Corporation
Furukawa-Sogo Bldg, 6–1, Marunouchi 2-chome, Chiyoda-ku, Tokyo
Swiss Credit Bank (Credit Suisse)
Kokusai Bldg, 1–1, Marunouchi 3-chome, Chiyoda-ku, Tokyo

Union Bank of Switzerland
Palace Bldg, 1–1, Marunouchi 1-chome, Chiyoda-ku, Tokyo
United Overseas Bank Ltd
Room 145, New Kokusai Bldg, 4–1, Marunouchi 3-chome, Chiyoda-ku, Tokyo

Wells Fargo Bank, N.A.
Fuji Bldg, 2–3, Marunouchi 3-chome, Chiyoda-ku, Tokyo

Appendix 3

EMBASSIES IN TOKYO

Afghanistan
Olympia Annex Apt, 31–21, Jingumae 6-chome, Shibuya-ku 400 7912

Algeria
Shibusawa Bldg., 1, Shiba Koen 21-gochi, Minato-ku 431 7481

Argentina
Chiyoda House, 17–8, Nagata-cho 2-chome, Chiyoda-ku 581 0321

Australia
1–14, Mita 2-chome, Minato-ku 453 0251

Austria
1–20, Motoazabu 1-chome, Minato-ku 451 8281

Belgium
5, Nibancho, Chiyoda-ku 262 0191

Bolivia
37–16, Ebisu 3-chome, Shibuya-ku 441 1667

Brazil
Aoyama 36–16, Ebisu 4–14, Akasaka 8-chome, Minato-ku 404 5211

Bulgaria
33–5, Yoyogi 5-chome, Shibuya-ku 468 3351

Burma
8–26, Kitashinagawa 4-chome, Shinagawa-ku 441 9291

Cambodia
7–17, Akasaka 8-chome, Minato-ku 401 0191

Canada
3–38, Akasaka 7-chome, Minato-ku 408 2101

Central Africa
4–15, Komazawa 1-chome, Setagaya-ku 422 3185

Ceylon
8–28, Aobadai 2-chome, Meguro-ku 463 0321

Chile
Belaire Garden, 2–11, Jingumae 4-chome, Shibuya-ku 404 8466

China
4–39, Motoazabu 3-chome, Minato-ku 408 5131

Colombia
9–10, Minami Aoyama 5-chome, Minato-ku 409 4289

Congo
Isurumi Bldg, 1–1, Tomigaya 1-chome, Shibuya-ku 469 8176

Costa Rica
6–15, Horinouchi 2-chome, Suginami-ku 312 4734
Cuba
6–2, Hiroo 2-chome, Shibuya-ku 409 6861
Czechoslovakia
15–6, Hiroo 2-chome, Shibuya-ku 400 3116

Denmark
Denmark House, 17–38, Aoyama 4-chome, Minato-ku 404 2331
Dominican Republic
2–28, Shiroganedai 3-chome, Minato-ku 442 6137

Ecuador
Azabu Sky Mansion,
19–13, Minami Azabu 3-chome, Minato-ku 442 6008
El Salvador
No. 1019, Yurakucho Bldg., 5, Yuraku-cho 1-chome,
Chiyoda-ku 211 1587
Ethiopia
2–13, Akasaka 8-chome, Minato-ku 401 3679

Finland
2–7, Roppongi 3-chome, Minato-ku 583 7790
France
11–44, Minami Azabu 4-chome, Minato-ku 473 0171

Gabon
16–2, Hiroo 2-chome, Shibuya-ku 409 5116
Germany
5–10, Minami Azabu 4-chome, Minato-ku 473 0151
Ghana
15–12, Higashi Gotanda 5-chome, Shinagawa-ku 445 4301
Greece
11–11, Jingumae 1-chome, Shibuya-ku 403 0871
Guatemala
17–1, Shoto-1-chome, Shibuya-ku 467 7276

Haiti
24–8, Minami Aoyama 4-chome, Minato-ku 400 3390
Holy See
9–2, Sanbancho, Chiyoda-ku 263 6851
Honduras
2–25, Minami Azabu 4-chome, Minato-ku 443 8785
Hungary
1–29, Nakameguro 1-chome, Meguro-ku 712 0801

India
2–11, Kudan Minami 2-chome, Chiyoda-ku 262 2391

Indonesia	
2–9, Higashi Gotanda 5-chome, Shinagawa-ku	441 4201
Iran	
10–32, Minami Azabu 3-chome, Minato-ku	473 4237
Iraq	
21–22, Higashiyama 1-chome, Meguro-ku	719 9147
Israel	
3, Niban-cho, Chiyoda-ku	264 0911
Italy	
5–4, Mita 2-chome, Minato-ku	453 5291
Ivory Coast	
Aoyama Tower Bldg., 24–15, Minami Aoyama 2-chome, Minato-ku	402 8371
Khmer	
7–17, Akasaka 8-chome, Minato-ku	401 0191
Korea	
2–5, Minami Azabu 1-chome, Minato-ku	452 7611
Kuwait	
13–12, Mita 4-chome, Minato-ku	455 0361
Laos	
3–21, Nishi Azabu 3-chome, Minato-ku	408 1166
Lebanon	
Azabu Tokyu Apt, 47, Azabu Mamiana-cho, Minato-ku	583 4248
Liberia	
1, Kioi-cho, Chiyoda-ku	264 0651
Libya	
Tokyo Daikanyama Tower Apt. 35–11, Ebisu Nishi 1-chome, Shibuya-ku	461 7872
Madagascar	
11–43, Akasaka 8-chome, Minato-ku	404 8511
Malaysia	
20–16, Nanpeidai, Shibuya-ku	463 0241
Mexico	
15–1, Nagata-cho 2-chome, Chiyoda-ku	581 1131
Morocco	
19–10, Shiroganedai 4-chome, Minato-ku	441 7951
Nepal	
17–1, Higashi Gotanda 5-chome, Shinagawa-ku	447 7303
Netherlands	
1, Shiba Sakae-cho, Minato-ku	431 5126
New Zealand	
20–40, Kamiyama-cho, Shibuya-ku	460 8711
Nicaragua	
2–3, Roppongi 4-chome, Minato-ku	401 0380

Nigeria
2–2, Shoto 2-chome, Shibuya-ku 468 5531
Norway
12–2, Minami Azabu 5-chome, Minato-ku 446 4711

Pakistan
Ikeyama Height, 22–33, Higashi Gotanda 5-chome, Shinagawa-ku 445 4511
Panama
2–9, Akasaka 9-chome, Minato-ku 403 3782
Paraguay
Akasaka Kokusai Kaikan, 10–16, Akasaka 8-chome, Minato-ku 408 7343
Peru
15–8, Minami Aoyama 1-chome, Minato-ku 403 9509
Philippines
6–15, Roppongi 5-chome, Minato-ku 583 4101
Poland
13–5, Mita 2-chome, Meguro-ku 711 5224
Portugal
Olympia Annex, 31–21, Jingumae 6-chome, Shibuya-ku 400 7907

Romania
3–1, Aobadai 2-chome, Meguro-ku 463 3395

Saudi Arabia
4–18, Motoazabu 3-chome, Minato-ku 408 5158
Singapore
Kasumigaseki Bldg., 2–5, Kasumigaseki 3-chome, Chiyoda-ku 581 9631
Spain
3–29, Roppongi 1-chome, Minato-ku 583 8531
Sweden
103, Roppongi 1-chome, Minato-ku 582 6981
Switzerland
9–12, Minami Azabu 5-chome, Minato-ku 473 0121

Tanzania
21–9, Kami Yoga 4-chome, Setagaya-ku 429 6807
Thailand
14–6, Kamiosaki 3-chome, Shinagawa-ku 441 7352
Turkey
33–6, Jingumae 2-chome, Shibuya-ku 401 2144

Union of Soviet Socialist Republics
1, Azabu Mamiana-cho, Minato-ku 583 4224
United Arab Republic
5–4, Aobadai 1-chome, Meguro-ku 463 4564

United Kingdom	
1, Ichiban-cho, Chiyoda-ku	265 5511
United States of America	
10–5, Akasaka 1-chome, Minato-ku	583 7141
Uruguay	
Akasaka Height, 5–26, Akasaka 9-chome, Minato-ku	403 4725
Venezuela	
11–23, Minami Azabu 3-chome, Minato-ku	444 7551
Viet Nam	
50–11, Motoyoyogi, Shibuya-ku	466 3311
Yugoslavia	
7–24, Kitashingawa 4-chome, Shinagawa-ku	447 3571

Appendix 4

SOME USEFUL SOURCES OF INFORMATION

The embassy of Japan (Commercial Section) in your country

Your own embassy in Tokyo (Commercial Section)

MITI (Ministry of International Trade and Industry), Tokyo

JETRO (Japanese External Trade Organization) in your country

The Japanese Economic Institute in your country

The export division of your own Department of Trade and Industry

Major clearing banks in your country and Japanese banks that are represented

Your local Chamber of Commerce at home and in Japan

Japanese Chamber of Commerce in your country

Japan Air Lines

Japan National Tourist Organization

Management consultants and securities companies with a specialist knowledge of Japan

Selected Bibliography

1 GENERAL: INSIGHTS INTO JAPANESE SOCIETY

RUTH BENEDICT, *The Chrysanthemum and the Sword*, (London: Routledge & Kegan Paul, 1967).

The work of an American social anthropologist, first published in 1946. A classic sociological study of its kind; well worth exploring.

PRUE DEMPSTER, *Japan Advances: A Geographical Study*, 2nd ed. (London: Methuen, 1969).

Survey of the geography of Japan with special attention to recent developments in farming and industry. Helpful maps and diagrams.

MARSHALL E. DIMOCK, *The Japanese Technocracy: Management and Government in Japan* (New York: Walker, 1968).

Study in the modernization process; how the Japanese technocrat combines modern performance with traditional values.

TAKEO DOI, *The Anatomy of Dependence* (Tokyo: Sophia/Kodansha, 1973).

A penetrating and rewarding study of the workings of the Japanese mind and mentality. A best-seller in the original Japanese edition.

HERBERT GLAZER, *The International Businessman in Japan* (Tokyo: Sophia/Tuttle, 1968).

A very helpful volume which attemps to answer the question: 'What is the image that Japanese businessmen and critics have formed of the foreign businessman in Japan?'

ROBERT GUILLAIN, *The Japanese Challenge: The Race To The Year 2000* (Philadelphia: J. B. Lippincott, 1970).

Translation from the French (1969). Keen observation based on long years of familiarity with Japan and the Japanese, as well as with East Asia.

HIROSHI IYORI, *Antimonopoly Legislation in Japan* (New York: Federal Legal Publications, 1969).

Scholarly study, but most helpful. A short history is followed by a review of the various aspects of the Antimonopoly Act, and the various exemption laws. Illustrated by Fair Trade Commission and court decisions.

EUGENE T. KAPLAN, *Japan: The Government–Business Relationship. A Guide for the American Businessman* (Washington, D.C.: US Department of Commerce, 1972).

Most instructive. Especially helpful for three industry studies (steel, automobile, computer) depicting government–business interaction, sometimes a success, sometimes a failure.

CHIE NAKANE, *Japanese Society* (London: Weidenfeld & Nicolson 1970).

Contribution by a foremost Japanese anthropologist. A fascinating account of the vertical structure of Japanese society, its implications and applications.

LAWRENCE OLSON, *Japan in Postwar Asia* (London: Pall Mall Press, 1970).

Reviews the war reparations agreements and the restoration of commercial relations; then moves into the late sixties when Asia's development came to the foreground.

Quality of the Environment in Japan (Tokyo: Environment Agency, 1972).

Condensed version of the 1972 White Paper on the Environment. Necessary source for the exporter of pollution–control equipment and related industries.

Staff of *Asahi Shimbun, The Pacific Rivals: A Japanese View of Japanese–American Relations* (New York and Tokyo: Weatherhill, 1972).

Collection of short essays by the staff of Japan's largest newspaper. A best-seller in Japanese. Interesting reading taking the pulse of postwar Japanese public opinion as moulded and expressed by the press.

EZRA F. VOGEL, *Japan's New Middle Class: The Salary Man and His Family in a Tokyo Suburb* (Berkeley: University of California Press, 1963).

Although depicting the situation at the end of the 1950s, this sociological study remains a major contribution to the understanding of the current consumer market and its behaviour patterns.

CHITOSHI YANAGA, *Big Business in Japanese Politics* (New Haven: Yale University Press, 1968).

Excellent contribution to the understanding of the government–business relationship from the viewpoint of a political scientist.

2 BUSINESS KNOW-HOW

JAMES C. ABEGGLEN, *Management and Worker–The Japanese Solution* (Tokyo: Sophia/Kodansha, 1973).

Reprint of the classic *The Japanese Factory* (1958), to which was added a comprehensive analysis of the employment system in the 1970s.

JAMES C. ABEGGLEN (ed.), *Business Strategies for Japan* (Tokyo: Sophia/Britannica, 1970).

A key volume describing exactly what its title purports: relationship between government and business, financing, marketing, personnel, etc., with a concluding chapter on 'The Problem of Entry'.

ROBERT J. BALLON (ed.), *Doing Business in Japan*, revised ed. (Tokyo: Sophia/Tuttle, 1968).

Introduction to the key aspects of the Japanese business world: industrial society, psychology, law, consumer, banking, accounting and management practices.

ROBERT J. BALLON (ed.), *The Japanese Employee* (Tokyo: Sophia/Tuttle, 1969).

Most helpful in understanding the Japanese approach to personnel and wage administration as well as industrial relations.

ROBERT J. BALLON (ed.), *Marketing in Japan* (Tokyo: Sophia/Kodansha, 1973).

The topic is treated under three central headings: Setting-up in Japan; the Japanese consumer; marketing strategy for Japan.

ROBERT J. BALLON and EUGENE H. LEE (eds), *Foreign Investment and Japan* (Tokyo: Sophia/Kodansha, 1972).

Review of the investment situation in Japan and its critical areas: corporate control; antimonopoly legislation; taxation; patents and trademarks; the management of foreign operations.

K. BIEDA, *The Structure and Operation of the Japanese Economy* (Sydney: John Wiley, 1970).

Overall review. Provides detailed insights into many lesser known practices. Via the index, a helpful source of reference.

TUVIA BLUMENTHAL, *Saving in Postwar Japan* (Cambridge, Mass.: Harvard University Press, 1970).

Lucid analysis of one of the most intriguing aspects of Japanese society–the capacity to save.

TERUO DOI, *Digest of Japanese Court Decisions in Trademarks and Unfair Competition Cases* (Tokyo: The American Chamber of Commerce in Japan, 1971).

An analysis of thirty-two recent cases. Appendix includes the Trademark Law and the Unfair Competition Prevention Law.

RONALD DORE, *British Factory–Japanese Factory. The Origins of National Diversity in Industrial Relations* (London: George Allen & Unwin, 1973).
Lengthy but extremely helpful comparative analysis. Via the index, an enlightening reference source on almost all aspects of personnel administration and industrial relations.

DAN FENNO HENDERSON, *Foreign Enterprise in Japan: Laws and Policies* (Chapel Hill: University of North Carolina Press, 1973).
Comprehensive study of the investment climate in present day Japan. Probes the depths of most problems encountered by foreign firms. Written by a lawyer.

The Industrial Policy of Japan (Paris: OECD, 1972).
Incisive analysis of a broad topic. Based on extensive documentation provided by the Japanese government.

Manual of Employment Practices in Japan, revised ed. (Tokyo: The American Chamber of Commerce in Japan, 1970).
Meant for the resident foreign executive confronted with the problem of managing a Japanese work-force. Periodically updated.

BYRON K. MARSHALL, *Capitalism and Nationalism in Prewar Japan–The Ideology of the Business Elite, 1868–1941* (Stanford University Press, 1967).
Illuminating study. Will help in the understanding of the mentality of present-day Japanese executives in their fifties.

Outline of Japanese Distribution Structures (Tokyo: The Distribution Economics Institute of Japan, 1973).
Indispensable guide. General considerations on the distribution environment and structure, followed by detailed analysis of the practices and channels for each major category of consumer goods. Illustrated by diagrams.

J. TOSHIO SAWADA, *Subsequent Conduct and Supervening Events* (University of Tokyo Press, 1968).
The second half of this volume deals with business practices in Japan, in particular the contract. Shows how the contractual relationship is essentially considered as "beyond" the positive law.

Y. TAJIMA, *How Goods are Distributed in Japan* (Orient International Business Books, 1971).
A simple and very logical introduction to the subject, including a historical perspective showing how distribution has evolved.

Tax and Trade Guide: Japan (New York: Arthur Andersen & Co., 1972).
The publisher is an international audit partnership; the publication is available to clients. Covers types and regulations of business organizations; labour and social laws; financial institutions; economic and government controls. Concludes with a detailed analysis of the taxation system.

YUKUZO YAMASAKI, *Digest of Japanese Court Decisions in Patentability and Patent Infringement Cases, 1966–1968* (Tokyo: The American Chamber of Commerce in Japan, 1970).
This is the third volume on the subject (available from the same publisher). Depicts the evolution in judicial thinking through a three- to four-page digest of forty cases. Index to the three volumes.

M. Y. YOSHINO, *Japan's Managerial system–Tradition and Innovation* (Cambridge, Mass.: MIT Press, 1968).
In-depth analysis starting with the pre-modern and prewar eras; considers present-day Japanese executives and their ideologies, the industrial structure, industrial groupings, the organization structure and decision-making.

M. Y. YOSHINO, *The Japanese Marketing System–Adaptations and Innovations* (Cambridge, Mass.: MIT Press, 1971).
Exhaustive study covering the postwar emergence of the mass-consumption society; the marketing behaviour of the large manufacturing firms; tradition, innovation and government policies in the distribution sector; and consumer financing.

3 PERIODICALS/ANNUALS

Basic Economic and Social Plan (1973–1977) (Tokyo: Economic Planning Agency, 1973).
The sixth postwar economic plan of the Japanese government. Basic document indicating the direction proposed and largely incorporated as the minimum in the long-range business planning of Japanese enterprises.

Economic Information File: Japan 1973 (Tokyo: World Economic Information Services, 1973).
Second edition of a recent annual. More specific and analytical than other current yearbooks. Special studies on regional development and Japan–China trade. Major industries are reviewed individually, with list of major Japanese and foreign companies.

Economic Survey of Japan (1972–1973) (Tokyo: The Japan Times, 1973).
Translation of the annual survey presented by the Economic Plan-

ning Agency to the government. Besides key economic data, presents the official thinking with regard to economic, social and international implications.

Economic Surveys: Japan (Paris: OECD, 1973).
Annual authoritative survey at the aggregate level.

Japan Economic Yearbook 1974 (Tokyo: The Oriental Economist, 1974).
Annual following the universal pattern of such yearbooks. Detailed current data on society in general and on each industry, as well as a list of major companies classified by industry. Useful reference.

The President Directory 1974 (Tokyo: Diamond-Time, 1973).
Annual. Commented listing and ranking of all major Japanese and foreign-capital affiliated corporations in Japan. Inspired by the *FORTUNE* annual listing.

White Paper on International Trade 1973 (Tokyo: Japan External Trade Organization, 1973).
An annual analysis of Japan's international trade. Detailed statistics by region, country and commodity, supported by comments on the international environment viewed from the Japanese angle.

White Papers of Japan, 1971–72. Annual Abstract of Official Reports and Statistics of the Japanese Government (Tokyo: Japan Institute of International Affairs, 1973).
Annual publication containing about ten-page abstracts of the White Papers published by various government agencies, as well as public opinion surveys, an outline of the political system and detailed organization charts of the Japanese government agencies.

Notes on Contributors

DR JAMES ABEGGLEN was a Ford Foundation Fellow in Japan in 1955–6; later he was with the Centre for International Studies at MIT, involved in research into the Mexican economy. He is Vice-President of the Boston Consulting Group Inc., and President of its Japanese offshoot the Boston Consulting Group KK, Tokyo. He is the author of *Big Business Leaders in America, Occupational Mobility in American Business and Industry, Management and Worker–The Japanese Solution,* and a number of other studies and monographs.

ROBERT J. BALLON, born in Belgium, first went to Japan in 1948. Since that time he has concentrated on the study of Japanese labour-management relations and Japan's role in international business. His books include *Doing Business in Japan, Joint Ventures in Japan, The Japanese Employee, Japan's Market and Foreign Business* and *Foreign Investment and Japan*. He is currently Chairman of the Socio-Economic Institute at Sophia University, Tokyo, and head of the International Management Development Seminars sponsored by this institute.

GEORGE FIELDS, president of Audience Studies (Japan) Inc., has spent more than twenty years in Japan and has been in market research for as many years. As a consultant researcher his particular grasp of the nuances of Japanese life and living has played a great part in the success of ASI's credibility worldwide. Mr Fields is Chairman of the Trans-Market Research organization and Executive Vice-President of INMARCO, ASI's parent company.

PROFESSOR HERBERT GLAZER first visited Japan as a civilian adviser on systems analysis to the US Seventh Fleet in 1959. He is now Professor of Marketing at the American University, Washington, D.C., and visiting Professor of Economics at the Socio-Economic Institute of Sophia University. His books include *The International Businessman in Japan*.

GENE GREGORY, a specialist in Asian affairs, has published widely on the Japanese economy. His career in Asia during the past twenty-five years has included diplomacy, business and journalism.

DAVID GRIBBIN is a former literary editor and copywriter and was, until last year, creative director of Collett, Dickenson Pearce & Partners' Tokyo office. He has recently established the London firm of Gribbin & Gribbin, a marketing consultancy specialising in Japan.

PROFESSOR YUJIRO HAYASHI is a professor at the Tokyo Institute of Technology and President of the Institute for Future Technology. A graduate in electro-chemistry, he has at different times been a technical official of the Prime Minister's Office, research official of the Economic Counsel Board, Counsellor of the Economic Planning Agency, President of the Economic Research Institute of the Economic Planning Agency, and Professor of Social Engineering at the Tokyo Institute of Technology. His publications include *Capitalism and Technology, Informationized Society, Social Engineering*, and *Human Welfare and Technological Innovation*.

GIL HOLDSWORTH was for five years general manager of Dodwell in Japan (Dodwell being one of the largest foreign trading companies in Japan). He is now director of Dodwell & Co. Ltd, responsible in London for the affairs of Dodwell in Japan. He is Chairman of the Japan Association in London, and of the Japan section of the London Chamber of Commerce. He is a member of the Japan Trade Advisory Group, which advises the British Overseas Trade Board, and he visits Japan regularly.

DR IWAO HOSHII, before acquiring Japanese citizenship in 1958, was known as Peter J. Herzog. He was born in Aachen, Germany, in 1905 and became a member of the Society of Jesus in 1924. He first encountered Japan in 1935 and then went on to graduate in law and political science (M.A., LL.B., Ph.D.) at Fordham University, New York. He joined the faculty of Sophia University, Tokyo, in 1940, remaining until 1957 when he joined the research division of Fuji Bank, Tokyo. Dr Hoshii remains closely involved in the bank's research work, along with other consultancy activities. His books include *The Economic Challenge to Japan, The Dynamics of Japan's Business Evolution, Japan's Business Concentration*, and *A Financial History of Modern Japan*, co-authored with T. F. M. Adams.

MICHAEL ISHERWOOD is manager of the general affairs department in London and assistant to the London director of Mitsubishi Corporation–the trading company of the massive Mitsubishi industrial and commercial group. In the eleven years he has been with Mitsubishi he has had a wide range of experience in different trading activities between Japan and Europe. He holds directorships in several subsidiary companies, and has been an active member of the Council of the Japan Society of London for the past ten years.

EUGENE H. LEE is Professor of International Business at the Socio-Economic Institute, Sophia University, Tokyo. He studied at Kansas University and graduated at the University of Washington both as J. D. (Doctor of Jurisprudence) and LL.M. (Master of Law)–specialising in Asian law. Later he studied Japanese commercial law as a Fulbright Scholar at Tokyo University. Throughout he has participated extensively in problems of management development and international business. He is also the author of numerous essays and papers.

SADAO OBA is the deputy general manager of Mitsui & Co. Ltd, London. He graduated from the Otaru College of Commerce in 1942, and has worked for Mitsui & Co. in Tokyo and its subsidiaries since 1948, specialising in business co-ordination, economic analysis and research. He joined the Mitsui London company in 1969 with responsibilities for general economic surveys and market research for the whole of Europe. He is a frequent contributor to Japanese and other publications, and a frequent speaker at business and management conferences. He is a co-author of *The European Economic Community and Japan*.

CHARLES SMITH was for many years Far East correspondent for the *Financial Times* in London. Now based in Tokyo, he is Far East editor of *the Financial Times*, a position he took up in 1973. It is largely through him that the *Financial Times* has built up its authoritative viewpoint of Japan and the Far East.

PROFESSOR YOSHIHIRO TAJIMA is acknowledged in Japan as perhaps the leading expert on distribution economics. He is a professor of marketing and distribution economics at the Gakushuin University, and founded the Distribution Economic Institute of Japan (an educational and research foundation). He serves on various government economic committees, and is an expert on foreign economic and marketing affairs. His book *How Goods are Distributed in Japan* is considered a definitive study, and he is the author of numerous other books and papers on related subjects.

FUMIO YAMAMOTO is manager of the overseas advertising division of Matsushita Electric Industrial Company, Japan. Since 1968 he has been concerned with advertising in numerous export markets–from the United States to India.

THE EDITORS

PAUL NORBURY is managing director of Paul Norbury Publications.

GEOFFREY BOWNAS is Professor of Japanese Studies and Director of the Centre of Japanese Studies, University of Sheffield.

Index